CONTENTS

PREFACE

SCOPE

Marketing Today's Fashion is an introductory text designed to acquaint students with the American fashion industry.

The fashion industries—from the production of raw materials to the distribution of finished goods—accounts for an estimated one-third of the world's economy. In the United States alone, Americans spend nearly 80 billion dollars a year on wearing apparel, and one out of every eight workers in the United States is employed in the fashion industry or its allied fields. As a result, there has been a tremendous increase in the formal teaching of Fashion Marketing on the secondary and post-secondary level. As more and more students gravitate toward these innovative programs, the need for an authoritative text for teaching the "business" aspects of the industry has increased.

This text is intended for students enrolled in a one-semester introductory course in fashion at a two- or four-year college or business school and for the growing number of similar courses that are taught on the secondary level.

STRUCTURE

The text has been divided into 6 parts, 15 chapters, and an appendix. Each chapter contains Objectives, Terms to Remember, Highlights of the Chapter, and Questions. Each part ends with a Bibliography.

A "Focus" feature has been included in the text to spotlight outstanding people, places, and things of the fashion business. The Focus approach is also used to examine the various career possibilities in the industry, incorporated into the body of the text at a point where that aspect of the fashion industry is discussed. Fashion trends, designers, and leading fashion retail stores also comprise the Focuses.

The subject matter of the text naturally focuses upon women's wear because of its preponderance in the industry. However, the integration of menswear, childrens' wear, and accessories into the general fashion picture by the industry is a *fait accompli.* The time has come to treat these three classifications similarly in the text of a fashion marketing book—not as separate entities, but as integral parts of wearing apparel. Marketing Today's Fashion has done exactly that.

ORGANIZATION

Part I provides the students with an understanding of fashion, its language, and its movements.

Part II provides a brief history of the evolution of the American fashion industry.

These first two sections set the stage for understanding present fashion producers and their methods. A description of America and Europe as design centers is given in Part III, followed by the role of the foreign and domestic primary markets and manufacturers in Part IV.

Once students are aware of how fashion is produced, they then learn how it is merchandised. Retailers—who they are and how they operate—and their auxiliary merchandising operations and methods of promotion are the subject of Part V.

Finally, a complete understanding of fashion includes analysis and understanding of the fashion consumer. Since consumer wants and needs change constantly, this serves as a catalyst for the future direction of the industry. These concepts are the subject of Part VI.

By organizing the material of the book in this sequence, and especially by including the historical perspectives of the fashion industry, a two-fold goal is achieved:

First, a view of the past, present, and future prepares the students with a keen understanding and appreciation of the business of fashion.

Secondly, the wide scope of the material gives the students an all-encompassing familiarity with fashion. This equips them with additional authoritive knowledge of the subject that is certain to help in their search for a successful career in the industry.

We gratefully acknowledge the generous help we have received from the many people in the fashion industry, in academia, and from our reviewers. We would also like to thank our production editor, Marian Hartstein, and in particular, our typist and kind and encouraging friend, Helen Zapolski.

Helena de Paola / Carol Stewart Mueller

1

UNDERSTANDING TODAY'S FASHION

To fully appreciate the nature and scope of the fashion business, it is necessary to begin by exploring the concepts which answer the following fundamental questions.

First, *what* is fashion? *How* is it defined? *What* is its special language or "jargon" of the trade?

Second, what are the theories which explain how and why clothing began? What social and psychological roles does clothing play today?

Finally, how does fashion move? Does fashion move in a mysterious and unpredictable way? Or, can the movement of fashion be analyzed and evaluated under systematic cycles and patterns?

Chapters 1 and 2 should provide the answers—as well as a deep look into the fundamental underpinnings of the exciting, dynamic, multifaceted business called fashion.

1

THE LANGUAGE OF FASHION

OBJECTIVES

After reading this chapter, you should be able to:

- Give a specific, all encompassing definition of what the word *fashion* means.
- Define the terms used as technical language or "jargon" by the fashion industry.
- Understand how the language of fashion is used by those in the fashion industry.

Fashion. A complex word. Meaning glamour and excitement to many; creativity and business opportunity to a few. To some it suggests a world of fantasy—a world of designers, models, and expensive clothes. For these people "fashion" is often undefinable—something mysterious and illusive; something not really related to them.

But the word fashion can be clearly defined. It does have specific and concrete meanings. Fashion means *acceptance.* It is a business which requires *innovation.* It is *reflective* of people and their environment. It means *imitation* and at the same time *self-expression.* Since the student of fashion should begin learning about fashion by defining it, each of these definitions of fashion is explained as follows:

DEFINING FASHION

Fashion Means Acceptance

From an academic viewpoint, *Webster's New Collegiate Dictionary*[1] defines *fashion* as "the prevailing style during a particular time." The definition includes "the choice or usage (as in dressing, decorating, or living) generally accepted by those who regard themselves as up-to-date and sophisticated." In his book, *Economics of Fashion,*[2] Dr. Paul Nystrom, an economics professor who was the first to apply economics to fashion, defined *fashion* as "nothing more or less than the prevailing style at any given time."

These two definitions describe fashion in extremely general terms referring to home furnishings, apparel, accessories, even a style of behavior. Since these references are too broad for the purpose of this text, the definition of fashion will be limited to the dress and personal decoration worn by men, women, and children. *Fashion,* then, is the prevailing style or groups of styles in dress and accessories worn by a group of people at a particular time. It follows, "whenever a style is accepted and worn by a sufficient number of people it is in fashion or becomes a fashion."[3]

As this definition implies, many fashions may exist at the same time. A fashion which is accepted by one group of people is not necessarily accepted by another. In the mid-sixties, pants became popular with young women. They were a fashion with that particular group. However, they were then not a fashion with older women. It was not until the 1970s that pant suits came to be worn by women of all ages. The young, though still addicted to pants, then discovered skirts. Below-the-knee length skirts once considered "old hat" by the young, became popular with that group. In many cases, young women were wearing them for the first time in their lives. By the mid-seventies, pants and skirts were equally popular but not necessarily with the same groups. The young had "discovered" the newness of skirts. The mature had "discovered" the comfort of pants. But both skirts and pants, since they were a prevailing style, worn by the majority of a group, were a *fashion.*

[1]By permission. From *Webster's New Collegiate Dictionary,* 1976, by G. & C. Merriam Company, publishers of the Merriam-Webster dictionaries.

[2]Paul H. Nystrom, *Economics of Fashion* (New York: Ronald Press, 1928), p. 4.

[3]Harriet T. McJimsey, *Art and Fashion in Clothing Selection* (Ames, Iowa: Iowa State University Press, 1973), p. 48.

Fashion Means Business

The acceptance of a prevailing style as a fashion automatically implies that consumers have *purchased* that particular garment or accessory. And since Americans purchase nearly 80 billion dollars worth of fashion merchandise a year, fashion acceptance translates into big business. As in all businesses, the goal of those in the fashion business is to make a profit. And like other businesses which depend on the ultimate consumer for profit, the fashion industry has become market oriented.

No longer does the fashion industry dictate what customers should wear. Today, the successful process of marketing a garment or an accessory *begins* with the customer. *First* the customer is analyzed to evaluate his or her wants and needs. *Then* apparel which will hopefully meet these wants and needs is produced and sold. This procedure is known as *fashion marketing,* and can be defined as directing the flow of fashion goods from producer to consumer in order to profitably satisfy consumer wants and needs.

Fashion Means Innovation

Consumer wants and needs are unending and constantly changing, challenging the fashion industry with the job of providing newness and variety in the fashion market place. To meet this challenge, the fashion industry constantly updates its present offerings of apparel with newer versions. This constant alteration of what styles are fashionable and what styles are not has led to criticisms which charge fashion as an economic waste! Vance Packard, consumer advocate and author, charges that the fashion industry is based on the principle of "planned obsolescence"[4]—definable as: the deliberate outmoding of merchandise by the subsequent introduction of other products.

In particular, Packard accuses the fashion industry of forcing the obsolescence of fashion merchandise by eliminating its desirability. For example, a perfectly wearable pair of shoes goes out of fashion simply because the industry has introduced a "new look."

The reply to this criticism is simple: People become bored easily. Human beings have an insatiable appetite for new products and the fashion industry is only responding to this basic need for variety and change. Moreover, the industry is providing a very important and useful economic function: by directing raw materials into finished goods, it creates employment and revenues.

[4]Vance Packard, *The Wastemakers.* Copyright © 1958. Reprinted by permission of the David McKay Company, Inc.

Fashion Means Reflection

The fashion business responds rather than initiates. This means that, in order to be successfully innovative, fashion industry changes must take place when changes in other areas occur. Fashion must respond to the current changes which a particular society or group is undergoing in its values, mores, and customs. As a culture undergoes changes which are *political, legal, social, technological,* or *economic*—the changes must be and usually are translated and reflected in fashion.

Examples of this responsive nature can be found throughout America's history. The colonists made the wearing of domestic fabrics a symbol of their desire to be *politically* independent from England.

The popularity of pants is credited to the changing roles of females in the society—a *social* change. *Technological* advances have led to the discovery of man-made fibers with the desirable "wash and wear," "double knit," and "permanent press" characteristics—revolutionizing the garment industry.

It has been proposed that the rise and fall of women's hemlines

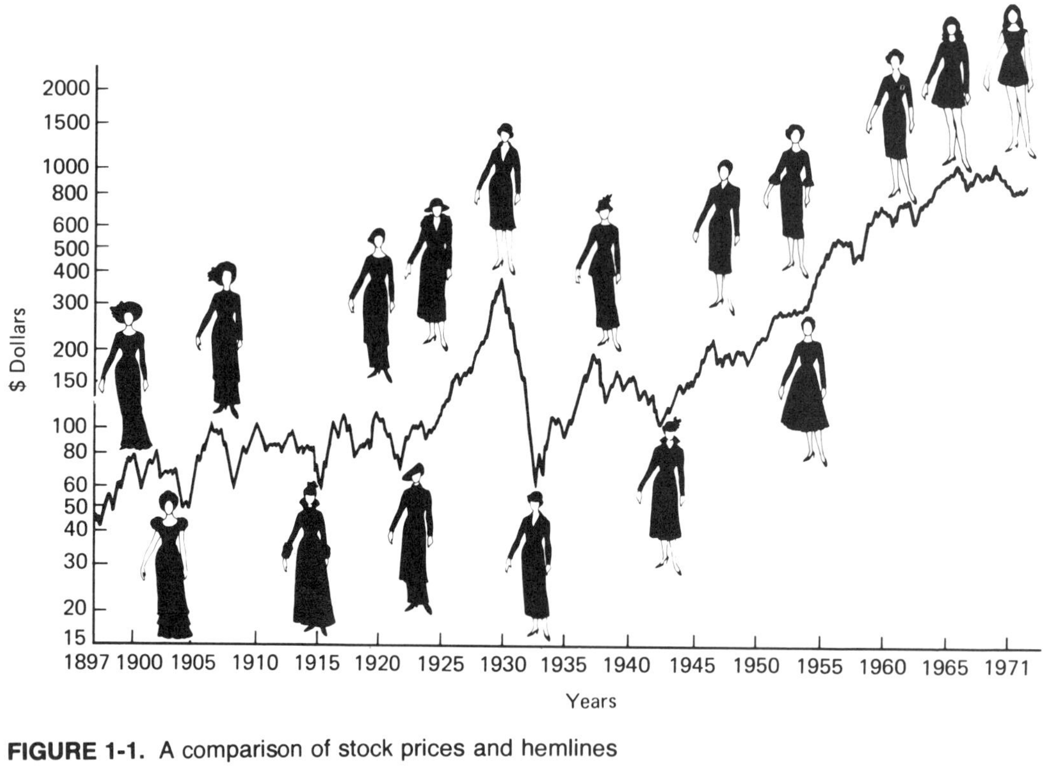

FIGURE 1-1. A comparison of stock prices and hemlines

depicts the *economic* health of the country and even the performance of the stock market (see Fig. 1-1). As hemlines move up, the economy expands. When hemlines fall the economic picture is bleak. Although there is no logical explanation for this occurrence, it is another illustration of fashion reflecting the times.

The concept of reflection can be reversed. By looking at how people dress and accessorize themselves, certain inferences can be made about the society. American dress is casual, comfort oriented, easy care, and mass produced. It may be implied therefore, that this country is a classless society and technologically advanced, embracing and emphasizing convenience and comfort in its life style.

Fashion Means Imitation

For a fashion idea to be successful it must be copied. In this country "success" means mass produced by manufacturers and mass purchased by consumers. Fashion involves producing and promoting new ideas and items which will have widespread appeal.

Historically, fashion emulation followed a straight and narrow path. Royalty created fashions copied by the lower classes. French designers created looks copied by American manufacturers. Today, imitation is still the key to the process, but those who initiate fashion have changed. Ideas to be copied now come from anywhere and everywhere as will be discussed later in the text.

Fashion Means Expression

Though fashion is an imitative process, it does not necessarily follow that everyone must look alike. Fashion is a general concept and people interpret a fashion by choosing a particular style reflecting their judgment and taste. Fashion then becomes a visible extension of one's personality. "You are what you wear—you wear what you are," may be an appropriate verbalization of this concept.

Sociologists and psychologists have done extensive research on role theory. In essence, people wear a variety of hats—such as father, husband, employee, sportsman, repair man—in order to function in society. To properly play each of these parts, different "uniforms" are worn. The fashion industry provides a varied selection of clothing and accessories to meet this demand for what might be termed "occasion dressing." When playing golf or going to work, a different outfit is worn for each assumed role.

Being fashionable is also a way of obtaining approval from others and gaining social status. Apparel and accessories provide a means of distinction, giving others a basis for evaluating a person. Sociologist Thorstein Veblen in his famous book, *The Theory of the Leisure Class,* calls this concept "*conspicuous consumption.*"[5] In summary, this means that a person wears certain clothes or purchases certain objects for the sake of improving his or her status in the eyes of others. These objects or articles of clothing and their extravagant quality are a means by which the wearer can communicate position and rank.

Although Veblen's book was written in the late 1800s, conspicuous consumption is still practiced by some people today. In a recent article in *The New York Times Magazine,* columnist Russell Baker states: "In New York at least, males of the moneyed class announce their wealth through their shoes. On meeting a New York man, one instantly looks at his feet for the buckles of Gucci, which declare: "rich."[6]

Fashion is also a way of expressing society's or an individual's attitude towards sex. By exposing and emphasizing different parts of the body erotic interest is stimulated.

In the early 1930s the low back or backless gowns were fashionable. In 1947 Dior emphasized the hourglass shape and small waistline. More recently the leg and thigh were focused on by the mini-skirt and "hot pants" (see Fig. 1-2). These changing styles seem to have one thing in common—sex appeal! Throughout history both men and women have chosen clothing which gains approval from the opposite sex.

It seems almost contradictory to use concepts such as conformity and self-expression together to define fashion. Yet both are correct. Conformity is seen through the silhouette that is popular at a given time. Self-expression is achieved through varying the elements of texture, color, detail, and trim. Quoting from teacher and author Harriet T. McJimsey:

> The desire for self-identification and self-expression is part of the universal human need for self-assertion and recognition. Conversely, there is the need for friendship and companionship, the desire to imitate people we admire and to conform to members within our own group. This desire to be like others conflicts with the wish to be different, to stand out from the group. Some compromise between imitation and originality is usual: this extent of the originality attempted depends on an individual's own sense of security, initiative and creativity.[7]

[5]Thorstein Veblen, *The Theory of the Leisure Class,* Mentor ed. (New York: New American Library of World Literature, 1963), p. 97.

[6]Russell Baker, "Talking Clothes," *The New York Times Magazine* (December 7, 1975), p. 6.

[7]Harriet T. McJimsey, *Art and Fashion in Clothing Selection* (Ames, Iowa: Iowa State University Press, 1973), p. 12.

1935 1947 1967

FIGURE 1-2.

From the foregoing discussion, a definition of fashion can now be summarized as follows: *The imitation and general acceptance of certain apparel and accessories which are produced and marketed by the fashion industry and are reflective of society's and individual prevailing values, attitudes, and beliefs.*

FOCUS ON THE INDUSTRY
DIANA VREELAND AND FASHION

The French word *doyenne* means the senior or highest ranking woman of a group. In the fashion business the *doyenne*- of fashion is Diana Vreeland.

Diana Vreeland is now Special Consultant to the Costume Institute of the Metropolitan Museum of Art. Prior to joining the museum in the early 70s, she enjoyed a brilliant editorial career which began in the 1930s and ended with her editorial retirement in 1971. During that time she was Fashion Editor for *Harper's Bazaar* and—her final editorial job—Editor-in-Chief of Vogue.

An individualist, her policy at these magazines was always to present the newest and most original in fashion. She loved the fashion period of the 60s. For her it was a time to break with tradition. Her philosophy was reflected in the bizarre fashions which she chose to appear on Vogue's pages. Very articulate, she is famous for coining words which, because they are so often quoted, sometimes became part of fashion's vocabulary. "Pizzaz" for instance, is a Vreeland word.

At the Metropolitan Museum of Art, Mrs. Vreeland has continued to display her brilliance and originality, creating several imaginative exhibits of contemporary as well as period costume. The exhibits have included a collection of fashions from the first thirty years of the twentieth century; an exhibit of the work of the leading Hollywood designers; and an exhibit of the costumes of Czarist Russia. These, as well as all the other exhibits she has created at the museum, have received much praise and acclaim.

It is to be expected that Diana Vreeland would have strong opinions on clothes and fashion. She feels it is terribly important for everyone to take the time to think about clothes—not an enormous amount of time—but certainly enough time to enable one to dress well every day of one's life. However, she also feels, clothes alone don't make the person. One's physical well being and mental alertness are of equal importance and every effort should be made to care for one's body and stimulate one's mind. As for fashion, *fashion is all-encompassing* to Diana Vreeland. It's something which enters into everything in a person's life, into everything one does, whether it's walking, talking, breathing, thinking, eating, sleeping—even loving. Those who know Diana Vreeland agree that, as the *doyenne* of fashion, fashion is certainly an all-encompassing force of her life.

DEFINING THE TERMS OF FASHION

As is true in any industry, the fashion business has a jargon or language all its own. When words or terms are used by those who work in the fashion industry, they have specific and technical meanings. Anyone

FIGURE 1-3. Diana Vreeland

learning the business of fashion must first become familiar with its special language.

Style

The term *style* refers to the characteristic inherent in a specific person, place, or thing. A singer sings in a particular style—rock, folk, or pop. Furniture may be chosen in many styles—among them Early American, French Provincial, or Contemporary. In apparel, the distinctive appearance of a garment through its shape, detail, and other visible design elements marks its style. This appearance immediately sets it apart from other styles.

Skirts are a style. Pants are also a style. But sometimes, certain characteristics are so pronounced within a large style classification, like pants, that those characteristics develop into their own style. There are styles within styles. For example, bell-bottom pants, straight-legged pants, and jeans have all become *styles* of pants. In essence, then, style refers to the visible characteristics of an item of wearing apparel. It does not refer to acceptance. It is incorrect to say that "pants are in style."

Pants are a style. It is proper to say that "pants are in fashion" or that "the fashion is for pants." Fashion refers to acceptance. Style refers to characteristics.

A basic style, though sometimes modified to conform to current fashion trends, always remains the same. For instance, the shirtwaist is a style of dress which features as its basic characteristics a partial or complete button-front closing, notched collar, and cuffed sleeves. The di-

FIGURE 1-4. Variations of the shirtwaist dress—a basic style

mensions of the sleeves and skirt may change and some other details may vary throughout different periods of fashion (see Fig. 1-4), but the basic characteristics which make up a shirtwaist style remain the same. The Empire style of the nineteenth century featured a high waistline, placed directly under the bustline as its major characteristic. Today, any dress or coat featuring this high placed waistline is identified as an Empire style. Blue jeans, introduced more than one hundred years ago during the gold rush of the 1840s, have changed very little since then. They are still made of denim, top-stitched, and riveted. Today, "jeans" is an accepted description for that style of pants.

Style, then, refers to the basic characteristics of an item of clothing. A style may grow or diminish in popularity throughout the years. It may be modified slightly to conform to the current fashion trends. But a style remains a style and its basic characteristics do not change.

In the fashion industry, the word *style* is also used by manufacturers and retailers in another way. A manufacturer gives each item produced a number for identification purposes. That item is then referred to as "style 00" or "style number 00." When store buyers order and reorder that particular item or design, they always refer to it as "style number 00." In this instance the word *style* is not used in reference to the characteristics of an item. It is simply taking the place of the word *item.*

Design and Its Elements

A *design* is simply a unique version of a style. For instance, though a shirtwaist is a style of dress, it can be interpreted in many ways. Its silhouette, fabric, and detail or trim can vary. These variations contribute toward its overall appearance, creating different versions of a shirtwaist style dress. Each version is called a *design.*

Silhouette, texture, color, detail and *trim* are the basic elements which form all design. Whether it be for architecture, automobiles, or wearing apparel, these elements contribute to the overall concept of design. They are the basic resources of all designers. When one of these elements is changed, the original design is altered and it takes on a different appearance, resulting in a new design.

Silhouette. The general outline or shape of a costume is its *silhouette.* There are three basic silhouettes. They are the straight or tubular line, the bell-shaped or curved, and the back fullness or bustle (see Fig. 1-5). Throughout the history of fashion, all costumes have related to these three basic silhouettes.

Texture. The appearance and the "hand" or feel of a fabric is called its *texture.* It is an important element, contributing toward the total concept of a design in the following ways:

FIGURE 1-5. Three basic silhouettes

The texture of a fabric contributes toward the *appearance* of a garment. For example, a rough, heavy tweed adds a casual dimension to a sports jacket, while a shiny satin offers sleek glitter to an evening dress. Either texture is an important factor in the appearance of each garment.

The texture of a fabric can contribute toward *performance* in a garment. Tweed is a fabric which "tailors" well, taking naturally to the precise sewing and pressing required in a sports jacket. For an evening dress satin "drapes" well, falling in soft folds while clinging attractively to the curves of the body. Both textures perform correctly during the construction and the wearing of each garment.

The texture of a fabric also contributes toward the quality of *color* in a garment. Light is absorbed by rough surfaces and colors become muted or dull. A tweed's rough texture reflects muted color, tonalities which are deemed fashionable and totally appropriate for a casual sports jacket. On the other hand, light is reflected from smooth surfaces, brightening colors and making them brilliant. Because of its smoothness, color in satin is rich and bright. This rich color adds another exciting dimension to the design of an evening dress.

Finally, the texture of a fabric contributes toward the *acceptance* of a garment. The way a garment looks and feels—its "eye appeal" and its "touch appeal"—are tremendous factors in its desirability. The soft, muted color and the rough texture of a tweed looks and feels appropriate for a sports jacket. The sleekness of satin flatters the figure while feeling luxurious on the body and to the touch. Both textures, the tweed and the satin, through their "eye" and "touch appeal," make a great contribution toward the ultimate sale of a garment, its acceptance.

Color. Color is a phenomenon of light which, in a visual sense, distinguishes one object from another. It specifically applies to such qualities as red, yellow, or blue, and because of its immediate impact can be the most important element in design. Many forces govern color preferences and they are all taken into consideration in the creation of a design.

One of these forces is emotional or psychological. Psychologists have done extensive research to determine the reaction of human beings to color. They have discovered that all colors are capable of working some kind of an emotional response. Peace, calm, excitement, violence, fear, and joy are some responses commonly experienced by people as they are exposed to various colors. Each color seems to have its own emotional impact. The "cool" blues and greens are calming. Orange and red suggest excitement and, because of fire, sometimes fear. And yellow, probably due to its identification with the bright sunshine, is considered a color of joy.

Color also has historical and traditional meanings. Purple has long been associated with royalty. White with brides, black with mourning. "Baby blue" and "baby pink" with infants. These colors are certainly not relegated to be worn solely by these groups, but they, and other colors, continue to have well-known, traditional connotations.

In fashion, forces of change cause color preferences to run in cycles. When pale colors have been popular, deeper shades begin to look "new." If color has been "hot"—bright and deep in its intensity—softer color interpretations seem to be a welcome change. These changes do not occur dramatically. They evolve over a period of several seasons, with colors deepening or lightening in successive steps. These color changes are part of a color "cycle."

Changes in color are made by experts in the textile and dress design fields. They understand all the forces which govern color preferences and they take all these forces, including the cycle of color, into consideration when preparing the colors for a season.

Detail. The various components or parts within a silhouette are called its *detail.* These parts include collars, sleeves, shoulder treatments, waist treatments, and the length and width of skirts and pants. By changing any of these details, the design of a garment can be transformed. If the change is in the skirt, the silhouette is also transformed.

These changes can be made by altering the dimensions of a detail. Collars can be widened, narrowed, or removed. Sleeves can vary in shape and length. Waistlines can be placed anywhere between the bustline and the hips, or totally eliminated. And the dimensions of a skirt can be changed in a myriad of ways, including its always controversial length.

Trim. Trims are decorative additions which are not part of the general construction of a garment. They include buttons, belts, buckles, stitching, embroidery, appliqués, beading, and edgings.

The type of trim which is used on a garment contributes a great deal toward the overall appearance and characteristics of the design. A nightgown immediately becomes "feminine" through the application of lace. Replace the lace with plain edging or remove it altogether and the nightgown retains its "tailored" look.

The choice of trim is often governed by the other elements of a design. Heavy fabric and rough texture naturally dictate heavy buttons. An emphasis on the waistline often suggests an emphasis on belts. Like silhouette, texture, color, and detail, trim is an important tool in creating a design.

Classics

Styles or designs which remain in fashion year after year are known as *classics.* They are simple in design and this simplicity insures their popularity since they easily integrate into current fashion. Minor

FIGURE 1-6. A classic—the Chanel suit.

changes, like a skirt length, are usually all that is necessary to up-date a classic, and its basic styling remains the same.

Though all classics are generally acceptable at all times, there are some that enjoy special acceptance, becoming preferred. The Chanel suit is a perfect example of a preferred classic (see Fig. 1-6). Designed after World War II by the famous French designer Coco Chanel, it features a simple cardigan jacket and a straight, slightly flared or pleated skirt. Throughout the years, some of its detail and trim has varied, but its silhouette has remained the same. It is just as wearable and as fashionable today as it was when Coco Chanel introduced it in 1954. And in some high fashion circles, an original Chanel suit takes preference over anything introduced into the current season.

The trench coat is another example of a classic. First worn by British soldiers fighting in the trenches during World War I, its popularity with men and women has existed for decades and will undoubtedly continue for many more.

Some other styles which are considered classics are the shirtwaist dress, the cardigan sweater, the navy pea jacket, and the blazer jacket. They are among many of those styles which remain consistently the same throughout periods of fashion. They require minor, if any, changes to acquire a contemporary appearance, thus earning the coveted label of "classic."

Fad

Though classics remain in fashion year after year, other styles or designs gain and lose their popularity within a brief period of time. These fashions are called *fads*.

Unlike classics, most fads are not simple in styling. Often they are extreme, causing people to tire of them quickly. The "hot pants" of 1971 were a fad. Though short pants, or "shorts," as they are popularly known, are an accepted item in sportwear, these brief pants were introduced for streetwear. They became very popular that spring and were worn anytime and any place, including for evening wear. By the fall their popularity had vanished as quickly as it arrived.

Sometimes fads, if they are well designed and answer a need, remain in fashion for an acceptable duration and may even go on to become classics. Back in the 1930s and 1940s, sunglasses were worn strictly for practical purposes: to protect the eyes from the glare of the sun when outdoors or at the beach. Only movie stars wore dark glasses indoors. During the early part of the 1960s wearing sunglasses indoors became a popular fad. Everyone wore them, on the head as a "headband" as well as over the eyes. The pretentious connotation began to disappear. Sunglass manufacturers quickly recognized the new trend and provided lenses safe for indoor lighting. Today, sunglasses are considered a basic accessory, necessary from a fashion as well as a practical point of view.

Accessories

Accessories are items which accompany a dress, suit, or other basic items of wearing apparel. Hats, gloves, jewelry, scarves, belts, handbags, and shoes are all considered accessories. Though most are necessary articles of clothing, they, and other items like them, also serve to complement a garment and are important in obtaining a complete or "total" look.

Designers, stylists, and fashion coordinators from other areas of wearing apparel work very closely with the accessory makers. They are keenly aware of the role the "right" accessories play in projecting current trends or looks. This close relationship automatically influences the trends within the accessory market. For instance, when the emphasis in dresses is on a narrow, defined waistline, wider belts are needed to point out that emphasis.

The popularity of an accessory shifts with apparel trends. Belts may be important when waists are defined, but they become obsolete should the fashion trend veer toward a straight or tubular silhouette.

Today, fashion is moving away from the fads and flamboyance of recent years. The return to classicism increases the emphasis on accessories. Stores across the country reflect this emphasis by featuring large, well-stocked diversified accessory departments.

Trend

The direction fashion is taking is called a *trend.* Many trends may exist at one time, each one experiencing various levels of acceptance. As a fashion gains popularity, it is called an *incoming trend;* as its popularity diminishes, it is called an *outgoing trend.*

Manufacturers and retailers capitalize on trends. Much of the success of their business is based upon their ability to recognize and predict current and future fashion trends. This prediction is called *fashion forecasting.* It is done by talented professionals who are knowledgeable in every aspect of fashion.

The life style, environment, occupation, financial and social status of individuals are factors which motivate tastes and buying habits of consumers. Prevailing economic and social conditions of the country are additional influencing factors. Fashion professionals research and evaluate these conditions to determine new developments within the fashion industry. Armed with this information, it becomes possible to recognize and predict current and future fashion trends.

The following analysis is a typical example of an industry fashion report—dateline November 1977. It illustrates how the previously defined fashion terms are integrated into the everyday vocabulary of the fashion professionals as they analyze and discuss fashion trends.

FOCUS ON THE INDUSTRY

A NEW TREND—THE SOFTENED SHAPE OF PANTS

Several years ago, designers began to veer away from wide bell-bottom pants, giving us styles which featured a modified flare or a straight-leg silhouette. Belt carriers and sharply creased waistline tucks were added for a menswear look and these rather classic trousers have been popular ever since. But the overall shape of clothing has loosened up and for spring '78, designers are now starting to change and soften the shape of pants.

The new pants are full on top and narrow at the ankle. Many styles are available in this new silhouette, but the majority of the designs have waist pleats or gathers as softening details. Lengths too have changed. No longer must pants cover the shoe, dragging along the pavement. The new pants are cropped above the ankle to show off a pretty high heeled shoe. Preferably, it should be a sandal—the new season's hottest accessory.

Fabrics do much to contribute to the softness of the new shapes. All are lightweight and supple and many are of a smooth and silky texture.

A few sneak previews of some very early Fall '78 lines have confirmed our opinion that this new fashion constitutes a lasting and important trend. Most designers are including the new pants as part of the "loose and baggy" story and none considers them a fad. The consensus of opinion it seems, is that pegged trousers are definitely here to stay.

TERMS TO REMEMBER

Fashion
Fashion Marketing
Style
Design and its elements
Classic
Fad
Accessories
Trend
Fashion Forecasting

HIGHLIGHTS OF THE CHAPTER

- Fashion means a general acceptance of a prevailing style at a given time.
- Fashion is a business whose goal is to satisfy apparel and accessory wants and needs of consumers.
- Fashion is innovative. It constantly varies the selection of fashion goods offered to consumers.
- The fashion industry has been charged with using "planned obsolescence of desirability" in order to give customers a variety of goods.
- Fashion reflects popular values of society. As these values change, so does fashion.
- Fashion means imitation. Ideas must be copied, mass produced and mass merchandised.
- Fashion offers a way to visibly express one's personality, role, and desired status in society.
- A style is specific characteristics of fashion.
- The elements of design are silhouette, texture, color, detail, and trim.

QUESTIONS

1. What is planned obsolescence? How can it apply to the fashion industry?
2. Fashion means acceptance. Explain this concept.
3. Define conspicous consumption. Give two examples of fashion apparel which connotes status.
4. What is the difference between a classic fashion and a fad? Give an example of each.
5. Fashion means imitation, yet not all who are fashionable look alike. Explain.
6. How does clothing express "sex appeal"?
7. Why is it important for the fashion business to "know the customer"?
8. Define and give three examples of accessories.
9. What is high fashion? What is its significance to fashion producers?
10. How is color used as an element of design?
11. Give an example of a present fashion trend.
12. Name the five elements of design.

2

THE WHY AND HOW OF FASHION

OBJECTIVES

After reading this chapter, you should be able to:

- Identify and discuss four theories which explain how and why clothing began.
- Describe the various roles and functions clothing performs today.
- Discuss the environmental factors which cause fashion changes.
- Cite the five principles which underlie fashion movements.
- Analyze fashion movements in terms of three processes.
- Explain the four stages of the Fashion Life Cycle.
- Describe how basic styling characteristics and merchandise characteristics affect the life cycle of fashion goods.

The successful marketing of merchandise—be it fashion or otherwise—is accomplished by satisfying the wants and needs of the customer. Therefore, an analysis of the desires, ambitions, background, life styles, and underlying motives which govern the behavior of that customer is essential for a merchant in order for him to develop a marketing plan.

From this perspective, students of fashion marketing must familiarize themselves with the role that clothing and accessories play in the satisfaction of these human wants and needs. Why and how did wearing apparel originate? Why and how did and does it continue to be used? What purpose does it serve? The answers to these and other questions will be discussed in this chapter.

CLOTHING: HOW AND WHY IT BEGAN

From the earliest recorded history, we have learned that humans were never content with an unadorned, uncovered body. Instead they chose to put upon themselves a variety of articles such as animal skins, teeth, leaves, and vegetable dyes. This crude form of dressing is still observable in the primitive societies of today, which leads many psychologists and anthropologists to conclude that clothing—from the simplest to the most lavish of costumes—does serve to satisfy *basic* as well as *specific* human wants and needs. Simply stated, where there is human life there is evidence of a *need* for some form of dress. Although this need premise is generally accepted, a difference of opinion arises when further analysis into how and why clothing originated is undertaken.

Three basic theories on the origins of clothing have been developed. Each theory contends that clothing materialized to satisfy a *single* human want or need. These theories are *the Protection Theory, the Modesty Theory,* and *the Adornment Theory.* Each offers plausible explanations for the origins and purpose of dress. But individually, each is inconclusive. The authors therefore propose a fourth theory, one which is multi-dimensional and proposes that dress cannot be traced back to a single need; but that it was devised to satisfy *several* human wants and needs at one time. In other words, *the Combined-Need Theory* contends that most dress is devised for the purpose of meeting more than one of the three human needs for protection, modesty, and adornment.

The Protection Theory

Probably the simplest and most practical explanation for wearing clothes is the need to obtain physical protection. Humans are relatively hairless and thin-skinned. Naked, they are quite defenseless against the elements, the environment, and other living creatures. Consequently, all humans have a basic and very real need for some type of shelter or protection.

In the beginning, caves, trees, huts, and so on, provided this necessary coverture; but these were stationary and clothing was an attempt to make protection portable. Animal skins were draped over the body providing warmth and insulation from the wind. Tree parts and vegetation were fashioned into body garments and headcoverings as a shield of relief from the sun. Leaves or bark were tied around the waist by males to protect otherwise exposed genitals. Bark and skins were wrapped around the feet to make walking more comfortable and prevent bites and stings from insects and other animals. Finally, since humans needed protection against their own species, they covered certain parts of their body, hoping to become more effective in battle.

Not all dressing was devised solely for physical protection. Some clothing was worn as "psychological armor" to provide humans with a defense against evil spirits. Certain articles of clothing and accessories were believed to have magical powers against demons and the "evil eye." Shells and other items were placed close to the sex organs in the belief that they would prevent "sterility and pain."[1]

During religious ceremonies and tribal rites, costumes also played an essential role in protecting individuals and property from the wrath of the gods.

Throughout history many articles of clothing have been devised for the purpose of protecting the wearer. Some examples are suits of armor, helmets, umbrellas, chastity belts, diving suits, rain coats, and—the ultimate in protection—the space suit used by astronauts. However, one does not have to be a fashion or history expert to realize that even among the earliest civilizations articles of wearing apparel were not solely protective in design. This led to the development of the second explanation on the origin and purpose of clothing: that the human species was and is motivated to cover the body out of a sense of shame or modesty.

The Modesty Theory

Modesty is defined as behaving properly in dress, speech, or conduct. In all societies and with most people, a failure to do so results in feelings of personal shame.

In dress, personal shame has been the most widely proposed rationalization for the origin and purpose of dress. It is the overriding concept of the modesty theory.

The causes of this shame are open to speculation. There are two schools of thought. The first school endorses the premise that humans are *born* with *inherent* shame, the second insists that they *learn* to be ashamed.

Inherent Shame. The advocates of *inherent shame* have humans *instinctively* covering certain parts of their anatomy because they are *inherently*

[1]James Laver, *Modesty in Dress* (Boston: Houghton Mifflin Company), p. 7. Copyright © 1969 by James Laver. Used by permission.

ashamed of them. In other words, they propose men and women are *born* with a shame instinct.

Proponents of this reasoning base their thinking on the Bible. They cite the story of the fall of man in the Book of Genesis. As the story unfolds, Adam and Eve eat the forbidden fruit from the tree of knowledge of good and evil. This act made them aware of their nakedness and for the first time, they were ashamed. As a consequence, they covered themselves with aprons made of fig leaves. When the Lord discovered their disobedience, he punished them by making coats of animal skins for each of them and by expelling them from the Garden of Eden. The shame and guilt of Adam and Eve's Original Sin was then forevermore inherited by all human beings.

Based on this story, it follows, then, that like Adam and Eve, humans cover their body—particularly the sex organs—out of an innate sense of shame.

Learned Shame. For centuries, inherent shame was universally accepted as the basis for modesty in dress. However, as the disciplines of psychology, sociology, and anthropology were developed, it became apparent that in this theory much about dress and behavior was left unexplained.

For example, no evidence has been found to support the notion that humans are instinctively ashamed of their body or that guilt feelings pertain only to nakedness. Nor is there any support for the notion that they feel compelled to cover their sex organs. In fact, there is much evidence to the contrary.

This evidence is found in both the primitive and the civilized worlds.

For instance, along the Amazon, the Botocudo Tribe women are ashamed to be seen without wooden plugs in their earlobes and lower lip, but are unaffected if their breasts are exposed. Among the Australian Aborigines, it is shameful to be seen eating, but perfectly all right to be seen naked. And in the Arab world, it is important for the woman's face to remain veiled—more so than any other part of her body.

In the Western world, there have been periods in history when it was considered "sinful" for a woman to expose her ankle or shoulder while at other times it was socially acceptable for unmarried women to expose their breasts. Today, men and women may appear at the beach in scanty bikinis without feeling a sense of shame over their nearly naked bodies and without fearing the disapproval of society. However, it is not likely that this attire would be considered by most as appropriate for street wear.

These examples lead to the conclusion that a sense of shame and modesty is not inborn, but is instead a *learned behavior;* that is, one governed by customs, traditions, and mores of a culture or a society at a particular time. If a certain part of the body is customarily covered up, then exposing it is immodest. If certain apparel is accepted as suitable for one occasion or place, then wearing it other times is inappropriate.

We must conclude, therefore, that modesty is the result of a socialization process; that people are *taught* proper attire and dress. Only then do they understand and live by the concepts of modesty and shame. It is not an inherited trait. "A sense of modesty is," according to noted anthropologist E. A. Hoebel, "merely a habit, not an instinct."[2]

Since modesty is a learned behavior, we may also conclude that it is unlikely that modesty was the original need which prompted primitive peoples to cover their bodies.

The Adornment Theory

The protection and modesty theories have established that early humans may have initially covered the body for protection and because of a sense of shame. These two theories, however, do not explain a third phenomenon—the preoccupation with the beautification and adornment of the body.

The urge for self-adornment has always been compelling. Even before men and women discovered materials to fashion into some form of apparel, they enjoyed decorating their bodies. Noted fashion historian James Laver emphasized this point when he wrote that "a delight in decoration was, of course, present even before clothes were invented."[3] Laver was referring to such uncanny techniques as body painting, tattooing, cicatrization, piercing, and body deformation—all devised by man to achieve a desired self-image (see Fig. 2-1).

Upon analyzing this preoccupation with beautification, many social scientists have come to the conclusion that *adornment* is the logical explanation for the origin of clothing. The original purpose of clothing they claim, was to enhance one's *self-concept* and *self-image,* rather than to protect or hide the body. Humans, they propose, want to call attention to themselves, thereby satisfying several conscious and unconscious ego needs. They list these needs as *self-beautification;* improving *sexual attractiveness;* and establishing *social status.* There are differing opinions, however, as to which of those particular needs dominates.

Self-Beautification. Most theorists propose self-beautification as the uppermost ego need. Though the definition of what is beautiful varies,

[2]E. A. Hoebel, *Man in The Primitive World: An Introduction to Anthropology,* 2nd ed. (New York: McGraw-Hill, 1958), pp. 248–249.

[3]James Laver, *Modesty in Dress* (Boston: Houghton Mifflin Company), p. 31. Copyright © 1969 by James Laver. Used by permission.

FIGURE 2-1. a) Tattooed native of Nukahiwa
Courtesy: American Museum of Natural History, New York

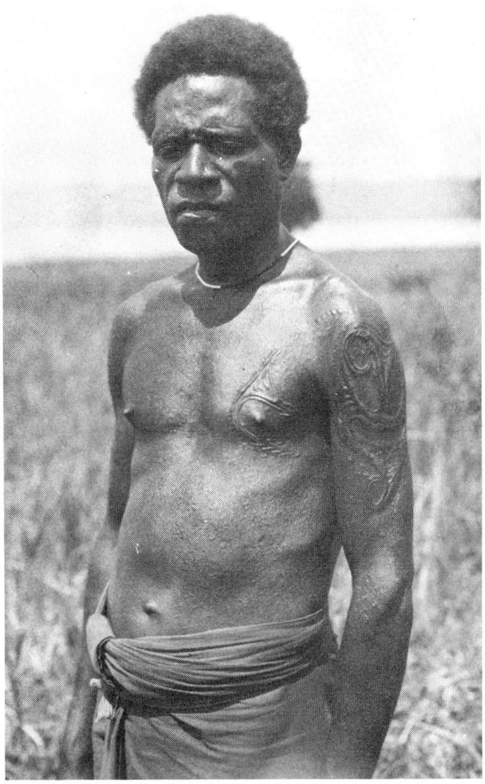

FIGURE 2-1. b) A native with body scarring—cicatrization
Courtesy: American Museum of Natural History, New York

aesthetic pursuits and a search for beauty are universal. To please themselves, humans have always pursued their own particular concept of beauty. By exposing some parts of the body and covering other parts they have been able to emphasize their desirable physical qualities and to hide their flaws. In doing so, their need for self-beautification is satisfied.

Sexual Attraction. Other sociologists feel that the ego need most satisfied by dress is that of *being sexually attractive.* Clothing has always played a role in sexual stimulation and the poet Robert Burton observes, "The greatest provocations of lust are from our apparel."[4]

[4]Quoted in H. M. Evans, *Man The Designer* (New York: Macmillan, 1973), p. 305.

FIGURE 2-2. Dancing girl of the Arokaiwas
Courtesy: American Museum of Natural History, New York

Different cultures consider different parts of the body sexually stimulating. Some of those cultures expose those parts of their bodies they find sexually exciting. Most cultures prefer to conceal the sexually stimulating portions of their bodies, considering complete nudity not nearly as alluring as suggestive concealment (see Fig. 2-2).

Social Status. Still a third group of scientists take the position that people are forever striving for social supremacy over other people and that man uses dress mostly as a means to display his *social status.*

For instance, by wearing lavish, expensive clothing, the wealthy use dress as a means of conveying to others their social and economic superiority.

Similarly, the dress of primitive groups can also convey the rank and power of persons within those groups. Among the American Indians, for example, braves may wear one or two feathers in their hair but only their chief may wear an elaborate headpiece consisting of many beautiful feathers.

Wearing desirable insignias and uniforms is another means of displaying a preferred status in society. They provide instant identification with a preferred group or social class and thereby generate self-pride and self-worth.

The above conclusions of the Adornment Theory, then, are that man devised apparel as a means of beautifying his body, attracting a mate, or obtaining social acceptance and superiority. All are plausible proposals. But like the Protection and Modesty Theories, when taken individually these conclusions are only partial explanations for the origin of clothes.

The Combined-Need Theory

Upon reviewing the Protection, Modesty, and Adornment Theories, it is apparent that each of the theories contains intelligent, justifiable, but incomplete explanations for the origin of clothing.

The Combined-Need Theory accepts some of the premises of these theories and uses these concepts to enhance the idea that *from the beginning,* clothing needs were *multidimensional.* Focusing on only one need to the exclusion of others seems incorrect. Clothing satisfies several needs concurrently.

The Combined-Need Theory borrows heavily from the work of psychologist *A. H. Maslow.* His theory, known as *The Hierarchy of Needs,* describes the human being as an ever-wanting animal whose behavior is determined by a priority of needs (see Fig. 2-3).

Everyone begins in need of satisfying level one. Once these needs are generally met then behavior is governed by the urgency to satisfy level two and so on up to level five. Thus a person's behavior is a result of functioning at a particular need level. He or she does not advance upward until the present level needs are met.

For example, if a person is at level four in terms of needs, then it is assumed the lower-level needs have been satisfied and that they no longer motivate that person's behavior.

In applying this concept to the origins of clothing it is reasonable to state that the motives for dress depend upon which level of need a person is functioning on. If climatic and environmental conditions are such that a person is in need of shelter and safety—levels one and two—then dressing will be practical and protective. It will be prompted by needs similar to those outlined in the Protective Theory. Since sex is also a need on level one, dressing might also incorporate the sexual attractiveness of the Adornment Theory.

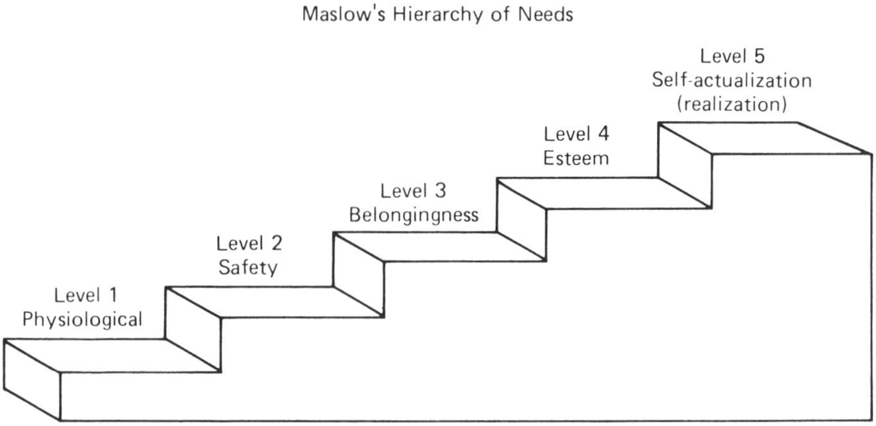

FIGURE 2-3. Maslow's Hierarchy of Needs

*Data for figure based on "Hierarchy of Needs" in "Theory of Human Motivation" from *Motivation and Personality,* 2nd ed., by Abraham H. Maslow. Copyright © 1970 by Abraham H. Maslow. By permission of Harper & Row, Publishers, Inc.

After these basic needs are met, either by clothing or some other means, then apparel will be chosen for reasons listed on level three. At this level, the wearer's choice of clothing will conform to that worn by his or her peer groups, providing that person with acceptance and a sense of belonging. The needs of this level are similar to the needs outlined in the Modesty Theory where acceptance is an important motive for modesty in dress.

Once these levels of need are met then the wearer moves up to level four where one can personalize and individualize one's appearance. By doing so, the wearer enhances his or her self-esteem and gains prestige from contemporaries on level four. This need to step to level four may be compared with the social status and beautification ego needs of the Adornment Theory. The step, however, can only be taken if the wearer is not ostracized by the groups on level three and if the basic safety and physiological needs on levels one and two continue to be met.

It is difficult to determine the role clothing plays in satisfying, self-actualization—Maslow's fifth and ultimate need. This is an internalized need dealing with maximizing one's potential in terms of creative ability. External factors such as appearance relate to the four lower levels of needs. However, if clothing helps to satisfy those lower level needs, then it allows a person to move upward and expand creatively within the highest level.

Today, most apparel does not perform merely one function. Nor does it satisfy one need. Instead it may protect, allow for conformity and provide a means of self expression—all at the same time. It appears to have had this multidimensional role from its inception. *Therefore, the origin of clothing seems most plausible if viewed as always having satisfied combined needs.* Fashion author Karlene Anspach summarizes several aspects of the Combined-Need Theory in the following quote:

> Theoretically, man's wants are unlimited. They vary among people and places, from time to time, but the urgency of wants does not appreciably diminish as more are filled. When man has satisfied his physical needs, his psychologically grounded desires take over. He demands high fashion clothing, foreign made cars and original paintings rather than food for hunger or clothes for warmth.[5]

ROLE OF CLOTHING TODAY

As societies develop and become more complex, the amount and variety of clothing available for use and consumption increases. When this occurs, dressing takes on added meaning. Not only do clothes satisfy personal needs but they also reflect predominant values of a people and a society at a given time. In this sense, today's clothing provides both psychological and sociological insight into people and their worlds.

Clothing Expresses Personality

Personality is defined as the set of unique behavioral and emotional characteristics possessed by an individual. It is the sum total of everything a person has inherited and learned and experienced.

The Combined-Need Theory states that, from the beginning, clothing satisfied several personal needs at the same time. This basic premise can now be expanded also to include a person's feelings, beliefs, attitudes, and moods. Thus, clothing becomes an accurate expression of personality—a visible, tangible extension of who we are and how we feel about ourselves.

Our choice of clothing can also help to compensate for negative feelings of *depression, insecurity,* or *rebellion.*

Until the present hatless generation, the old cliché "nothing perks up a woman like a new hat" had merit and is an appropriate illustration of how apparel offsets *depression.* For some people, today's "picker-upper" might be designer labeled merchandise—one of the present status symbols.

[5]Karlene Anspach, *The Why of Fashion* (Ames, Iowa: Iowa State University Press, 1967), p. 3.

An initialed Gucci handbag can also compensate for *emotional insecurity* by giving the wearer an immediate identification with success. Psychologists have discovered that the use of clothing as a "fashion security blanket" is so compelling that people are even willing to suffer physical discomfort for it.

Clothing can also be used to make a statement of disapproval and *rebellion.* The unkempt look and "dressing down" syndrome so popular with the youth of the late 60s is an example of the use of clothing to broadcast rebellion. It was a way to vent feelings of fear, frustration, and anxiety against a much disputed Viet Nam war and other policies of the Establishment.

Clothing Communicates

Since clothing makes up a major part of one's appearance, it plays a vital role in the impressions people make on each other. First impressions, quickly made and largely determined by appearance, are usually based on the wearer's clothing.

In this sense, clothing is a form of non-verbal communication. In many ways it speeds up and enhances the communication process. For instance, because of an easily identifiable uniform, a flight attendant, police officer, or teammate can be recognized quickly and spoken to in specific terms.

Of course communication can be adversely affected when people are stereotyped because of their appearance. For example, a job applicant may not even get an interview because he or she walks into an office dressed in jeans.

Though most people may consider it wrong to judge a book by its cover or a person by his clothing, marketing experts recognize packaging as an important element in consumer purchasing decisions. It may very well be that clothing—our outer packaging—plays the same important role in influencing others and affecting the way they react to us.

Clothing as a Dimension of Time

Historically, clothing of the past has been identified regionally. Apparel worn by different groups was typically identified as Grecian, Roman, Egyptian, and so on. Today, designations which refer to places or nationality do not seem appropriate. Fashion apparel in the modern world is no longer a function of place but a function of *time.*

Fashion historian James Laver suggested that the "victory of time over place"[6] occured in the 1400s at the end of the Middle Ages. He

[6]James Laver, *Modesty in Dress* (Boston: Houghton Mifflin Company), p. 3. Copyright © 1969 by James Laver. Used by permission.

FIGURE 2-4.

suggests it was the rise of the French Court and the prospering bourgeoisie which accounts for this change.

> Such an event, such an acceptance of change, is the beginning of modernity. It is the emergence of the mobile modern world from the static world of the early Middle Ages. . . . no longer did people dress according to their nationality or even according to their position in society but according to the year.[7]

From then on it became easier to *date* a person than to determine his nationality. That is, by looking at apparel, one could more easily determine the period in history in which it was in fashion than the country in which it was worn. For example, by looking at Figure 2-4, it is apparent that this type of dress was popular in the 1920s. Certainly the

[7] *Ibid.*

look was not limited to one country, but rather was an accepted fashion worn by most of the modern world.

Clothing not only helps in identifying a period in time, it also helps become accustomed to change and successfully learn to cope with its consequences.

By introducing new styles of clothing, the fashion industry encourages change and emphasizes the future over the present and past. These time zones become easily recognizable through apparel. If people are futuristic about their wardrobe, they are considered to be progressive and moving in the right direction. If they wear styles that are current, they are considered correct. However, if they wear outdated styles they may be subject to ridicule, scorn, and even considered backward in their thinking. In the words of Paul Nystrom: "To be out of fashion is, indeed, to be out of the world."[8]

Clothing as a Symbol

One means of distinguishing the human species from other animals is through its use of symbols. Humans can comprehend the meaning of words and pictures and translate thoughts into various mediums. They may write poetry, sculpt, draw, or design a garment. In each case the finished product *symbolizes* a thought translated.

One such example of the symbolic use of clothing is seen in the dress of the Amish people. Their beliefs lead them to reject modern technology and its secular trappings for after-life spiritual rewards. Because their religion automatically rejects anything new, they wear the basic, unadorned clothing of their ancestors. This dress has become a symbol of their religion and their views.

This example should not imply that symbolism is limited to a unique group of people. Consciously or unconsciously, everyone translates his or her values and beliefs into his apparel.

Conscious effort was made by many blacks in the 60s to affirm their African heritage through fashion symbols. The diminishment of this effort was recently discussed in *The New York Times*:

> The African influenced fashions that came into vogue with many black people in the late 60s—first as political and cultural symbols—then as fashion items—recently seem to have all but disappeared from the city streets.[9]

[8]Paul H. Nystrom, *Economics of Fashion* (New York: The Ronald Press, 1928), p. iii.

[9]"African Fashions: Less and Less a Political Statement," *The New York Times* (March 16, 1976), p. 53.

The 1920s and its emancipation of women was symbolized by the bob haircut, a de-emphasis on the female body, and shockingly short skirts. Later in the 1960s, the liberated leg and mini skirt were illustrative of women's new-found freedom. Finally, women all over adopted pant suits which were as much a symbol of desired female equality as they were a symbol of casualness and comfort.

From these examples, it can be assumed that all apparel contains some kind of symbolism reflecting the predominant spirit and way of life of the times. "The dress of a nation reflects the core of beliefs of the nation and becomes a collective symbol of social identity."[10] In this sense what we wear symbolizes both our individual and societal values.

Clothing Channels Creativity

An increase in leisure time and affluence can be a mixed blessing. Of course relief from the drudgery of work and from financial burdens is welcomed. But what is to be done with the extra time and money? A lack of activity can become a primary cause of boredom and discontent.

Although some may argue that fashion is a superficial pastime, it can help channel activities and prevent boredom. It is an excellent means of self-expression; it offers an opportunity to experiment with new things; and it can be an outlet for the imagination.

All this is particularly so today when attitudes about fashion are totally unrestricted. As we move away from strict interpretation of what is proper and improper in attire, the opportunity to create and experiment with fashion increases. Dressing can become a pleasurable creative pastime. Designer Carol Horn expresses it best when she says:

> It's all right to experiment, it's all right to play. If someone takes clothes too seriously, it just means they spend a lot of money. It's more fun to develop your own style, your own potential.[11]

FACTORS INFLUENCING FASHION CHANGE

If there is one absolute constant concerning fashion, it is the fact that it is always changing. As pointed out in Chapter One, the causes for this continuous change can be found in the political-legal, social, technologi-

[10] Karlene Anspach, *The Why of Fashion* (Ames, Iowa: Iowa State University Press, 1967), p. xiv.

[11] Bernadine Morris, "Three Good Sports", *The New York Times Magazine* (Feb. 29, 1976), p. 36.

cal, economic, and seasonal environments. Within these general contexts, there are several specific factors which seem to directly govern both the amount and type of change in fashion. Some of these factors inhibit fashion change while others accelerate it.

The Political-Legal Environment

The methods a government uses to conduct its affairs and the formal rules it enacts make up the political-legal environment of a society. Within this environment, three factors affect fashion: sumptuary laws, foreign policy, and trade regulations.

Sumptuary Laws. A sumptuary law is traditionally defined as a law which prohibits lavish dress by regulating personal expenditures on extravagant and luxurious items. For the purpose of this text, the authors have enlarged upon that definition to include laws which control nudity.

There have been and continue to be several motives behind the passage of all types of sumptuary laws. These motives generally reflect the prevailing *social, religious,* and/or *moral* beliefs of a given time.

Historically, most sumptuary laws were used to maintain class distinction. For example, in previous centuries, French and English royalty decreed that only they could wear ermine, brocade, and other similar rich furs and fabrics.

At other times, however, the laws were religious in nature. During the 1600s, the elders of the Puritan Church in Massachusetts preached against "love of fashion" and, through their influence, laws restricting opulent dress were passed.

Sumptuary laws were also used to uphold prevailing moral standards. During different periods in history, puritanical beliefs against "nudity" outlawed garments which exposed the arms, legs, and even an ankle.

Today, passage of sumptuary laws seem to be motivated by two issues: *morality* and *environmental control.*

As in the past, the subject of nudity continues to be a moral issue. The unrealistic bans against exposing an ankle no longer exist, but many local governments continue trying to maintain prevailing moral standards by stemming the increasing trend toward extreme nudity. In those cities and states, the topless look and other similar revealing fashions are prohibited.

Laws have also been enacted to prevent the use of furs and skins from animals considered to be in danger of extinction. It is illegal for any United States citizen to purchase apparel and accessories made from the cheetah, leopard, alligator, or other animals listed by the government as an endangered species.

All sumptuary laws are, by nature, restrictive. By regulating materials and styles and limiting them to one particular group or forbidding them from society entirely, these laws encourage a more conservative style of dress. In terms of fashion change, therefore, sumptuary laws *inhibit* the movement of fashion.

Foreign Policy. The relationship between a country and the world community is another factor affecting fashion change. When a country encourages travel, business expansion, and interdependence with other nations, that country is exposed to foreign fashion inspiration and foreign goods. With more ideas and materials at hand, the fashion creativity of that country expands. A non-isolationist foreign policy, then, *accelerates* fashion movement. On the other hand, when a country is *isolationist* in its foreign relations, that policy *inhibits* fashion change.

Trade Regulations. The enactment of trade agreements between countries can also influence fashion change. When a country encourages trade with nations by reducing tariffs and increasing quotas, these favorable conditions stimulate trade and increase the import of foreign made goods. As these foreign goods arrive, they contain new ideas which introduce and *accelerate* fashion change. However, if a country partially or fully restricts the import of foreign fashion goods, fashion change slows down and is *inhibited.*

An excellent example of how favorable trade relations can accelerate fashion change is the recent exchange of ideas between this country and the Soviet Union. In 1976, the first American blue jeans ever to be sold to Russia appeared in Russian department stores. They became the rage, selling at exorbitant prices. Russia, meanwhile, loaned the United States unusual historic costumes for the Russian Costume Exhibit at the Metropolitan Museum in New York. The exhibit helped to stimulate the popularity of the "peasant look" which was being introduced at that time.

The Social Environment

The way a society functions in terms of its structure, customs, and values provides the backdrop for fashion and fashion change. As social patterns undergo restructuring and re-evaluation, that change is often reflected in a corresponding change of life styles and, of course, dress. Some of the aspects of our society which have been the subject of recent radical change are: religion; class structure; levels of education; increased mobility and leisure time; the changing role of women; and a changing ideology or value system.

Religion. The amount of influence religion exerts on individuals usually affects their attitude toward fashion. Since religious leaders stress the importance of spiritual concerns over material ones, religion is viewed as an *inhibitor* of fashion change. Religion relies on traditions, customs, and habits, and in general resists change or, at best, accepts it slowly. As the religious influence in a society wanes, attitudes toward fashion and change become more positive. Today, a more casual attitude toward dressing for religious services is but one example of the lesser role played by this institution in governing fashion.

Class Structure. Over the past two-hundred years, the distinctions separating the upper, middle, and lower classes have blurred. With the redistribution of wealth the middle class has emerged as the largest and most important group in terms of buying power and in the successful adoption of new fashion. This *democratization* has *accelerated* and increased the demand for fashion goods and the rate of fashion change.

The correlation between the distribution of *wealth and fashion change* is explained by author Quentin Bell:

> . . . . fashionable changes can only occur when wealth is so distributed in a society as to allow more than one class to afford the luxury of sumptuous dress. There must, in addition to the ruling class, be a middle class, and this middle class must have the power, financial and political, to vie with that above it, to imitate its dress and defy its sumptuary laws.[12]

When the size and affluence of the middle class increases, fashion change occurs even more rapidly—it *accelerates.* Should there be an economic downturn, and the size and affluence of the middle class decreases, fashion change moves at a slower pace—it is *inhibited.* Consequently, the *economic* changes which take place in society and which relate to the middle class serve as important barometers for the fashion industry.

Levels of Education. Another factor which contributes to fashion change is education. In addition to increasing income, a higher level of education also increases aesthetic values and fashion tastes. With more money to spend and an increasingly sophisticated interest in fashion, the educated customer looks for new ideas and new fashion thus *accelerating* fashion change.

Increased Mobility and Leisure Time. In the last three decades, the average work week has declined sharply for many American workers.

[12]Quentin Bell, *On Human Finery,* p. 113. Reprinted by permission of Schocken Books, Inc., New York. Copyright © 1976.

This increased leisure time has been enhanced by increased mobility. The automobile, a system of national roadways, and the jet plane have turned leisure time into travel and vacation time.

These developments have increased the need for travel and vacation apparel. New fashions to meet that need are constantly being developed and introduced. Thus, the increase in mobility and leisure time has become a contributing factor toward *accelerating* fashion change.

The Changing Role of Women. Since three-fourths of the fashion merchandise produced in this country is for women, the role of this group in society greatly affects the fashion business.

Today, women are being given greater responsibilities and freedom. As their experiences and roles become more diverse, their fashion tastes, needs, expenditures, and purchasing power change accordingly. For example, more and more women are combining motherhood and housework with careers. Part of their additional income is spent on new wardrobe needs. As the role of women continues to evolve and change, this and other similar requirements and expenditures will emerge to favorably stimulate the fashion business and further *accelerate* fashion change.

Changing Ideologies. The kind of values that are important to a society at a given time directly influence taste and dress. Often, these prevailing values are embodied in persons who are admired, in groups who receive unusual amounts of attention and publicity, and in items or materials which are greatly sought after. These individuals, groups, and things in turn affect prevailing styles of behavior and dress.

Probably no one person received as much recognition in the last fifteen years as Jacqueline Kennedy Onassis. As first lady, her influence on fashion was profound. "The Jackie Kennedy look" came into being: a casual, understated fashion image. Part of the look attributed to Mrs. Kennedy included the pillbox hat and the bouffant hair-do (see Fig. 2-5).

At about the same time, an unknown rock group from England exploded onto the American scene. In addition to leaving a musical legacy, the Beatles are credited with changing the appearance of most young men in the mid-60s by popularizing longer hair styles and the Edwardian look.

After a while it was not a group of four singers who exemplified American values but that portion of the population known as "youth." In the turbulent mid-60s, they set the trends for a life style and much of fashion. Their "youth quake" was best expressed by blue jeans, love beads, and Army surplus clothing.

In turn, this group and its values gave way to the "back to nature" movement of the early 1970s which emphasized natural products and hand craftsmanship. After the turbulent 60s, this movement prefaced

FIGURE 2-5.

the trend toward quieter, less volatile fashion. By the mid-70s, the return and acceptance of soothing, quiet "classic" fashion was complete.

Since changes in values and ideologies have occurred rapidly in the past few decades, corresponding changes in fashion have been *accelerated.* If the status quo had remained intact for long periods of time, as in previous generations, then fashion changes would have been *inhibited* and occurred more slowly.

The two reports that follow illustrate how the fashion industry analyzes the social environment for an indication of how fashion is reflecting that environment. The first report examines the turbulent 60s and the second the rather complacent late 70s. Each deals with the social phenomena of their particular time: the youth quake of the mid-60s and the fashion freedom and absorption with self of the late 70s. Although the reports examine two eras with very different social environments, the technique used to analyze the relation between fashion and those social environments is identical in its approach.

FOCUS ON THE INDUSTRY

THE TEMPER AND TEMPO OF FASHION

Fall 1965

Gone is the "haughty" couture fashion customer. She disappeared with high heeled pointed shoes. Here instead is the young school girl . . . the young collegian . . . the young career girl . . . the young suburbanite . . . the young matron . . . all with diverse needs, cultural backgrounds, environment, tastes. The young junior may have a passion for the look of the London Mod. The career girl may be that marvelous customer who understands, accepts, and actually reveres the clean architectural neatness of Courrèges. The young matron may still yearn for a soft and feminine look, but wants it served with the all-important young approach. Each is adamant in her likes and dislikes. Each is very much her own type. And each is forever on the lookout for "my" look—"my" type. It's important for the retailer to recognize this search for individuality and perhaps to understand why it exists. But most important, it is imperative that the retailer recognize all these individuals as his fashion customers of toda;y.

The inspiration for all this is the temper and tempo of the times—quick, jet-paced, urgent, up-to and beyond the minute. Op art. Pop art. James Bond. Nureyev. Bogart. Moon rockets. Man rockets. Jackie

Kennedy. Barbra Streisand. The Beatles. The Mets. And Arthur's. These are all NOW! They equate with youth, movement, verve, zip, the current, and the avant-garde. In addition, each stands dynamically alone as an individual concept, idea, person, thing. And so it is with fashion. The "tomorrow is today," the "raciness" and the "individuality" which exist around us also key the current fashion story.[13]

Thirteen years later, a similar analysis. This time, one of fashion for Spring 1978.

FOCUS ON THE INDUSTRY

THE TEMPER AND TEMPO OF FASHION

Spring 1978

The fashion revolution of the 60s was responsible for radically changing the look of fashion. But its most lasting by-product was the permanent dissolution of the power structure within the directive forces of the fashion industry. By the time the youth quake simmered down at the end of the turbulent 60s, fashion's long established dictatorships—particularly those in Paris—had lost their power. Since then, people have worn what they pleased—vehemently rejecting unappealing fashion in spite of the dictates of the powers-that-be. In short, fashion has become *democratized.*

These are quiet times. Since the 60s America has indeed settled down. New movements have sprung up, but most are concerned with the self. Men and women are busy improving and discovering themselves. Yoga, meditation, psychiatry, jogging, tennis, and a host of similar activities are the self-absorbent interests of Americans today.

Both the preoccupation with self and the quiet of our social environment are very much reflected in fashion. Like the times,

[13]"The Temper and Tempo of Fashion . . . Fall 1965," *Fall 1965 Fashion Book* (New York: Allied Stores Corporation, 1965), excerpted and reprinted by permission.

clothes are relaxed—easy to wear. Fabrics are soft. Colors pretty. But, bent upon "doing their own thing," women will be wearing these pretty clothes in an exciting eclectic mix. Wearing what they want, wherever they want. Moreover, they'll choose clothes that will flatter. Clothes that will show off their "body beautiful" and their much cared-for healthy self. All in all, a delightful picture of what the contemporary woman will look like and be like in the spring and summer of 78.

Technology

Probably the one factor responsible for increasing the rate of all types of change in our country, has been the strides made in technology. No aspect of our lives has remained unaffected. However, four areas of technological improvements directly relate to fashion change. These are: mass media; textile technology; newer methods of production; and newer methods of distributing fashion goods.

Mass Media. As we will learn in Chapter 5, before the 1800s fashion information travelled very slowly. Fashion news took weeks and sometimes months to reach various cities and countries. As mass communication and transportation systems developed, the time span for disseminating information was dramatically shortened.

Today, transcontinental messages are received within seconds of the time they were transmitted. Through satellite, visual pictures and TV, programs can be shown simultaneously throughout the world.

Technology has also increased the number of people that can be reached. Through readily available newspapers, magazines, television, and radio, an overwhelming number of Americans of all economic backgrounds are immediately informed of important national and world events.

This up-to-the-minute reportage is also used to disseminate fashion information, and because today's fashion news travels to so many so quickly, fashion trends are immediately absorbed. This rapid absorbance often encourages fashion obsolescence, stimulating a demand for fashion change. The mass media, therefore, serves as an important factor toward the *acceleration* of fashion change.

Textile Technology. By improving the utilitarian and fashion characteristics of textiles, and by introducing new production methods, new fashion looks can and often do appear. One such improvement which revolutionized certain areas of wearing apparel was the introduction of stretch fabrics. These fabrics immediately replaced the traditional ones in ski-wear, hosiery, and intimate apparel. Machine double knits and bonded fabrics are two other excellent examples of past innovative successes. By developing fabrics such as these, technology stimulates and *accelerates* fashion change.

Improved Clothing Manufacturing Methods. The majority of steps in apparel production methods are mechanized, and in some cases, also automated. New technological advances which improve these methods have been and continue to be introduced. Sewing machines are now in use which are capable of sewing over 5000 stitches a minute. New cutting techniques have been developed that are saving both time and money. With these improvements, a greater variety of less costly merchandise is produced.

Consumers are stimulated into buying by the proliferation of these less expensive fashion goods. As they do so, they increase the movement of the goods and thus *accelerate* fashion change.

Methods of Distribution. Having merchandise readily available for the consumer is an important element of the marketing process. This is particularly true for fashion goods since today's consumer, informed about new styles and fashion trends, wants those goods immediately.

Technology has played a major role in bringing goods quickly to the consumer. Because of the improved air, rail, and highway transportation systems previously discussed, a manufacturer can ship goods rapidly and safely to retail customers throughout the country.

Merchants have also been able to meet consumer demand more efficiently by using computers for inventory control. Purchasing decisions can be made more accurately and quickly with these computerized systems. Improvements in the receiving and marking of merchandise have also speeded up the all important process of getting the goods onto the selling floor.

All these technological improvements in the distribution of fashion goods have resulted in the faster movement of merchandise and have greatly *accelerated* fashion change.

The Economic Environment

Technological improvements such as the ones previously discussed can only occur in an economy which is highly developed and self-sufficient. Therefore, the economic condition of a country greatly affects not only the fashion industry but all aspects of consumer and industrial life. There are, however, certain economic conditions that have a direct bearing on the rate of fashion change. These are the availability of resources, business expansion, consumer income, and the use of credit by the consumer.

Availability of Resources. In an economic context, resources are all the ingredients necessary to operate a successful business. In order to manufacture fashion merchandise, producers need raw materials, labor, production facilities, production equipment, and capital. If any *one* of these elements is lacking or is in short supply, fashion change will be *inhibited.*

As will be discussed in Part II, during its early development, America was most fortunate to have acquired an abundance of all the resources necessary to produce fashion merchandise. However, the present position of the industry is not invulnerable to losing one or more of these essential resources. For instance, skilled labor is in diminishing supply. Therefore, the industry must actively search for and train individuals who have the background and skills necessary to work in the fashion business. Furthermore the industry must continue to replenish the other resources necessary for fashion production because only then can it function efficiently and *accelerate* fashion change.

Business Expansion. In today's economy, a business or an industry must grow to survive. In the fashion industry, part of that growth revolves around rapid style change and fashion evolution.

In order to encourage change, larger and more efficient production facilities must be opened. More retail outlets must emerge for the distribution of the finished goods. The growth of these facilities *accelerates* fashion change.

Consumer Income. Important as it may be for consumers to desire new looks and styles, it is more important that they be able to afford them.

Fashion change is directly associated with consumer income. When consumer income is up, fashion change is *accelerated.* When consumer income is down, fashion change is *inhibited.*

Fortunately, over the last one hundred years, American consumer income has generally been up. It has kept pace with and—over the long run—managed to outdistance inflation. This is especially true of the portion of consumer income known as *discretionary* income. This type of income is the amount of money available to spend on luxury items and leisure time activities. Since the majority of fashion purchases are "luxury" items, and discretionary income has been available to buy them, over the past century the pace of fashion change has been *accelerated.* However, should there be a galloping inflation, recession, high unemployment, or depression—then the rate of fashion change would be *inhibited.* For this reason, consumer purchases of apparel and accessories have become an important economic indicator of the health of this country's economy.

Use of Consumer Credit. The rise in incomes and the dispersion of wealth has created the uniquely American phenomenon, consumer credit. Although other countries are introducing the "buy now-pay later" system, no country has extended consumer credit as has the United States.

Today, well over 50 percent of all department store sales are "charged." The customer does not have to have or save up the purchase price of a desired item. Instead, he or she can wear the merchandise literally before it is paid for and while it is still in fashion.

With availability of credit, consumer purchasing power has increased tremendously, stimulating the demand for fashion goods. Available consumer credit, therefore, serves as a positive factor toward the *acceleration* of fashion change.

The Seasonal Environment

Many people refer to changes in fashion as fashion seasons. Even if climatic conditions are fairly stable in an area, the industry has successfully maintained fashion change based on the four natural seasons, on climatic weather conditions, and on artificial seasons.

The Four Natural Seasons. There is virtually no place in the continental United States where the temperature and weather conditions are constant. Most Americans live in geographic areas which experience a change in temperature during the fall, winter, summer, and spring seasons. Generally, these people need a larger wardrobe to correspond with those seasonal changes.

Although some progress has been made by the introduction of "three-season" and "all-season" textiles and by the multiconcept of the "layer look," most manufacturers offer styles which are meant for wear during a specific season—styles which are inappropriate for all seasons. For example, the fabrics and styling of spring lines are geared for moderate temperature wear. Even the lightest weight long sleeved wool dress, comfortably worn in spring, is going to be extremely uncomfortable when temperatures reach 95°.

Because of these seasonal conditions, therefore, fashion must—of necessity—be varied. The seasons, then, serve as a great *accelerator* for fashion change.

Climatic (Weather) Conditions. There are many fashion producers who specialize in fashion apparel and accessories that are designed for wear under certain climatic conditions. Rainwear, beachwear, and snow gear are the three dominant categories.

By meeting specialized climatic needs, these manufacturers stimulate consumer spending. A customer, for instance, feels justifiably compelled to purchase a raincoat, an umbrella, or a pair of rain boots for protection against inclement weather. By increasing both the amount and type of apparel purchased by the consumer, these producers stimulate fashion change. Thus the weather, through this unique industry, helps to *accelerate* fashion change.

Artificial Seasons. By designing clothes geared for a specific purpose, manufacturers have literally created three other "seasons" to add to the four natural ones. These are back to school, holiday, and cruisewear. The specific characteristics of these lines are described in Chapter Nine, which covers American manufacturers, but the motives behind the introduction of these seasons is added business through specialized merchandise.

These artificial seasons are not separate manufacturing seasons as much as they are separate *selling* seasons. For example, the back-to-school lines are shown and produced by manufacturers with their regular fall merchandise. But they are introduced in the stores in July and August, slightly ahead of the goods for fall. In any case, these contrived "seasons" serve to *accelerate* fashion change.

HOW FASHION MOVES

Fashion is constantly changing—but those changes take place *within* fashion *movements. Fashion movements* pertain to the overall direction of fashion. For example, a trend toward longer skirt lengths or softer, more feminine clothes is a fashion movement. A movement of that type will last several years. Seasonal fashion changes—new colors, fabrics, styles, or trim—will be expressed within that existing fashion movement.

Fashion movements do not occur in a haphazard or mysterious manner. In fact, by analyzing past fashion movements, one is able to see that most movements emerge with a predictable regularity and—sometimes—in a predictable sequence. For instance, a fashion movement toward softer, more feminine clothes may be safely predicted to follow an era of tailored, classic fashion.

This predictability is due to the fact that—regardless of the causes or the direction of a fashion movement—there are five basic principles which underlie all fashion movement. And, in all types of movements, one or more of these principles applies.

The Five Basic Principles That Underlie All Fashion Movement

1. Fashion Movements Are Evolutionary. Overall, fashion does not move rapidly. It follows a progressive pattern where change is introduced slowly, not radically.

An example of this phenomena may be seen in the raising and lowering of skirt lengths. Hemlines literally inch their way up or down, depending on the fashion period.

In recent history there has been one notable exception to this principle of the evolutionary movement of fashion. This unique event occurred in 1947 at the end of World War II. Because of the war and restrictions on the use of fabrics, fashion change had been at a standstill for several years. It had not continued along at its normal evolutionary pace. That year, French designer Christian Dior introduced his now famous "new look." It featured small waists, long, flowing skirts—a total departure from the austere, tailored, war-time garb worn by most women. Yet, even though the look was *revolutionary*, it was totally accepted (see Fig. 1-2). Women are ready for it. The look was one which they would have been wearing had the normal evolutionary process of fashion change been uninterrupted by the war. But unless such special circumstances occur again, it is correct to assume that Dior's "new look" will remain the only modern exception to this basic fashion principle.

The premise of this principle is best expressed by the following quote: "Fashion change is always gradual unless there is an abrupt dislocation of economic conditions or social values."[14]

2. Fashion Cycles Run to Extremes. This second principle deals with the lifespan of a fashion movement. Once a trend is set in motion it will not end until an extreme interpretation of that trend is reached. French designer Paul Poiret is credited with best summarizing this thought by saying, "All fashions end in excess."

For example, in 1906, just prior to Poiret's emergence as an influential designer, women were crammed into wasp-waisted corseted clothes which emphasized the bustline and derriere. When this fashion movement reached an uncomfortable extreme, Poiret introduced a relaxed look, eliminating corsets in favor of bras.

A more recent example of this principle is the mini skirt lengths of the late 60s. When they could go no higher, skirts started on their way down until a few seasons later, they covered and then passed the knees.

Be it silhouette, skirt lengths, or overall fashion themes, a fashion movement must run its course—reaching an extreme—before another can take its place.

Combining these first two principles, McJimsey further states "Fashions change so gradually that as they move in one direction, one is scarcely aware of how much has occurred until an extreme has been reached."[15]

[14]Harriet T. McJimsey, *Art and Fashion in Clothing Selection* (Ames, Iowa: Iowa State University Press, 1973), p. 25.

[15]*Ibid.*, p. 59.

3. Fashion Repeats Itself. The third premise of all fashion movement is that looks repeat themselves.

As later elaborated upon in Chapter 7, a good designer is constantly delving into the past for inspiration. A designer can revive past trends by studying his or her own and other designers' previous work, and by reviewing historical costumes and art history.

A recent example of fashion repeating itself through historical inspiration was Saint Laurent's 1976 revival of the peasant look. The styling of the clothes duplicated traditional folk costumes worn by Russian peasants and gypsies, and by northern and southern Europeans. The peasant look came at a time when women had been wearing classic tailored clothes and were ready to turn to more feminine fashion. The look fulfilled this need, becoming particularly popular for evening.

4. Fashion Change Never Ceases. Fashion change is and has been ongoing as long as fashion has existed. The reason for this is simple. There is no ultimate in design. Whatever look or style is currently being featured is not the final word.

This principle is the heart of the fashion business. No designer or manufacturer, no matter how perfect his work, would want to think of it as his last and ultimate design. Something past or current can always be improved upon, varied, or replaced.

At the same time, to a customer, something new is always more appealing. No customer, no matter how classic or perfect an item may be, would want to consider its design as final and irreplaceable. Therefore to designer, manufacturer, and customer alike, there is no "ultimate" for this would imply the end of change. And without change, fashion and the business of fashion would cease.

Fortunately fashion changes are continuously encouraged by the industry and the consumer alike. Because of that encouragement, fashion never stands still.

5. Repeat Time of Fashion Is Decreasing. As previously discussed, the entire pace of life and change has increased. Today, events become "history" with amazing swiftness. Consequently, the length of time it takes for a fashion movement to be revived or to repeat itself is decreasing.

In terms of fashion, one excellent example of decreased repeat time is in the time it takes for the prevailing silhouette (the overall shape of apparel) to be replaced.

Research shows that in the decades prior to 1947, a silhouette's life span was approximately thirty-five years. However, in post World War II years, the silhouette has been changing on the average of between every seven to ten years.

This fifth principle does not alter the first four principles of fashion movement. It simply implies that those principles must be viewed as functioning within a relatively shorter time span.

Analyzing Fashion Movements

To all involved in the profitable marketing of fashion, the reasons for analyzing the movement of fashion are twofold. First, it provides the ability to identify and determine the life span of current trends. Second, and more important, it provides the ability to identify and predict future trends. In the fashion business—where "wrong guesses" can be notoriously expensive—it is mandatory to be equipped with these abilities in order to be successful.

This thought was emphasized by Prof. Paul Nystrom when he wrote: "It would seem that a necessary step towards better merchandising of fashion goods would be to get more information about these fashion movements; in other words, to substitute facts for guesses, reasoning for hunches and a bit of science for the prevailing mystery regarding fashion."[16]

Predicting fashion correctly can and should be done within the context of the previously listed five general principles which underlie all fashion movement. There are three other specific categories which provide more detailed information on the movement of fashion. These categories are: *The Adoption Process; The Fashion Life Cycle;* and *Basic Styling and Merchandise Characteristics.* By researching each category separately and then combining the results, the guesswork when analyzing fashion movement can be eliminated.

The Adoption Process. This category refers to the *flow* of fashion from one class or group to another. It explains with whom fashion originates, and how it moves from acceptance by a few to acceptance by many.

Understanding the adoption process is an important key to monitoring fashion movement correctly because it describes the *sequence* of acceptance for new fashion trends.

The oldest process of adoption has become known as *trickle-down.* Under this process fashion originates with those at the top of a society and moves to the classes below. At first royalty unilaterally determined fashion for everyone. Then, the titled and noble class joined royalty as contributors to fashion trends. Still later, the entire group referred to as the upper class began and endorsed new fashions.

[16]Paul Nystrom, *Economics of Fashion* (New York: Ronald Press, 1927), p. 57.

Today, social class structure is not as rigid as it once was. But this should not imply that the trickle-down process is not currently working. Yesterday's aristocrats and upper class—those with title and money—have been replaced by new arbiters of fashion: the *Fashion Elite.*

The Fashion Elite is composed of three groups: (1) the *creators,* (2) the *reporters,* and (3) the *wearers* of high fashion.

The *creators* of high fashion are the leading fashion designers of America and Europe. They create the fashion reported and worn by other members of the Fashion Elite.

The *reporters* of high fashion are, of course, the editors and publishers of leading fashion magazines and newspapers. This second group has the power to endorse and publicize those fashion trends they deem most important. Consequently, they are powerful members of the Fashion Elite.

The *wearers* of high fashion, the third and last group, are usually moneyed people who can afford to indulge in expensive high fashion. Most have a built-in celebrity status—as members of society or the sports, entertainment, and political worlds—but that in itself does not make them influential fashion arbiters. There are many celebrities who are not fashion leaders. The fashion leaders are those who display unusual, *news-making* fashion taste.

The influence of these celebrities, however, exists only through and because of the attention and focus given to them by the media. Once the media establishes their fashion creditability, this third group becomes the group of the fashion elite which *displays* what is considered important fashion looks.

Sometimes those at the top of society admire and subsequently copy fashion from the classes beneath them. This second adoption process has been labeled *bottom-up.* It is not a new process. Marie Antoinette, for example, though at the very top of society as Queen of France, loved the costumes worn by shepherdesses and had them copied for her own use.

One very important point must be made about the bottom-up process: Its movement seems to follow a distinct pattern from the lower class to the upper class or fashion elite, and then to the middle class. In other words, in order for a bottom-up fashion to gain the widespread acceptance of the majority, it must be legitimatized by first gaining approval from those at the top.

Some modern day examples of the bottom-up movement include the poor boy sweaters, the Afro look, and—more recently—American blue jeans.

Finally, the adoption process can be analyzed from a *horizontal* perspective. This approach recognizes that adoption of a fashion by individuals or groups with the same social status does not occur at the same rate. The acceptance of a look more often hinges on peer group acceptance. A person who is a member of a particular group and who has popularity among its members initiates the look which is in turn copied by his or her peers. These individuals are not part of the fashion elite as described earlier. Instead they are friends, acquaintances, or group leaders of their own peers. They are, however, as influential as the fashion elite in getting their group interested in and into adopting a particular look.

In addition to following a social pattern, in this country fashion also follows a geographical one as it flows from group to group. Under this rule, looks are first accepted on the east and west coasts. There, they are worn by people in major cities like New York and San Francisco. Fashion looks then spread to the suburbs and then they finally move to the Middle West. This cross-country trek applies to the adoption of all types of fashion whether it be trickle-down, horizontal, or bottom-up.

The Fashion Life Cycle. The movement of a fashion becomes even more understandable when it is translated graphically into a sales curve termed the fashion life cycle. All fashions, over time, pass through four stages: *Introduction; Growth; Maturity;* and *Decline* (see Fig. 2-6). Each stage of the cycle is characterized by several distinct features.

In the *Introduction Stage,* the sales of a new fashion follow a gradual upward sloping pattern. Distribution of the goods is limited to those retailers who are innovative and whose customers desire the very latest looks.

The price of these goods is generally the highest in this first stage. This is attributable to expensive initial production costs and—because of possible consumer rejection—to the high degree of risk associated with

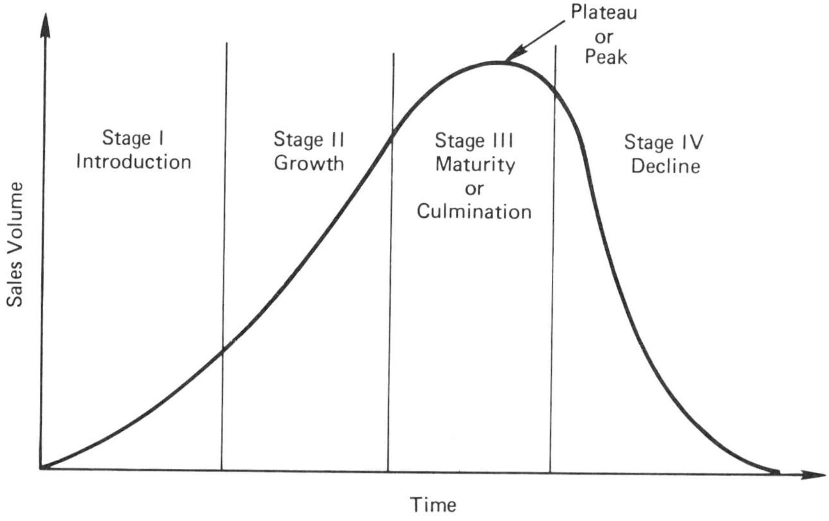

FIGURE 2-6. The fashion life cycle

innovative fashion. A high initial price tag thus becomes a common feature of this stage.

Trade publications and top high fashion magazines feature introductory stage fashions on their pages. This coverage and favorable commentary often gives the necessary impetus to move the fashion into stage two, the *Growth Stage.*

In the second phase, the fashion is popularized. Spurred by consumer interest and demand, manufacturers begin to copy the look to meet rapidly rising sales expectations. This in turn causes a decline in the selling price of the fashion, which serves to further stimulate sales during the Growth Stage. It also encourages increased distribution by retailers. All, including those retailers who initially were cautious, adopt the new fashion and mass merchandise it. Thus, the sales during this period increase rapidly and the look gains widespread acceptance. This acceptance is reported and confirmed by broad coverage from general readership publications, including the mass market magazines.

By the time a fashion reaches the third stage, *Maturity,* its sales potential is reached and a leveling off of volume occurs. This stage is characterized by a peak or plateau depending on how long the stabilization of sales continues. If customers do not repeat purchases of a look, then a peak will appear. If, however, customers buy various interpretations or collect several styles which are influenced by the current fashion look—then a sales plateau will occur. How long a fashion remains in stage three will depend on how quickly customers become bored with a current look and desire to replace it with a new one.

When this occurs, the sales pattern for the current fashion will begin to show a sharp drop, entering into the *Decline Stage,* or step four. In this stage, price reductions, discounts, and markdowns abound as manufacturers and retailers alike try to move out their stock and reduce inventory levels. Virtually no production or reordering of the fashion occurs. A decreasing number of customers buy what remains of the stock, motivated mostly by the often exceptional "bargain" prices.

By the *Decline Stage,* all the media has literally abandoned the fashion. Like the manufacturers, the retailers, and the consumers, it is already picking up on a new fashion which is entering the introductory stage. Thus, at any given point in time, several fashion looks can be depicted on the curve, as each moves along the stages of its own fashion life cycle.

Basic Styling Characterists and Merchandise Characteristics. Earlier, it was established that fashion movements refer to overall fashion trends and that these movements have a life cycle. Within the life cycle of these movements however, shorter life cycles exist. These shorter life cycles belong to the *basic styling characteristics* of a fashion and to the *merchandise characteristics* used in expressing that fashion.

In a fashion trend, there are *four basic styling characteristics.* These are Silhouette; the Fashion Look; Zones; and Color and Texture.

As mentioned earlier, in determining the *silhouette* or shape of women's apparel, only three distinct forms emerge: the bell-shape; the tube; and the bustle or back fullness. All wearing apparel can be classified under one of these three silhouettes. Currently the fashion life cycle of a silhouette lasts approximately seven to ten years.

Between the post-World War II period and today, only two silhouettes have reoccurred for daytime wear: the bell shape and the tube. It appears that modern life styles are not conducive to adding the back fullness of a bustle to garments except for evening and bridal wear (see Fig. 2-7).

Fashion journalist James Brady claims that he can most graphically describe the predominant *fashion look* by using six terms. He maintains that fashion is either pretty or ugly; short or long; tight or loose. Under his theory, these six elements can be combined in various combinations to accurately describe the look of fashion.[17] It can be "pretty, long, and loose" or—for that matter—"ugly, short, and tight." Other fashion reporters may prefer to use more elaborate, "fashion" terms—but Mr. Brady's descriptive technique gets right to the point and seems to serve the purpose.

All fashion looks, however, regardless of how they are described, have a very definite lifespan. A fashion look lasts approximately three to five years which is half as long as the fashion life cycle of a silhouette and may be analyzed accordingly.

Fashion historians have also uncovered the fact that a current look emphasizes one particular part of the body at a time—making it a focal point. The emphasis is placed either on the breasts, waist, hips, buttocks, legs, arms, or on the overall circumference of the body. In order to analyze fashion movements correctly, it should be determined which part of the body is receiving current emphasis, since future fashion will focus attention upon a different part.

A shift in emphasis occurs only after a part of the body has been emphasized to the extreme. For instance, interest will move away from a cinched waist when it cannot be tightened any further; as the waist is loosened, fashion interest will look for another part of the body to dramatically emphasize.

In the last few decades, the approximate length of time zones are emphasized has varied. Some—like the emphasis on the legs by the mini between the mid-60s and the early 70s—last about seven years. Others last longer. The emphasis on the bustline—the post-war phenomena which spurred the sale of pointed and padded bras—began in the 40s and lasted throughout the 50s.

[17]James Brady, *Super Chic* (Boston: Little, Brown, 1974), p. 49.

FIGURE 2-7. The back-fullness silhouette
Courtesy: Buckner's, Roosevelt Field, Garden City, New York

Color and texture are styling characteristics which generally complete their fashion life cycle in one season. Specific colors and textures from a given season will change in the next. The bright, lightweight fabrics of the summer, for example, will change to dark woolens in the fall.

However, there are broad color and texture trends which generally remain in fashion for one and sometimes as long as three or four years. Although new colors and textures are introduced each season, they are kept within these broad predominating trends.

Each type of fashion merchandise also has its own *merchandise characteristics*, which in turn have their own life cycle. The time span of these cycles varies, due to the unique characteristics of the merchandise.

For instance, *accessories* are a classification of goods which move through the fashion life cycle quickly. Merchandise such as jewelry, belts, and handbags, while keeping within the context of the current fashion trend, changes its dominant look from season to season. For example, if fashion emphasizes the "natural" look—handbags may be made of canvas for spring, straw for summer, and suede and leather for fall and winter.

Price also contributes to the short fashion life cycle of accessories. Accessory prices, in relative terms, are often lower than other types of fashion goods. Many customers find that they can vary and update their wardrobes frequently, but inexpensively, by purchasing new accessories.

On the other hand, *outerwear* has a much longer fashion life cycle. Purchases of such items as coats and capes can generally be postponed until there is a noticeable change in overall fashion such as the rise or fall of hemlines. Drastic changes of this type usually take several seasons or even years to develop, thus lengthening outerwear's fashion life.

Other classifications of wearing apparel, from *sportswear* to *formal attire*, also exhibit variations in their fashion life cycles and these are based on the styling characteristics previously mentioned.

By analyzing the movement of fashion from the perspective of the five general principles, as well as in terms of fashion life cycles as they pertain to general fashion trends and to styling and merchandise characteristics, a detailed picture emerges which erases most of the mystery and unpredictability from the movement of fashion.

TERMS TO REMEMBER

Protection Theory
Modesty Theory
Adornment Theory

Combined-Need Theory
Sumptuary Laws
Trickle-Down Process
Bottom-Up Process
Horizontal Adoption Process
the Fashion Elite
the Fashion Life Cycle

HIGHLIGHTS OF THE CHAPTER

- There are four theories which explain the origin of clothes. They are: The Protection Theory, The Modesty Theory, The Adornment Theory and The Combined-Need Theory.
- Each theory explains the origin of clothes using a different social, psychological, or religious premise. The Combined-Need Theory is based on Maslow's Hierarchy of Needs.
- Clothing today means many things to different people. It can be an extension of their personality, it can be a means of non-verbal communication, it can delineate time, be a symbol of ideals and values, and it can be a means of creative expression.
- Fashion is always changing. Changes are brought about by influences in the political-legal, social, technological, economic, and seasonal environment in which we live.
- There are five principles which govern all fashion movement. They are: fashion is evolutionary, cycles run to extremes, fashion never ceases, fashion repeats itself, and repeat time is decreasing.
- Fashion adoption moves in three directions; trickle-down, bottom-up, and horizontal.
- There are four phases to the fashion life cycle: introduction, growth, maturity, and decline.
- There are four basic styling characteristics. They are: silhouette, the fashion look, zone, and color and texture.
- Specific types of merchandise have varying fashion life cycles.
- Fashion does not move in mysterious, unpredictable ways. By using the five general principles, the fashion life cycle, and by looking at styling and merchandise characteristics, fashion can be clearly analyzed and understood.

QUESTIONS

1. Cite the premise on which each of the four theories about the origins of clothes is based.
2. Give an example of how clothing can be an expression of one's personality.
3. What role does clothing play in the communication process?
4. What is meant by Laver's quote, "fashion is a victory of time over place"?
5. How has clothing been used to symbolize religious and political beliefs?
6. How is clothing an outlet for imagination?
7. Define sumptuary laws. Give an example of a modern sumptuary law.
8. How does U.S. foreign policy and trade regulations affect fashion?
9. Mention some changes that have occurred in terms of leisure time, role of women, class structure, increased mobility, and changing ideologies. Show how each change has an impact on fashion.
10. Cite specific technological advances which have accelerated fashion change.
11. What kinds of economic factors affect fashion? How?
12. Seasons, real and artificial, play a role in fashion changes. Discuss.
13. Show how fashion changes have recently been evolutionary not revolutionary.
14. What does "fashion cycles run to extremes" mean?
15. What are the three basic silhouettes?
16. How many silhouette cycles have existed since World War II?
17. How does fashion "trickle-down"? How are fashions adopted from "bottom-up"?
18. Who are today's fashion elite?
19. What is meant by the term, "fashion look"?
20. What are the specific pricing and promotional characteristics of fashion in each phase of the fashion life cycle?
21. How do accessories differ from outerwear in fashion movement?

BIBLIOGRAPHY

Anspach, Karlene, *The Why of Fashion.* Ames, Iowa: Iowa State University Press, 1967.

Beckman, R., "Clothes Make the Person," *Psychology Today* (April, 1974).

Bell, Quentin, *On Human Finery,* 2nd ed. New York: Schocken Books, 1976.

Charles-Roux, Edmonde, *Chanel.* New York: Alfred A. Knopf, 1975.

Dorner, Irene, *Fashion.* London: Octopus Books, 1974.

Evans, Helen M., *Man the Designer.* New York: Macmillan Company, 1973.

Flugel, J. C., *The Psychology of Clothes.* London: Hogarth Press, 1930.

Hamburger, Estelle, *The Fashion Business, It's All Yours.* San Francisco: Canfield Press, 1976.

Hawes, Elizabeth, *Fashion Is Spinach.* New York: Random House, 1938.

Jarnow, Jeanette A., and Beatrice Judelle, *Inside the Fashion Business,* 2nd Ed. New York: John Wiley and Sons, 1974.

Laver, James, *Costume.* New York: Hawthorne Books, 1963.

Laver, James, *Modesty in Dress.* Boston: Houghton Mifflin, 1969.

McCardell, Claire, *What Shall I Wear?* New York: Simon and Schuster, 1956.

McJimsey, Harriet T., *Art and Fashion in Clothing Selection.* Ames, Iowa: Iowa State University Press, 1973.

Nystrom, Paul H., *Economics of Fashion.* New York: Ronald Press, 1928.

Picken, Mary Brooks, *The Fashion Dictionary.* New York: Funk and Wagnalls, 1973.

Roach, Mary Ellen, and Joanne B. Eicher, *The Visible Self: Perspective on Dress.* Englewood Cliffs, N.J.: Prentice-Hall, 1973.

Robinson, Dwight, "Style Changes: Cyclical, Inexorable and Foreseeable," *Harvard Business Review* (November–December 1975).

Rosenbaum, Gene, *Is Your Volkswagen a Sex Symbol?* New York: Bantam Books, 1973.

RUDOFSKY, BERNARD, *The Unfashionable Human Body.* New York: Doubleday, 1971.

RYAN, MARY, *Clothing: A Study in Human Behavior.* New York: Holt, Rinehart and Winston, 1966.

TOLMON, RUTH, *Guide to Fashion Merchandise Knowledge,* Vol. I. New York: Milady Publishing Corp., 1973.

TROXELL, MARY D., *Fashion Merchandising,* 2nd ed. New York: Gregg Division, McGraw-Hill, 1976.

VEBLEN, THORSTEIN, *The Theory of the Leisure Class,* Mentor ed. New York: New American Library of World Literature, 1963.

WILCOX, RUTH, AND ROY WILCOX, *Dictionary of Costume.* New York: Charles Scribner's Sons, 1969.

WINGATE, ISABEL, KAREN GILLESPIE, AND BETTY MILGROM, *Know Your Merchandise,* 4th ed. New York: McGraw-Hill, 1975.

YOUNG, AGNES, *Recurring Cycles of Fashion.* New York: Cooper Square Publishers, 1966.

II

THE BACKGROUND OF TODAY'S FASHION INDUSTRY

In Part I, we learned how the fashion industry corresponds to the various changing elements in society. Nowhere is this more apparent than in the historical development of this country's fashion industry.

Cloth production began in the mid-1600s when, for *political* reasons, settlers were forced to find ways to make their own fabrics and clothing. Those years—between 1640 and the American Revolution—became known as the Homecloth Period.

After winning political freedom, the country sought to obtain *economic* independence from England by concentrating much of its resources on the development of a textile industry. As they succeeded, they established more than economic autonomy. The birth of the textile industry also marked the beginning of its Industrial Revolution, changing the country from a land of agriculture into a nation of manufacturers.

Equipped with the know-how of producing unlimited amounts of piece goods, America was in an excellent position to mechanize its production of wearing apparel. By the middle of the 1800s, because of the invention and adoption of the sewing machine, and the fortuitous, coincidental rise in our immigrant population, America's now famous "factory made" clothing industry automatically and logically evolved.

Part II thus traces the growth of the American fashion industry from the time of simple cloth production through the emergence and establishment of ready-to-wear.

3

ESTABLISHING AMERICA'S TEXTILE INDUSTRY

OBJECTIVES

After reading this chapter, you should be able to:

- Recognize how the country's early textile industry provided an indispensable foundation for the development of America's great fashion industry.
- Tell about the colorful beginnings of America's fashion industry.
- Grasp the significance of how, through their mechanization, the early fashion industries were responsible for the initial economic expansion and industrialization of the United States.

The origins of America's textile industry date back to the early 1600s and the English colonization of the New World by two quite dissimilar groups of immigrants. The fortune-seeking southern colonies found it profitable—and were therefore content—to grow tobacco and exchange it with England for her manufactured goods. The colonists who settled in the north, however, sought political and religious freedoms and were determined to become independent of England and supply themselves with all their needs. Though growing food crops was necessary for survival, the goal of these colonists was complete self-reliance through the establishment of fishing, shipping, fur trading, and textile industries. Thus the seeds for the industrialization of the North and the agricultural development of the South were sown early in our country's history.

THE HOMECLOTH INDUSTRIES, 1607-REVOLUTION

The Beginning of Homecloth

The first step for organizing a cloth industry took place in 1640 when, disturbed by their dangerous dependence on England for textiles, the General Court of Massachusetts and Connecticut proclaimed an order for the colonists to manufacture wool and linen at home. In order to obtain the necessary raw materials, the raising of flax, hemp, and sheep was also mandated. Equipped with these raw materials, the settlers were then able to apply the talent and knowledge they had acquired in England for clothmaking.

To implement their orders, the government required everyone—unless they were otherwise usefully occupied—to spin[1] yarn for the settlements' weavers. The simplest of cloth in the drabbest of colors was the result. But it served to provide the families with the clothing they needed for protection against the winter elements.

Eventually the industrious activities of the New England colonists came to England's attention, and by the beginning of the 1700s it became obvious that her colonies were threatening to become her competitors. To curtail this competition, England imposed strict trade and manufacturing restrictions upon the resourceful colonists, but these impositions only served to strengthen the colonists determination for economic independence, and the home industries, by then firmly entrenched, flourished and grew.

By the time of the Revolution in 1776, the use of homespun cloth had become both patriotic and fashionable. In fact, wishing to make a significant patriotic statement, the 1768 Harvard graduating class wore suits made of homespun cloth to their commencement and, a year later, Yale graduates did the same.

Fabrics of the Home Industries

Homespun, a rough but popular *wool,* was made and used by the poor and the middle class for almost all of their clothing. However, *linen,* which comes from the flax plant, was the most widely used fiber. Flax was easy to grow and the colonist could turn it into cloth within the boundaries of his home. It became so synonymous with both table and bed clothes, that today, these cloth household needs continue to be re-

[1]Spinning—the drawing out, twisting, and winding of loose filaments of fiber into thread or yarn.

ferred to as "linens," though they are predominantly made of cotton and synthetics.

Though most of the colonists' needs were taken care of by the homespun industry, there was still a market for *imports.* The imports offered the wealthy the cottons and silks which were not yet manufactured in America. Among the lower classes, imports purchases were rare and limited to those times when the need arose for a good wool or a fine chintz or silk for a wedding or "Sunday Meeting" dress or coat. Kept for years, these once-in-a-lifetime investments were handed down to be altered and worn by succeeding generations.

FOCUS ON FASHION

OTHER POPULAR COLONIAL CLOTHS

Linsey-woolseys and oznaburgs are, like most of the fabrics of the period, now obsolete. Others, like calico, chintz, damask, denim, gingham, taffeta, and velvet, are still fashionable today.

Calico. The fabrics imported from India were called by the name of the town they came from. Calico was a popular printed cotton from the city of Calicut. When America's cotton industry began, all printed cottons continued to be called "calicos," regardless of origin.

Crewel. The patterns and colors of crewel embroidery were inspired and copied from the beautiful ornate cotton prints imported from India. A loosely twisted wool yarn called "crewel" was used for the embroidery, giving the work its name.

Darnick. This checked linen was the most popular fabric for curtains during the colonial period.

Duffel. A warm wool coating with a tufted or knotted nap, it was widely used by hunters and outdoor workers. The word "duffel" eventually became synonymous with sportsmen's equipment and though today's "duffel" bag is generally made of cotton canvas, it retains the name once applied to all outdoor gear.

Linsey-Woolsey. This warm, lightweight fabric was a mixture of linen and wool. Made by every family in the colonies, it was a winter staple for the entire family.

Oznaburg. This homemade cheap, coarse linen fabric was widely used for the clothing of farmers, the working class, and slaves.

Quilting. The "patchwork" quilt is an American invention. It began when precious pieces of left-over cloth were used as patches on wornout blankets. They were eventually called "crazy quilts" because, after being patched repeatedly, they resembled the crazed surfaces of cracked ice. In time, as cloth became more plentiful, the design of the patches were regulated, sewn together in original patterns and used as a decorative top layer of fabric in quilts.

It is interesting to note how well the homecloth industries served America. Started in 1640 to meet the dire needs of the Massachusetts settlers, they continued to provide most of the clothing worn by Americans until well after the Revolutionary War, when the first successful cloth factories were built. During that time, the home industries also provided the Americans with a marvelous tool for dissent. Time and time again, when England imposed restrictive, unjustifiable Acts against the colonies, the colonists were able to retaliate by boycotting English goods, utilizing the products of the home industries in their place.

THE MECHANIZATION OF THE HOME INDUSTRIES

The first cloth factory was built in Rowley, Massachusetts by John Pearson in 1643. He erected the first fulling mill,[2] which produced finished[3] wool cloth. However, during the pre-revolutionary period, the amount of fabric supplied by this and the few other hand operated cloth factories which followed was negligible in comparison to the country's needs.

When the Revolutionary War ended, the United States found itself lacking all types of manufactured products, especially clothing. Since it had little industry outside the home and had not yet reestablished trade with England and other European countries, it turned back to the home industries for its clothing needs. Fortunately, the industries were thriving. During the war, American women devoted all their time and effort toward home production, providng clothing for all the people, including the militia. Records and diaries of these small wartime enterprises exist today. Among these amazing reports are statistics indicating that

[2]Fulling—a process which cleans and presses woven woolen cloth creating "finished" cloth.

[3]Finished—cloth which has gone through the fulling process.

over 13,000 wool winter overcoats were produced for Revolutionary soldiers by the home industries. Peacetime demands became, by comparison, relatively simple and the women gladly undertook the job of continuing to provide the country's clothing needs until trade was resumed, and the prized imported goods were again available.

When trade with England resumed, however, it was more beneficial to England than to the United States. This imbalanced dependency on English manufactured goods troubled many American government officials and leading businessmen, and they began offering incentives to encourage new industry—particularly in the production of textiles.

But it was soon obvious, that America could not compete with the growing influx of English imports. The textile products of England's mechanized industry were not only cheaper, they were also of a better quality. America's home industry had neither the machinery nor the skilled labor necessary to produce comparable goods. To compete with England, it would have to get both.

Converting to Machinery

When America recognized the need to mechanize her textile industry, she sought to emulate the successful methods of England. Through a series of inventions, England had developed superior textile producing machinery. These inventions changed what was once a hand industry into one run by power, giving England her Industrial Revolution. By acquiring similar inventions, America hoped to accomplish the same.

FOCUS ON THE INDUSTRY

English Inventions That Revolutionized Her Textile Industry

1733 *John Kay* invented the *flying shuttle* which freed one hand of the weaver as the shuttle was cast from one side of the loom to the other by pulling a cord.

1769 *Richard Arkwright* developed a *spinning machine* which spun cotton by pulling it through rollers. This was an important invention since, till then, cotton thread was so weak it could only be used as a crosswide thread with stronger linen for the lengthwise.

1770	*James Hargreaves* invented the *spinning jenny,* a device that spun several threads at one time. First used in America in 1775.
1779	*Samuel Crompton* invented the *mule jenny,* combining the best characteristics of Hargreave's spinning jenny and Arkwright's spinning machine. It produced a fine, strong silky cotton thread.
1785	*Edmond Cartwright* invented the *power loom* which wove fabric by machine.
1785	*Thomas Bell* invented *cylinder printing* using engraved rollers which transformed printing on cloth from a hand to a machine industry.

Samuel Slater—Father of American Manufacturing. Unfortunately for America, England was determined to keep her superior position in the world's textile market, and forbade the export of textile machinery as well as the emigration of any person knowledgeable in the construction or running of these machines. The American government, hoping to discover American or recently immigrated talent, offered rewards to anyone able to produce any of these inventions. A 1789 Philadelphia newspaper account of one of these rewards found its way to England where it was read by a young man named Samuel Slater.

For seven years the 21-year-old Slater had been an apprentice in a cotton mill in Darby, England where he learned to run Richard Arkwright's cotton spinning machine. Eager to strike out on his own, but aware that his extensive textile experience could prevent him from leaving England, he left for New York without notifying anyone.

Shortly after his arrival, he heard of a Rhode Island man who was looking for an engineer-inventor. Moses Brown was so impressed with Slater that he offered him all the profits if he would come to Pawtucket, Rhode Island and perfect Brown's machinery. But Slater found the machinery so inadequate that he duplicated the Arkwright cotton spinning machine he knew so well (Fig. 3-1), relying totally upon his remarkable memory.

Samuel Slater completed his spinning device in 1790, introducing the first successful manufacturing machinery into the United States.

Although the spinning machine was a great step forward, there were still other areas in the production of cloth that had to be mechanized. All unspun cotton had to be imported. A way to clean American cotton was still to be discovered. And cloth was still being woven on hand looms.

FIGURE 3-1. Samuel Slater built a version of England's cotton spinning machine totally from memory
Source: *The Copp Family Textiles,* published by Smithsonian Institution Press, p. 58.

Eli Whitney Invents the Cotton Gin. In 1793, the introduction of the cotton gin made it possible to separate American cotton from its seed quickly and efficiently. The invention had a great impact on the economy of the entire country. New England replaced expensive imported cotton with the much cheaper cotton of the South. The South meanwhile, became immensely wealthy as it expanded its cotton agriculture and its exports.

With an unlimited supply of cotton and with the machines to spin it, the final device America needed for mechanizing its textile industry was the power loom.

Francis Cabot Lowell—Manufacturing Innovator. In the early 1800s a Bostonian, Francis Cabot Lowell, travelled throughout England and Scotland studying all phases of textile manufacturing. He returned in 1812 and, with two partners, set up a business in Waltham, Massachusetts. Like Slater, Lowell had a remarkable memory and was able to duplicate the construction of British power looms and manufacturing methods. Working with Paul Moody, a skilled mechanic, he succeeded in erecting an *improved* version of the English power loom. By 1814, his mill in Waltham became the first American factory to process cotton from its raw state to finished cloth entirely by machine.

Building the First Mills

America's conversion to machines gave it the first of the three key elements it needed to mechanize its textile industry. The other two, power and labor, would prove to be readily available.

Water was the power used to run the machines, and once again, it was Samuel Slater who showed America how to harness that power. He built the first mechanized mill in Pawtucket, Rhode Island, using the power supplied by the running water of a nearby river. Soon mills were being built—mainly by Slater's former employees—wherever rivers ran.

By copying Slater's methods, America built the foundation of this country's textile industry. That accomplishment earned him the title "Father of American Manufacturing."

Mills continued to be built throughout the 1800s, interrupted only by the Civil War. Some of the early ones are still in existence today. The well-known Wamsutta Mills began to manufacture cloth in Massachusetts in 1847. The Cranston Print Works goes back even further. It was founded by William Sprague as a sawmill and gristmill in 1620, over three and a half centuries ago. Two hundred years later, his descendants converted it into a cotton mill. By 1856 the company was said to be the largest in the world. Though the Spragues lost control of the company in 1888, the Cranston Print Works Company of Rhode Island remains a quality cloth print producer today.

The history of most mills paralells that of Slater's and Lowell's. They were built by men who saw a future in the production of textile, for themselves and for the country.

"Manning" the Factories

As Samuel Slater and Francis Lowell opened their mills, they patterned their production techniques after those in the English mills. In time, they began to change some of these techniques, introducing new ones that satisfied their special needs.

When the first mills were built, America's population was relatively small. The leading occupation was agriculture, which engaged the family as a unit. When Slater began to gather his labor force from the surrounding rural areas, the New England farms had become increasingly difficult to cultivate. Slater was able to use these unfavorable conditions to his advantage, offering these families work at his mill.

The workers were often recruited through local newspaper advertisements. The ads called for families with "five or six children" and for "widows with children." They offered Sunday School "to improve the mind." Those who responded were generally poor people with little hope for the future—but the ads seemed to offer them assurance of, at the very least, food and lodging.

By the mid-1830s, over half of the mill workers were families working under Slater's Rhode Island System of manufacturing—the *"family type."* The other half were employed under the method developed by Francis Lowell—popularly known as the *"boarding house"* type.

When power looms were introduced into the mills by Lowell, he deliberately avoided instituting the "family type" method of employment. His business as well as his humane instincts rejected the premise of child labor, with its permanent village of poor families. He wanted able and intelligent adults to run his large power looms.

Most of Lowell's mills employed young women between the ages of 18 and 22 who lived in boarding houses near the mills. In contrast to the other mill villages with their congregation of poor families, Lowell's factory towns were pleasant places, consisting of groups of well-kept boarding houses filled with young women who were pleased with the opportunity to be employed.

The operating success of the Waltham System, however, was not due solely to its "boarding house" system of labor—but to three other innovative factors. First, the owners made sure to maintain working capital. Second, they combined all operations in one plant. And third, they limited themselves to producing one type of cloth.

Both the Waltham and the Rhode Island systems of manufacturing were important in establishing the mechanization of the textile industry.

GROWTH OF THE COTTON AND WOOL INDUSTRIES

Before machines, America's "textile industry" (composed of home manufacturers) produced fabrics made primarily of wool and of linen. After its conversion to machinery, the "industry" expanded to include cotton. Almost immediately, cheaper cotton replaced linen in many areas of wearing apparel and home furnishings—decreasing the production of linen substantially. Cotton and wool became the major fibers of the newly mechanized textile industry.

"King Cotton"

The establishment of Samuel Slater's mill in Pawtucket and the invention of the cotton gin occurred within two years of each other. New England went into the business of manufacturing cotton cloth, while the

South went into the business of supplying raw cotton. Its fertile land and the huge world market for raw cotton were two of the inducements which contributed to the South's decision, but the greatest inducement of all was slavery.

The economic advantages of slavery promised to make the South rich. Cultivating the cotton fields required little training of the slaves. If the South converted to factories, it would have taken considerable time and effort to train the slaves.

As the cotton industry flourished so did the slave trade. In time, the South would discover the immeasurable damage that slavery caused to all involved. In addition to the grievious suffering of the black people, it also impaired the industrial and social development of the South.

After the Civil War, the South was economically ruined. There was no industry. All manufactured goods had to be imported from Europe or the North. Though the South returned to the cultivation of cotton, leading Southerners stressed the need to become self-sufficient and urged the establishment of cotton mills. Northern and English textile machine manufacturers also encouraged Southern textile manufacture, and invested large sums of capital in the new firms.

By 1870, the manufacture of cotton cloth was firmly established as one of the country's top industries. At that time, the textile "converter" was introduced. The largest and most famous of these was the Cranston Print Works. Functioning very much like a converter of today, these firms bought unfinished fabrics (greige goods) from mills, chose designs, supervised the printing and, finally, sold the finished product.

The Wool Mills

Copying the successful manufacturing methods of the established cotton industry, woolen mills began to grow in size and multiply in number. By 1840 there were 1420 woolen mills in the United States. Originally, 90 percent of these mills were established in New England and the middle states, but as the West opened up, they moved with the pioneers. By 1870 over half the wool mills were in other areas of the country.

The mills produced fabrics which best suited America's needs, an approach particularly helpful to the growing number of menswear manufacturers. Though most fine woolens were imported, the manufacturers were able to rely upon the domestic mills for adequate supplies of good medium quality wool fabrics.

By 1870, American sheep could supply all the quality raw wool the industry needed and its factories could function independently, performing all the steps required to transform greasy raw wool into handsome finished fabric.

So much of the political and economic background of America is directly related to the textile industry that the history of both becomes inseparable. The manufacure of cloth was America's first industry, and it gave the country economic independence. As the American textile industry grew, it stimulated and developed many other industries and areas of commerce in the United States. Today, it is considered the largest and most advanced in the world and continues to contribute enormously toward the strength and stability of the American economy.

TERMS TO REMEMBER . . .

spinning
fulling
finishing
textile converter
homecloth
flax
linsey-woolsey
home industries
Slater's mill
spinning jenny
power loom
Rhode Island system
Waltham system

HIGHLIGHTS OF THE CHAPTER

- The American textile industry began over 400 years ago when New England colonists decided to produce their own cloth in order to become economically independent of England.
- Almost all the cloth in pre-Revolutionary War days was produced in the home, and after the war, America was able to supply itself with home produced fabrics until trade with England and Europe resumed.
- Aware of the success of the mechanized English textile industry, America tried to copy its machinery and manufacturing methods,

using the talents of young English immigrants who built copies of these machines in America.

- The most famous of these was a mechanical and mathematical genius, Samuel Slater, who, in 1790, built a replica of the Arkwright spinning jenny that was used to spin cotton, linen, and wool yarn.
- The most revolutionary American invention was Eli Whitney's cotton gin. Invented in 1793, it cleaned the cotton, making it utilizable for American mills.
- The power loom provided the final device in the mechanization of textiles, built in America in 1814 by another manufacturing genius—Francis Lowell.
- Water was the power used to run the machines and the center of the industry was concentrated in New England and the Middle Atlantic States of the North.
- Two systems of manufacturing were used, devised by Samuel Slater and by Francis Lowell. Slater's Rhode Island Method was known as the "family" type because it used families, including children, for labor. The more successful system was Lowell's, also known as the Waltham Method—or "boarding house" type. It employed productive young women who lived in boarding houses owned by the mills.
- The success of the Waltham System was also due to three other factors: maintaining working capital—combining all operations in one plant—and limiting production to one type of cloth.
- Cotton and wool became the major fibers of America's newly mechanized textile industry, outdistancing linen. The manufacture of cotton began in the early 1800s in New England mills while the South concentrated on growing cotton. After the Civil War, southern mills for textile manufacture were established.

QUESTIONS

1. When did the colonial settlers make their first attempt to manufacture cloth? What prompted it?
2. What were the homecloth industries? What were the two most widely used fibers of these industries? Why?
3. How did England react to colonial attempts to manufacture cloth?

4. Where did America get its fabrics immediately following the Revolutionary War? Why were these sources unsatisfactory?
5. What was the most important factor needed to industrialize America's textiles?
6. Who was Samuel Slater? Why was he important to the development of American textile industry?
7. Describe America's most famous invention for the cotton industry. What effect did it have on America's textile industry?
8. What machine did Francis Lowell introduce to America? What did it do?
9. Name and describe other machines introduced in the 1700s.
10. What were the three key factors in the development of a mechanized textile industry?
11. Name and describe the two methods of manufacturing used in the mills. Who were their originators?
12. What four factors contributed to the success of the Waltham System?
13. Where and when did the manufacture of cotton begin? Why?
14. What is a converter? Which was the most famous and largest in the 1800s?
15. How did the cotton gin affect the South economically? Socially and industrially?
16. Historically, how, when, and where did the wool industry mark its beginning?

4

THE BIRTH AND GROWTH OF AMERICAN READY-TO-WEAR

OBJECTIVES

After reading this chapter, you should be able to:

- Tell how ready-made clothing was first introduced in the United States.
- Explain why the sewing machine had such an impact on the American ready-to-wear industry.
- Describe the development and growth of the country's ready-to-wear industry and its colorful New York City garment center.

Until the early 1800s, all Americans wore clothing that was "made to order." Most people dressed in clothes sewn by the "woman of the house" who, in most cases, was an amateur seamstress. The affluent minority bought the services of the professional dressmakers and tailors. But everyone, rich and poor alike, wore clothing that was made on an individual basis. Clothing was, in essence, a "custom-made" business.

THE FIRST READY-MADES, 1830s–1850s

Clothing the Sailors, Slaves, and Laborers

The first large-scale production of ready-made clothing began in 1830 in New Bedford, Massachusetts, the country's largest whaling port.

Visiting sailors, mostly men without wives and permanent homes, depended upon the city's tailors to outfit them with their sailing clothes.

Unfortunately, the length of a sailor's leave was short. To eliminate the normally long wait which accompanied made-to-order clothes, tailors began to make and stock simple shirts, trousers, and coats for the sailors.

Other manufacturers and dealers of sailor's clothing soon emerged throughout the Boston and New York area. The most famous of these is Brooks Brothers, the well known men's clothier and the nation's oldest clothing store. Founded in 1818 as a tailor shop by Henry Sands Brooks, Brooks Brothers began to produce sailor's ready-mades in 1830. In time it expanded its assortment of ready wear. In 1859, after ready-made men's clothing had become acceptable to the American public (see Fig. 4-1), Brooks Brothers was a large emporium proudly advertising a "large and

FIGURE 4-1. Broadway and Grand Street, 1857-70
Courtesy: Brooks Brothers

complete assortment of ready-made clothing and furnishings goods of superior style and make."

In the 1840s, ready-made clothing for slaves was introduced. In the past, slaves had always made their own clothes, but with the cotton boom, the Southern plantation owners needed their labor on the fields. From 1840 until the beginning of the Civil War in 1861, the manufacture of slave clothing was a large, profitable business in many southern cities as well as in New York and Philadelphia.

The next large demand for ready-mades occurred in 1849 when men headed west for the California gold mines. Chicago and St. Louis dealers supplied work clothes to those traveling west by land, while New York outfitted those California-bound by sea.

FOCUS ON THE INDUSTRY

THE BIRTH OF BLUE JEANS

During the Gold Rush of '49, one of the many who hoped to strike it rich was a young immigrant named Levi Strauss. In 1850 he headed west with little except a roll of tenting sailcloth as insurance against California's much publicized housing shortage. Strauss was unsuccessful in his search for gold. But he did find miners who were desperately in need of work clothes. Resourcefully, he turned his roll of tent canvas into work pants and began the first and most famous blue jeans business in the world.

After experimenting with sailcloth and duck, Strauss imported a French cotton which was stronger and far more suitable for work pants. Called *serge de Nîmes,* it was shortened to *de Nîmes* which, in turn, was Americanized into *denim.* Joined by double stitching and rivets, denim gave jeans one of its most prominent style characteristics. Each of those characteristics was introduced by Strauss for strictly utilitarian purposes: denim for strength, double stitching and rivets for reenforcement at points of wear.

Within ten years, Strauss developed a flourishing business, one which saw his pants and overalls become the popular uniform of farmers and cowboys as well as miners and other laborers.

Women began to wear jeans in the 1930s after discovering their comfort for horseback riding and other active sports. During the 40s, teenagers adopted jeans and their popularity with this age group continued to increase becoming—during the youth revolution of the

60s—their anti-establishment symbol. At that time, jeans also became a "bottom-up" fashion, embroidered, jeweled, and otherwise embellished by high priced manufacturers for their older, affluent high fashion customers.

Today, jeans are an integral part of just about everyone's wardrobe. Men and women alike. They're made by dozens of manufacturers, including name designers like Gloria Vanderbilt, Calvin Klein, and Ralph Lauren. The fact that they still exist is proof of the value of Levi Strauss's marketing concept. In the 1800s, he stitched up blue cotton denim pants to fill a need—and created a classic of today (see Fig. 4-2).

Clothing the Men and the Boys

Because the first ready-made clothing was produced for sailors, miners, and slaves, it developed an inferior connotation and was socially unacceptable. Shops which catered to sailors became known as "slop shops," a reference to the ill-fitting, rough quality of the clothes.

There were, however, some tailor shops that offered imported ready-mades of a quality superior to those sold in "slop shops" and they slowly gained acceptance. By mid-century, "off-the-rack" men and boys ready-to-wear had gained some measure of respectability.

Once the stigma of ready-mades eased, the early manufacturers of sailor, worker, and slave clothing converted part or all of their produc-

FIGURE 4-2. Classic Levi's, created over 100 years ago by Levi Strauss, are at a peak of popularity today
Courtesy: Natalie Best for Copley Newspapers

tion to the new ready-to-wear for men and boys. As these suppliers joined the custom tailors in the business of producing menswear, they established America's ready-to-wear industry. Many expanded their retail business to include the wholesale market. On the other hand, some who entered the industry as wholesalers expanded into retailing, thus beginning the policy known as *dual distribution. Dual distribution* refers to the sale of goods by a manufacturer at both the wholesale and retail level.

With the increased production of ready-mades, more American men were offered a desirable, cheaper alternative to expensive custom-made clothing, and the popularity and demand for men's ready-made clothing grew.

Much of this demand was due to America's increased immigration. As the population grew, ready-made clothing seemed to be the only way to meet growing clothing needs. New production techniques could produce several ready-mades in the time it took to prepare a single custom garment. Instead of "one at a time," garments were cut several at a time. Construction was farmed out to sewing contractors by the tailors and owners of the shops. In turn, the contracting firms utilized the sewing services of farm wives—a technique long employed by the Army.

These then, were the beginnings of America's clothing industry. It was, however, an industry where all the sewing was still laboriously and slowly done by hand.

MECHANIZING THE INDUSTRY—THE 1850s

Many historians cite three developments as responsible for bringing about America's Industrial Revolution: Whitney's cotton gin, the factory systems developed by Slater and Lowell and, finally, the invention of the sewing machine. Without this final invention, ready-to-wear could not have been fully mechanized.

FOCUS ON THE INDUSTRY

ELIAS HOWE AND THE SEWING MACHINE

By the early 1800s, most of the processes used in the production of clothing had been mechanized. The one exception was sewing.

Intrigued with mechanization, many Americans had devoted much time and effort toward the invention of a sewing machine. All tried to imitate hand sewing—using a single thread. In 1834, Walter Hunt built a device which formed an interlock stitch with *two* threads but, unable to perfect the device, Hunt abandoned it.

Ten years later, a young mechanic named Elias Howe, Jr. became obsessed with the same double thread principle and after two years of hard work developed a machine which was similar but superior to Hunt's.

On September 10, 1846, Howe was granted a patent. Unfortunately, Howe was unable to sell his machine; it was vehemently rejected by tailors who feared that it would somehow cut into their business.

Discouraged, Howe sent his invention to England where it was purchased by a "William Thomas, Corset Maker." Thomas promised to obtain an English patent for Howe, making an oral agreement to give Howe three pounds for each machine that was sold. But the corset maker never kept his word. Though he made over a million dollars on Howe's invention, Howe never received a cent.

While Howe was in England trying to market his invention, his sewing machine had been copied and manufactured by others in America and was being successfully sold. One of its enterprising marketers was Issac M. Singer, the founder of the Singer Sewing Machine Company. In 1854, a desperate and destitute Howe sued Singer and two other firms for patent infringement; the courts decided in favor of Howe's patent and Howe was finally recognized as the original inventor of the sewing machine (see Fig. 4-3).

A financial agreement was made whereby Howe allowed Singer and the others to continue manufacturing the machine. Howe died thirteen years later at the age of 49, but between his legal victory and his death, his invention earned him over two million dollars in royalties.

With Howe's sewing machine, America now had all the ingredients necessary for the establishment of a mechanized ready-to-wear industry.

Machines Enter the Factory

When the sewing machine was brought into the factory in 1852, the production of clothing was revolutionized: A seamstress machine-stitched a man's shirt in one hour and fifteen minutes, a job which normally took her almost fifteen hours to perform by hand. Brooks

FIGURE 4-3. a) Elias Howe's sewing machine, 1845
Courtesy: Smithsonian Institution

Brothers produced a coat in three days instead of six. Hoop and crinoline makers eliminated hand sewing problems, radically speeding up production. And manufacturers of women's cloaks slashed retail prices as the new machines substantially reduced operating costs.

Innovations and Improvements for Cutting and Sewing

As factories expanded and multiplied, other new machines mechanized every facet of cutting and sewing. From 1842 to 1899, over 7,335 patents were issued on sewing machines and accessories alone. It has been only within the last thirty years that the zigzag stitch has been made widely available on machines manufactured for home consumption. Yet this and other innovations, were put into use in factories a scant thirty years after Howe patented his simple sewing machine.

1874 – Machine makes pleats and ruffles.
1877 – Machine stitches bone stays into corsets.

FIGURE 4-3. b) Isaac M. Singer's adaptation of the Howe sewing machine
Courtesy: Smithsonian Institution

1883 - Machine stitches, cuts, and trims in one operation.
1891 - Machine produces zig-zag stitch.
1892 - Electrical round knife cutting machine—based on circular saw premise—cuts six layers of cloth at one time.
1893 - Electrical vertical knife cutting machine cuts forty layers of cloth at one time.
1897 - Electrical vertical knife cutting machine improved to cut up to one hundred layers or 1 1/2 inches of cloth at one time.
1899 - Machine automatically stitches and cuts buttonholes.
1914 - Pressing machine invented.

GROWING PAINS OF THE INDUSTRY, 1860s–1880s

Prior to ready-mades, size was not a problem since everything was made to order (cut from the measurements of the individual and fitted directly on the body). With the introduction of ready-mades however, sizing became an issue.

Sizing the Men

The first attempt to standardize sizes of menswear was made by the United States Army Clothing Establishment, organized in 1812 to provide soldiers with unifroms. The clothing was cut from patterns which had been developed by a master tailor, but the few sizes could not properly fit ten thousand men and uniforms in the first half of the 1800s were either too short, too long, too tight, or too loose.

During the Civil War over a million chest and height measurements were taken for uniforms. After the war, these measurements plus those acquired from other studies enabled manufacturers to develop and perfect accurate patterns.

By the 1870s, men could purchase ready-made suits off the racks and be assured of a relatively good fit—simply by giving their chest measurements.

Sizing the Women

After the introduction of machine sewing in the factories of the 1850s, the manufacture of men's clothing quickly became an important part of the economy. It was not until 1860, however, that the United States officially recognized the manufacture of women's clothing.

That year, the Eighth Census of the United States introduced a report on the "women's clothing industry." It listed 188 establishments employing 5739 people and producing a total of over seven million dollars worth of goods. All these companies produced cloaks, mantillas, or crinolines—simply because they came in one size and fit almost all women. The art of *grading* patterns for women (duplicating a style in various sizes) had not yet developed into the sophisticated science it had become in the men's industry. Manufacturers were still unable to produce well-fitting women's merchandise in a variety of sizes.

In 1863, Ebenezer Butterick, the founder of the Butterick Pattern Company, developed a concept for grading patterns.

To introduce the patterns to the public, Butterick published *The Metropolitan,* a magazine illustrating the latest styles. Women were able to purchase the paper patterns by mail or at their favorite shop.

The Butterick pattern quickly became a major fashion innovation as well as a technical one. Fashions which were once too difficult and complicated for cutting and sewing at home were now available to the home sewer. Ready-made manufacturers also began to use Butterick's concepts for the purpose of developing and evolving patterns of their own.

FIGURE 4-4. One of the first women's ready-to-wear ads, circa 1880s
Courtesy: Smithsonian Institution

The Growth of Women's Wear

After pattern making was developed, women's dresses began to appear on ready-to-wear racks. At first they were inexpensive, to meet the demands of the immigrant women. As manufacturers improved upon their patternmaking and sewing techniques and fit was perfected, the ready-made stigma began to diminish. Soon, they were "trading-up", producing merchandise for the growing, fashion-conscious middle class. By the 1880s, B. Altman and Company of New York and other prestigious shops and department stores were advertising *"Ladies Dresses (ready-made)"* in their catalogues (see Fig. 4-4).

ESTABLISHING MASS PRODUCTION

Division of Labor

Makers of the first ready-mades, eager to produce in quantity, but pressed for skilled labor, used the limited talents of the local women to sew the simpler items while tailors produced the complicated ones. This innovative procedure became known as the *division of labor* and it proved to be a highly efficient method of production.

When the sewing machine was introduced, production steps were divided even further. Workers were trained to sew on just one part of the garment—a collar or a cuff—in a technique called *specialization.* In the 1880s, the *task system* became another method of dividing labor using a team of workers—a baster, operator, finisher, and presser—to work on each garment.

The Producers

Manufacturers. The first manufacturers began as retailers and the background of most was similar. The majority were German and Austrian Jews who, after emigrating to America, gravitated toward the same business they knew in their homeland. Gradually they expanded their retail operations into manufacturing.

The manufacturers of high priced quality women's coats were motivated by a concern for quality rather than cost, and preferred to use expert craftsmen under the slower "task system." But with manufacturers of medium-priced goods—such as men's shirts, for example—cost was the most important consideration. By having as many as thirty workers handle one shirt under the "specialization" method, they could produce a profitable, moderately priced, quality product.

The majority of manufacturers had large plants for their manufacturing and selling operations. The designing, sample making, cutting, sewing, pressing, and selling of a garment took place under one roof. This type of operation was known as an *inside* shop and, until the 1880s, most manufacturers operated in this manner.

Jobbers and Contractors. In time, many plants found it profitable to farm out some of the sewing and pressing. A plant of this type became known as a *jobber*. It gave those tasks to one or more *contractors*, paying them a specific amount for work done on each garment. Because the work performed for the jobber by the contractor was done outside the premises, the contractor's factory was known as an *outside* shop.

The choice between an inside or an outside shop by a manufacturer was often governed by quality considerations as well as profit. To control quality, high priced goods were generally made in an inside shop. Medium priced goods, where cost was an additional consideration, were usually produced with the help of the outside shop.

Between 1880 and 1890, contractors became a dominant force in the industry. Most were Russian and Polish Jewish immigrants and though some were located in a number of large eastern cities, the majority were in New York's lower East Side.

The term "jobber" was also used to identify firms who distributed the lines of several manufacturers. This type of "jobber" emerged when eastern manufacturers found it difficult to reach the many small retailers who were cropping up throughout the expanding country and chose instead to distribute their goods by selling large quantities to one firm in one large area. These firms—or "jobbers"—carried large assortments from several manufacturers and with a "one-stop" seasonal buying trip local merchants could adequately replenish their stocks.

As transportation improved, manufacturers were able to service retailers directly and many of these "jobbers" disappeared. At the present time some do exist in the fashion industry, but they usually deal with low priced goods and are generally found in the low end markets.

THE WORKERS AND THE SWEATSHOPS

The great waves of immigrants who came to America during the late 1800s and early 1900s provided workers for the clothing industry. The largest group began their arrival in the 1880s. They were Russian and Polish Jews, and historically they contributed the most to the industry's development. Entire families, including women and children, went to work in the needle trades.

The Italians arrived about the turn of the century, but in their case, it was mainly their women who, with their dressmaking skills, entered the industry.

Like most immigrants, all these people were intent on bettering themselves and were willing to work hard and put in long hours. Unfortunately, their willingness to sacrifice was shamefully capitalized upon.

The term *sweatshop* originated in England and was first used in America during the early 1800s when the production of sailor clothing began. It referred to the "slop" shop dealers who gave out work to local women, making a profit on their labor—or "sweat." As the industry grew, it was then applied to contractors.

The working conditions of the contracting shops were awful and "sweatshop" soon took on the added connotation as any place of business with unsanitary conditions, excessively long hours, and extremely low pay.

Many of the contractors "set up shop" without much capital. They rented dilapidated lofts and used the front room for the "sewing factory" and the rest of the flat for living quarters.

As many people as possible were crowded into these filthy tenements and their unsanitary conditions became breeding grounds for tuberculosis and other diseases.

Wages and working hours were just as appalling. The average paycheck was three dollars a week for a ten-hour, six-day work week.

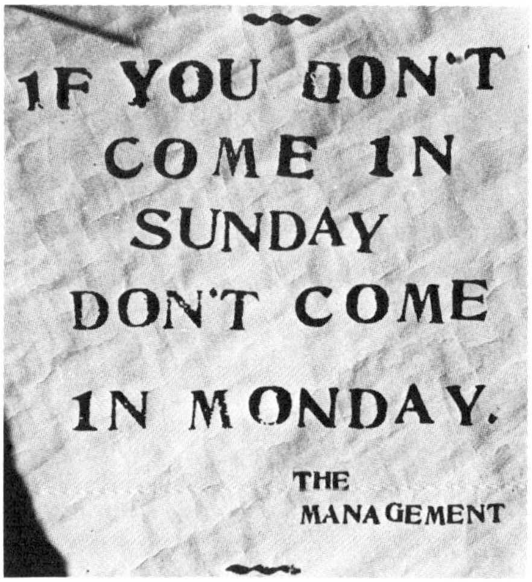

FIGURE 4-5. Courtesy: International Ladies' Garment Workers' Union, New York

During the busy season the work week was stretched even further and employers would force their workers to come in by posting warning signs (see Fig. 4-5) which threatened them with a loss of their jobs.

These conditions not only existed in the "outside" shops of contractors, but in the "inside" factories as well. The most infamous of these sweatshops was the Triangle Shirtwaist Company where, in 1911, a fire took the lives of 146 people.

FOCUS ON THE INDUSTRY

THE TRIANGLE FIRE

The Triangle Shirtwaist Company was the industry's largest manufacturer of women's shirtwaist tops. The company was located on the eighth, ninth, and tenth floors of the Asch Building (next to what is now New York University in Greenwich Village).

It employed 500 workers, most of them young women who worked crowded together on the eighth floor, surrounded by cardboard boxes of flammable cloth clippings. To prevent the workers from stealing a shirtwaist or sneaking out before closing time, all the doors leading to the stairwells were kept locked.

On the afternoon of March 25, 1911, eyewitnesses told of seeing smoke coming out of the eighth floor. Then they saw that one after another, bolts of dark cloth were being thrown out of the windows. As they approached the building to inspect the fallen bundles they saw that the bundles were not cloth. They were young women.

The fire began in one of the cloth-filled boxes, and in minutes the smoke and flames had spread to the ninth and tenth floors above. Unable to open the bolted doors, the girls ran to the fire escapes and elevators. The fire escapes collapsed from overloading, hurtling bodies to the courtyard below. The elevators were filled immediately by people on the top floor and bypassed the floors below. Though firemen arrived within minutes their ladders were useless; the ladders could not reach to the eighth floor.

Some girls, immediately overcome by smoke, were found still sitting at their machines—charred. The others—trying to escape the flames—jumped to their death. A newspaperman at the scene described the tragedy in his column:

"Thud—dead! Thud—dead! Thud—dead! I call them that because the sound and the thought of death came to me each time at the same instant."[1]

A half hour after it started, the fire was out. In that half hour, 146 died—mostly girls—with 124 of them jumping to their death.

The two owners of the company escaped unharmed. They were indicted on charges of first and second degree manslaughter and brought to trial. Both were acquitted. The shock of the acquittal created public outrage and a cry for reform.

A special factory Investigating Commission was formed in June, 1911. Inspectors were sent into factories, tenements, and shops—anywhere sweatshop conditions existed. Their findings publicized the horror of the sweatshop and led to corrective legislation.

The site of this now infamous fire is commemorated by the following plaque:

Triangle Fire

On this site, 146 workers lost their lives in the Triangle Shirtwaist Company fire on March 25, 1911. Out of their martyrdom came new concepts of social responsibility and labor legislation that have helped make American working conditions the finest in the world.

International Ladies' Garment Workers' Union
March 25, 1961

The Unions

Appalling working conditions in the clothing industry prompted the workers to organize.

On June 3, 1900, eleven delegates from seven small locals met in New York, representing less than 2,000 cloakmakers. They established the now great International Ladies' Garment Workers' Union—the ILGWU.

By 1910, the union had won many important reforms and recognition for itself.

The other union of the industry—the Amalgamated Clothing Workers—was formed in 1914, representing men's clothing workers.

[1]Leon Stein, *The Triangle Fire* (Philadelphia: J. B. Lippincott Company, © 1962), p. 19.

The reforms achieved by these unions had a profound effect on the sweatshop worker. In 1924 Dr. Louis Levine wrote that the immigrant "had been transformed into an industrial citizen who begins a new and constructed struggle for the democratization of his work-shop and for the Americanization of his home."[2] This transformation spurred the workers to seek other goals and "these unions were the *first* in the American labor movement to bring economic experts into the service of labor, to organize departments of research and investigation, to carry on special educational activities." He credited "their spectacular struggle for a living wage and for constitutionalism in the industry"[3] as a factor toward awakening the "social consciousness" of America to the plight of the working person—an awakening that was to influence the entire labor movement of the country.

Today, the unions of the clothing industry are praised and respected by all for their support of educational and social reforms and their early progressive policies.

THE INDUSTRY BLOSSOMS

After the 1880s, the industry grew at an incredibly fast pace. Three factors are said to have contributed to its growth: *immigration, economic depressions,* and *simplification* in women's clothes.

Immigration, described earlier in this chapter, spurred the development of the clothing industry by providing the industry with its main source of workers, while adding to the demand for all types of wearing apparel.

Economic depressions helped the industry by converting men to "ready-mades" when they found that quality comparable to that in custom-made clothing was available at half the cost. The depression of 1873 also gave birth to a new industry: "pants-makers." To economize, men bought ready-made pants for their contrasting custom jackets.

Because of the elaborate styling in women's apparel, women's wear developed at a much slower pace. It was only after the 1890s, when the *simplification* of women's fashion began, that mass-produced clothing for women was successful.

The item most responsible for popularizing women's wear was the shirtwaist top. It was introduced in 1891 to be worn under suits. Working women found that by having several of these tops, they could add to

[2]Louis Levine, *The Women's Garment Workers* (New York: B. W. Heubsch, 1924), Preface, p. vii.

[3]*Ibid.,* Preface, p. ix.

FIGURE 4-6. The Gibson waist, as popularized by the famous illustrator, Charles Dana Gibson, is illustrated above and on page 93
Courtesy: Smithsonian Institution

the versatility of a few suits. In time, the suit jacket was discarded for the "shirtwaist and skirt."

The shirtwaist fashion was immortalized by Charles Dana Gibson, the creator of the "Gibson Girl." A popular illustrator, Gibson painted beautiful young women who were dressed in a shirtwaist and skirt. In time, the tops came to be called "Gibson Waists" (see Fig. 4-6).

For twenty years—from 1892 to 1912—the shirtwaist costume was the uniform of American women. In addition to its versatility, two other factors contributed to its popularity. The first was its *non-restrictive qual-*

CHAS. J. HIRSCH.
I. C. LEVI.
THE... LATEST "GIBSON" WAIST
IN ALBATROSS.
OPEN FRONT or BACK.
No. 440.
THE Latest "Gibson" Waist, made of all-wool Atlantic Mills Albatross. Front has the latest broad-shoulder effect and trimmed with small velvet buttons. French back, Bishop sleeve and cuff stitched. Center plait with small buttons.
In all the leading Spring shades.
Packed one in a box.
Price, $1.50 EACH.
Elk Brand
Trade Mark
Registered
TERMS:
3% 10 DAYS. NO DATING.
PROMPT DELIVERIES.
ELECTROS FURNISHED FREE.
CHAS. J. HIRSCH & CO.,
160-162 WOOSTER ST., NEW YORK.

FIGURE 4-7. In 1911 dress manufacturers were born as blouse makers switched to making one-piece shirt-waist dresses

ity. Working women enjoyed its comfort and considered its simplicty a badge and symbol of their new-found freedom. The other was *mass production.* Though women were psychologically ready for its look, its success would have been impossible without mass production. Manufacturers produced millions in a variety of styles, fabrics, and prices, making them widely available to all.

In 1911, as an outgrowth of the shirtwaist top fashion, the *shirtwaist dress* (see Fig. 4-7) was introduced. At that time, there were no dress manufacturers—only those who produced separates, suits, and coats. As business slowed down, blouse manufacturers switched to the one piece shirtwaist dress, and dress manufacturers were born.

By the 1920s, women's clothing had changed radically from the small waists and respectable ankle-length skirts of the pre-war period to the emancipated "flapper look" of the 20s.

Thus, the simplification of fashion was complete. Astute manufacturers welcomed the change, well aware of the important relationship between simple styling and mass production.

By 1929, 3500 dress manufacturers had joined the industry, and sales rose to 900 million dollars. Eighty percent of all American ready-to-wear manufacturers were in New York City and the majority of them had moved to the industry's present location in mid-town Manhattan, establishing the world famous "garment center" along the now-famous "Seventh Avenue." In less than forty years—from 1890 to 1929—the colorful, exciting wearing apparel industry of today had blossomed.

TERMS TO REMEMBER . . .

dual distribution
contractors
jobbers
inside shops
outside shops
specialization or "piece work"
task system
sweat shop
"slop shop"
the Triangle Shirtwaist Company fire
ILGWU
ACW
shirtwaist

HIGHLIGHTS OF THE CHAPTER

- The first ready-made clothing to be produced in America was made in the 1830s and 40s for sailors, slaves, soldiers, and laborers.
- Denim blue jeans were devised by Levi Strauss, an immigrant peddler who outfitted miners with work pants during the 1849 California Gold Rush.

- The sewing machine was invented in 1843 by Elias Howe; in the 1850s the sewing machine transformed the clothing industry from a hand industry to a mechanized one.
- Because of poor fit and its "working class" origins, at first ready-mades were rejected by the middle and upper classes. But by the 1860s, fit and workmanship were corrected and manufacturers and retailers of better ready-to-wear for men and boys prospered.
- The first ready-mades for women, produced in the 1850s, were hoop petticoats and cloaks (capes). The development of women's graded patterns made it possible to produce sized women's clothing and in the 1870s ready-made suits and dresses were introduced.
- The *division-of-labor* premise introduced mass production. Two methods were used to divide labor: *specialization* assigns a worker to work on only one part of a garment, and the *task system* gives a team of workers the responsibility for completing an entire garment.
- A manufacturer who designs, sews, and sells his product under one roof runs an *inside* shop. A jobber is a manufacturer who designs and sells a product but gives the sewing out to a contractor. A contractor is one who does the sewing for a manufacturer for a fee; his establishment is known as an *outside* shop.
- The large immigration of the 1800s increased the demand for ready-to-wear and provided the industry with its workers, thus speeding the industry's development.
- The *sweatshop* was a clothing factory with unsanitary conditions, long hours, and low pay. The fire at the Triangle Shirwaist Factory sweatshop on March 25, 1911, killed 146 people. It shocked the country into passing reform legislation for the abolishment of sweatshop conditions.
- The International Ladies' Garment Workers' Union and the Amalgamated Clothing Workers Union, founded in 1900 and 1914 respectively, launched improvements in the wage and working conditions of the industry.
- The period between 1870 and 1920 marked the establishment of America's ready-to-wear industry. Immigration, economic depressions, and the simplification of women's clothing were the three factors which spurred the development and establishment of the industry.

QUESTIONS

1. Where, when, and for whom were the first ready-made clothes made? Why did middle-class men reject them?
2. How did blue jeans originate?
3. What was the professional background of the manufacturers and retailers of the first successful clothing for men and boys?
4. What is dual distribution?
5. Give a brief biography of the man who invented the sewing machine.
6. After the invention of the sewing machine, what were the other ingredients America had which made the development of a mechanized clothing industry successful?
7. What factors contributed toward the perfection of fit in menswear?
8. What were the first ready-made items produced in women's wear? What prevented early manufacturers from expanding into other areas of womens' wear? How and when were those problems resolved?
9. Define division of labor. What is specialization? The task system?
10. What is the difference between a manufacturer, a jobber, and a contractor? Describe and differentiate between an "inside shop" and an "outside shop."
11. What immigrant group became the early manufacturers and retailers? Who were the other two groups which followed to provide the industry's labor and when did they arrive? Of these three groups, which contributed most to the industry?
12. Describe a typical sweatshop. Why did they flourish? Why did the Triangle Fire serve as a catalyst for industry reforms?
13. Why were unions formed? How did they help the workers? The industry?
14. What is one of the requisites for mass production? What was the first sized ready-made item for women to be mass produced and sold in volume? Why was it so successful?

BIBLIOGRAPHY

APPLETON, NATHAN, AND SAMUEL BATCHELDER, *The Early Development of The American Cotton Industry.* New York: Harper & Row, 1969.

COOPER, GRACE ROGERS, *The Copp Family Textiles.* Washington, D.C.: Smithsonian Institute Press, 1971.

DANISH, MAX D., *The World of David Dubinsky.* New York: World Publishing Company, 1957.

FENNELLY, CATHERINE, *Textiles in New England 1790–1840.* Old Sturbridge Village Booklet Series, Old Sturbridge, Inc., Mass. 1966.

GLOVER, JOHN G., AND RUDOLPH L. LAGAI, *The Development of American Industries.* New York: Simmons-Boardman Pub. Corp., 1959.

GREEN, CONSTANCE MCL., *Eli Whitney and the Birth of American Technology.* Boston: Little, Brown & Company, 1956.

GRONER, ALEX, *The History of American Business and Industry.* New York: American Heritage Publishing Co., 1972.

JOHNSON, LAURENCE A., *Over the Counter and on the Shelf.* New York: Bonanza Books, 1961.

KITWELL, CLAUDIA B., AND MARGARET C. CHRISTMAN, *Suiting Everyone.* Washington, D.C.: Smithsonian Institute Press, 1974.

LEAVITT, THOMAS W., ed., *Hollingsworth Letters: Technical Change in the Textile Industry 1826–1837.* Cambridge, Mass.: M.I.T. Press, 1969.

LEVINE, LOUIS, *The Women's Garment Workers.* New York: B. W. Huebsch, Inc., 1924.

LITTLE, FRANCES, *Early American Textiles.* New York: The Century Company, 1931.

MITCHELL, BROADUS, *The Rise of Cotton Mills in the South.* New York: DaCapo Press, 1968.

NYSTROM, PAUL H., *Economics of Fashion.* New York: Ronald Press, 1928.

PARTON, JAMES, *History of the Sewing Machine.* New York: Reprinted from Atlantic Monthly May 1967 Issue, International Ladies' Garment Workers' Union, 1967.

PETTIT, FLORENCE H., *America's Printed and Painted Fabrics.* New York: Hastings House, 1970.

Signature of 450,000, International Ladies' Garment Workers' Union Booklet. New York, 1965.

STEIN, LEON, *The Triangle Fire.* Philadelphia: J. B. Lippincott Company, 1962.

WARE, CAROLINE, F., *The Early New England Cotton Manufacture.* New York: Houghton Mifflin Company, 1931.

WHITE, GEORGE S., *Memoir of Samuel Slater.* Philadelphia, 1836.

III

CREATING TODAY'S FASHION

The celebrities—*the stars*—of the fashion business are its fashion designers. This part studies the designers of today. It prefaces that study, however, with a look into the background of modern fashion design which began in France over four centuries ago.

Over the centuries, the role of the designer grew into one of dictatorial proportions. But in the last two decades, that role has been remarkably changed. Fashion has been democratized and the dictatorial rule of the fashion designer is gone. The loss of their dictatorial powers has not, however, diminished the position of the designer. Present day designers have developed into *marketers* of fashion—expanding into many areas of design and becoming well-known personalities who successfully *sell* fashion. Karl Lagerfeld, ready-to-wear designer for the French firm *Chloe,* stressed the multi dimensional role of contemporary designers when he said, "When people ask me what I do, 'designer' seems inadequate. I tell them that I'm in the fashion business. But that is what happens with ready-to-wear. You become an enterprise."[1]

[1]Bernadine Morris, "A Designer Gets Ahead of Himself," *The New York Times* (September 21, 1976), p. 42.

5

ORIGINS OF MODERN FASHION DESIGN

OBJECTIVES

After reading this chapter, you should be able to:

- Explain where and how modern fashion design began.
- Understand France's early impact on fashion.
- Recognize the names and achievements of the great fashion designers and fashion personalities of the past.

The theories on the origin of clothing and fashion have been elaborated upon in Part I. An oversimplified summary of these theories suggests that when man covered his body with leaves as protection—*clothing* was born; when he chose one leaf over another because of its appearance—*fashion* was born; and when he assembled the leaves on his body so they pleased him aesthetically—*fashion design* was born.

Although this hypothetical version of the birth of fashion design appears farfetched—designing clothing probably began as primitively and as effortlessly as this account suggests. As man became more civilized, *fashion design* developed, reflecting his increasing sophistication. However, it was not until two hundred years or so ago, that the *business* of designing clothes evolved. Until then there were no fashion designers—only dressmakers and tailors whose suggestions and ideas were often edited by their customers.

The history of the creative or designing aspects of the fashion business is made up of people and personalities. In learning about their lives and accomplishments, the development of the industry automatically unfolds.

FRANCE—THE FIRST FASHION CENTER

Until the thirteenth century, the fashions of each country differed from one another. Dress was a form of national costume, and consequently an international fashion influence did not exist.

During the late 1200s, France emerged as an important European center of culture and learning. Although her reputation grew steadily for the next 400 years, it was during the reign of Louis XIV which began in 1661, that France's world-wide reputation peaked. Under Louis XIV, the expansion of cultural achievement was encouraged as part of his scheme to politically dominate the Western world.

The King's ambitious plans included the building of a magnificent palace in Versailles, a suburb of Paris. The palace served as his home, military headquarters, and as the social and political center of France. Sparing no expense, the palace was landscaped and decorated with the finest furnishings and art. The splendor of Versailles became legendary and served as a showcase of luxury and the "fashionable" life. The elaborate clothing preferences of Louis and his court were widely copied by the wealthy throughout Europe.

To meet the growing interest in and need for beautiful fabrics, tapestries, and ribbons, the King established textile production in Lyons and other French cities, and a lace works in Alençon. This was the beginning of France's fashion industry and marked her start as the fashion capital of the world.

ESTABLISHING FASHION LEADERSHIP

The First Fashion Leaders

During the next century, the monarchs who succeeded Louis XIV and the women of their royal courts, continued to encourage and support the French fashion industry. Two of the most famous were Madame de Pompadour and Madame du Barry. As mistresses of Louis XV, both dressed extravagantly and were noted fashion leaders of their time.

They were followed by the most influential fashion leader of the century, Marie Antoinette. As wife of Louis XVI she was Queen of France until her execution in 1793.

Because of her absolute passion for clothes, Marie Antoinette was known as the "Queen of Fashion." Her huge and lavish wardrobe occupied three of the palace's large rooms. Unfortunately, her clothes were so important to her that she refused to flee France without them. Traveling with several huge wardrobe trunks, she was easily spotted and arrested by the revolutionists. Her attachment to her clothes literally cost her her head!

The First "Name" Fashion Designer

The clothes of the rich and titled were made in shops owned by former dressmakers and tailors whose outstanding ability and good taste enabled them to direct the design and construction of the lavish garments. They were called *couturiers* and received little personal recognition.

But during the 1770s, a talented couturière named Rose Bertin became famous for her flair for choosing flattering fabrics, colors, and trims for her aristrocratic customers. Her fame brought her to the attention of Queen Marie Antoinette, then a shy and uncertain sixteen-year old. Under Bertin's guidance, the young queen was transformed into France's leading fashion personality.

One of Bertin's great achievements was to persuade the Queen to simplify her elaborate dress by adding more practical wool and cotton costumes, similar to those worn by shepherdesses. These imitations of lower-class apparel delighted the Queen. They became immensely pop-

FIGURE 5-1. Elaborate hairdressings made popular by Marie Antoinette in the 1780s were designed by the world's first designer—France's Rose Bertin

ular with her court and are an early example of a *bottom-up* fashion. Another well-remembered Bertin innovation is the elaborate hair-do's and wigs which so typify the late 1700s (see Fig. 5-1).

Bertin also counted foreign royalty among her clients, and she sent exquisitely dressed "fashion dolls" as far away as Russia and Turkey for the approval of her titled clientele. As a salute to her genius, the French government honored her with the official title "Minister of Fashion."

The Revolution forced Bertin to flee France, but she returned in 1800 and reestablished her business. Unfortunately, she never regained the prominence she enjoyed under Marie Antoinette, and she died in obscurity in 1813. Though her fashion credits are many, Rose Bertin is remembered as the first person to gain recognition from the public as a famous "name" designer.

FOCUS ON THE INDUSTRY

FASHION DOLLS—PARISIAN COMMUNIQUÊ

When the rest of the world began to copy French fashion, news and illustrations of the latest styles were eagerly sought. However, in the late 1700s, fashion magazines and newspapers did not exist. Women relied on word of mouth and a unique means of communicating the latest fashions—fashion dolls.

Fashion dolls were approximately eighteen inches high, had cloth bodies and china heads and hands. French dressmakers dressed them in an exact replica of the latest fashions—from the most elaborate Bertin hair-do to the tiniest miniature accessory.

The dolls originally circulated within France, but as French fashion influence spread, they were sold abroad. After the styles were copied and the dolls became outmoded they were given to children as playthings and very few, if any, of these eighteenth century fashion dolls now exist. In the early 1800s the introduction of the fashion magazine replaced the need for these unique fashion dolls.

Early Trend Setters

The Empire Look. After the Revolution, the French fashion industry fell apart. The ostentatious fashions of Marie Antoinette were banned and the new regime chose J. H. Leroy to design clothing reflecting the politically free atmosphere of France. Leroy based his designs on the ancient classical style of the Greeks.

A more elaborate version of this look was later wholeheartedly endorsed by the Emperor Napoleon and his wife, Empress Josephine. It was appropriately named the "Empire Look" (see Fig. 5-2). For about twenty-five years, it remained the accepted fashion of Europe and

FIGURE 5-2. Simple, high-waisted styles, called Empire gowns and patterned after ancient Greek costumes, flourished in France's post-Revolutionary early 1800s

America, helping France once again to establish herself as the fashion leader of the world.

At the height of its popularity, the look caused great concern as women were literally "dying" to be in fashion. The low cut, tiny sleeved dresses were made of very sheer fabric, worn over flimsy slips. Once on, the dresses were often dampened so they would hold their pleating by clinging to the body. This practice caused many a wearer to become ill and some even to die of pneumonia.

Beau Brummel and the Dandies. Besides Empress Josephine and Leroy, very few fashion leaders emerged during the early 1800s. The one notable exception was an Englishman named *Beau Brummel.*

Men of wealth had always been fascinated with dress. Often they appeared more opulent than women since they were great users of ruffles, laces, and elegant fabrics. In the nineteenth century these men were grouped by their fashion preferences and known by such names as beaus, spivs, and incroyables (incredibles). One groups—the "Macaronis"—who were partial to rosettes and feathers became immortalized in the old chant: "Yankee doodle went to London, riding on a pony, stuck a feather in his cap and called it macaroni."

But the most influential group of the time were the "dandies", headed by Beau Brummel. Because of his keen interest in dressing and his extreme fastidiousness Brummel was the undisputed leader in men's fashion from 1796 to 1816.

Brummel was a perfectionist when it came to dress. It is said that he even went so far as to employ two glovers—one to fit the hand, the other to fit the fingers. It took him over two hours to tie his cravat to his satisfaction, and he bathed three times a day—an unheard of practice in those days.

His greatest contribution to men's fashion was the replacement of silks, ruffles, and lace with elegant but simple wools; and an emphasis on expert cutting and tailoring. Because the English had years of experience working with British woolens, a by-product of this change was England's emergence as the world's leader in men's fashions—a position she maintains even today.

ESTABLISHING HAUTE COUTURE

Charles Frederick Worth—Beginning the French Couture

Though Bertin and Leroy were successful as "name" couturiers, their businesses functioned more like dressmaking establishments than the couture houses of today. The person credited with beginning the French couture, Charles Frederick Worth, was (curiously enough) not French, but English.

The "Father of the French Couture" learned about the fashion business at the early age of eleven when, forced to help support his family, Worth acquired salesmanship and tailoring skills in various London shops. At the age of twenty, he decided to go to Paris, becoming a salesman in a ladies' dress shop. There, he met his wife and began designing clothes for her. Worth's designs caught the attention of the shop's customers and this led to a successful partnership in the business. In 1860, Worth opened his own establishment, The House of Worth.

Because his creations were in such demand, Worth chose to dress only clientele with the "right" social status and rejected customers who would not do "justice" to his designs. His most important client was the wife of Napoleon III—Empress Eugenie.

To maintain his selectivity, Worth never advertised. Instead, each season he prepared hand-colored portfolios for each of his customers. This was but one of the many Worth "firsts." Another idea he is credited with and which he started by dressing his wife, was the use of live mannequins (models) to display his creations. Worth was also the first to select and supply fabrics for a design. Previously, customers supplied their own.

The House of Worth is credited with setting the major fashion trends of the mid to late 1800s. The most famous of these was the crinoline. By using a stiffened fabric to hold out the extremely wide skirts, Worth eliminated steel hoops and uncomfortable petticoats (see Fig. 5-3).

Worth's influence was profound; he has been called the "first fashion dictator" of modern times. After his death in 1895, the House of Worth was operated by his heirs, and although dressmaking activities stopped in 1930, the famous Worth fragrances are still successfully marketed today.

PAST DESIGNING GREATS OF THE FRENCH COUTURE

After Worth opened his couture house in 1860, others followed his lead. Between the turn of the century and the 1960s, France remained the undisputed mecca of fashion design. Among the many well known French designers, several emerged as "greats." Most of these designers were *revolutionaries,* rejecting the accepted fashion standards for their own radical new ones. The remaining few "greats" can be classified as

FIGURE 5-3. Worth introduced layers of crinoline petticoats to replace the cumbersome steel and bone hoops of the 1850s

traditionalists. Their innovations were more subtle, introducing gradual but nevertheless influential fashion change.

The French Revolutionists

These fashion revolutionaries were designers who were tuned in to the quickened pace of the twentieth century. Their greatness came from their ability to recognize the changing needs of women and to translate them into fashion.

Paul Poiret. When this designer opened his salon in 1904, women were uncomfortably poured into S-shaped corsets which emphasized their bustline and derriere. *Paul Poiret* considered this form of dress not only unhealthy, but passé. He felt it was time to "free the body" from this "kangaroo" shape so he introduced a simple tubular silhouette and replaced the hideous corsets with his new invention: the brassiere.

Poiret's revolutionary design concepts and campaign against the corset was welcomed by free-thinking women everywhere. Until 1914 he was, as he called himself, "King of Fashion."

Poiret's clothes were exotic with oriental overtones. One of his most famous shapes consisted of a "lampshade" tunic with a circular *wired* hem which was worn over a narrow hobble skirt (see Fig. 5-4).

Many of Poiret's friends were artists. By asking them to paint his collections, he was instrumental in elevating fashion illustration to an art form. Poiret also encouraged his friends to design fabrics and several of the ones he used are outstanding examples of classic Art Deco which was popular at that time.

Though Poiret was the first 20th century revolutionist to "free the body," he did not continue to evolve with this trend. In time, Poiret's fashions became hopelessly out of step with the times and the great designer's influence quickly diminished.

The period after World War I was an important one in the women's liberation movement. All over the western world women were fighting for equality and the right to vote. One means of expressing this new freedom was through appearance and dress. Curls, frills, and flounces were out. Short haircuts, tubular flat-chested silhouettes and *simplification in design* were in.

Coco Chanel. The most powerful personality behind this new look was *Coco Chanel.* From the beginning of her career in 1909, Chanel rejected Poiret's elaborate designs, maintaining that couturiers were not "artists," they were "furnishers." She believed women should dress *simply* and *comfortably.*

The first time she put her theories into practice was during World War I. French women could not successfully take over the jobs of the fighting men and still wear ornate fashions and hobble skirts. In her small shop Chanel offered an alternative style of dress: men's pullover sweaters, sailor jackets, and straight skirts. The new "working costume" was a success and so was Chanel.

Chanel was often inspired by the everyday clothes worn by working people around her, borrowing from a mechanic's blouse, a ditchdigger's scarf, and the white collar and cuffs of a waitress for ideas.

The first designer to use wool jersey in women's wear, Chanel revolutionized the textile industry. Originally, the fabric had been produced for use in men's underwear, but men found it too "scratchy." However, the jersey appealed to Chanel who found it perfect for the kind of comfortable and understated apparel she had in mind.

FIGURE 5-4. Poiret's famous tunic of 1912 was stiffened with hoop for its "lampshade" effect

She was also the first to make costume jewelry socially acceptable. She popularized the use of "fake" jewels by lavishly using rope upon rope of imitation pearls and other fake stones to enhance her simple, understated clothes. The simplicity of her designs made them easy to copy in the factory and she is credited with being the designer who had the greatest effect on the early development of American mass production.

FIGURE 5-5. Mademoiselle Gabrielle Chanel, the great French couturière, photographed in the drawing room of her salon in the late 1950s.

Until her retirement in 1939, Chanel was one of the world's most influential pre-war designers. Her retirement was not permanent, however. In 1953 she was prompted into a comeback by her distaste for post-war fashions. In opposition to the cinch-waisted, full-skirted styles being presented by Dior and other designers, she reintroduced her *simple, comfortable* shapes (see Fig. 5-5). By 1959, her famous Chanel suit had become the "uniform" of well-dressed women everywhere.

Chanel died in 1971 at the age of eighty-eight, but under the talented designer Philippe Guiborge, her business continues producing clothes which reflect the classic look of Chanel. The famous numbered Chanel fragrances also continue to be produced, including the legendary No. 5, named by Chanel for her lucky number. In 1977, the current management at Chanel departed from Chanel's preference for numbers by introducing the latest Chanel fragrance as *Cristalle.*

In Part I we determined that fashion reflects the social and economic conditions of a given time. The great designers are those who best reflect the spirit of those times. In that context, most fashion authorities agree that Coco Chanel was the century's most "influential and revolutionary designer because she brought simplicity and freedom to women's clothes."[1]

Besides Chanel, there were two other important designers who had a revolutionary impact on the fashions of the 20s and 30s. They were Madeline Vionnet and Elsa Schiaparelli.

Vionnet. The design concept of Madeline Vionnet was quite different than that of Chanel. It was revolutionary; her greatest contribution was her invention of intricate bias cuts (fabric cut on the diagonal of the grain line). She also believed in retaining the natural lines of the body and rejected corsets, padding, or stiffening which might distort the anatomy.

Vionnet was in business several years before her bias cut made her famous in 1922 and she continued to design until 1939. Born in 1877, Vionnet was in her late nineties when she died in 1975. Though Vionnet's dressmaking techniques differed from those of Chanel, both introduced a contemporary approach to fashion. In his autobiography, *Christian Dior and I,* the great post-war designer credits Chanel and Vionnet with being the creators of modern fashion.

Schiaparelli. While Chanel and Vionnet designed easy, soft clothes, this designer's look was quite different.

Elsa Schiaparelli was an Italian who began her Paris career in the early 30s by knitting beautiful sweaters. Her subsequent couture collections seemed to mirror the chaotic times. She used unusual and shocking colors; "shocking pink" was her invention. She introduced "mad" prints, buttons, and accessories, and an upturned shoe became one of her most famous hat designs. She was the designer for those who advocated "hard chic," who wished to be "shocking," and as such became quite successful.

Schiaparelli is also credited with introducing the *boutique* into the couture business. She decided to sell some of her unusual accessories, sweaters and other less expensive items of clothing in a corner of her salon. After the war her boutique concept was copied by other French couturiers.

At the start of World War II, Schiaparelli closed her business. She never returned to fashion but continued to enjoy a successful perfume business. Elsa Schiaparelli died 1973 at the age of eighty-three.

During and immediately after World War II, the influence of the Paris couture was interrupted and fashion remained unchanged. But by

[1]Bernard Roshco, *The Rag Race* (New York: Funk and Wagnalls, 1963), p. 210.

1947, the Paris couture was on its way to recovery. That fall, Christian Dior introduced the New Look in his first collection. Instantly the dress of women all over the world was revolutionized and Paris' position as the world center of high fashion was restored.

Dior. The New Look (see Fig. 5-6) that Christian Dior presented was a radical departure from the existing silhouette. He eliminated shoulder pads, cinched the waist and—unhampered by former wartime cloth restrictions—widened and lengthened the skirt.

The initial reaction was explosive and controversial, but women welcomed its luxurious feminine look and eventually, the New Look was overwhelmingly accepted.

Christian Dior died in 1957 at the age of 53, ten years after he started his business. In those ten years, he developed his organization into one of international scope. After his death, designer Yves Saint

FIGURE 5-6. Christian Dior's revolutionary "New Look" of 1947 made him the leading designer of the post-World War II years

Laurent took over the firm's designing duties, but after a few seasons, he was called to serve in the French military service. Marc Bohan became the firm's design director and under him, it has continued to produce luxurious, beautiful clothes.

Though Christian Dior's revolutionary New Look made him the most famous post-war designer, fashion authorities agree that, until the youth revolution of the 60s, the designer who had the most overall influence on post-war fashion was Christobal Balenciaga.

Balenciaga. Unlike Dior, Christobal Balenciaga's clothes were understated and tailored, relying on cut and shape for design. Through the use of interfacings and linings, his sculptured shapes were built into his clothes.

His concern for shape and form led him to introduce new shapes, earning him the name "prophet of silhouette." One of his most influential silhouettes was the 1957 chemise. Its tubular shape was the forerunner of the popular straight "shift" of the late 50s and early 60s.

The rest of the couture was tremendously influenced by the work of the man they called "The Master" and they followed his lead. Because of that influence, he is credited with creating the major trends of the 50s and 60s (see Fig. 5-7).

To Balenciaga, fashion and elegance were inseparable. Disillusioned with the new young revolution in clothes, he retired in 1968. He died in Spain, his birthplace, in 1972 at the age of seventy-seven.

The French Traditionalists

While the revolutionists dramatically influenced fashion, several other designers earned an important position in the French couture. These were the traditionalists and the most famous two made their major impact during the pre-war era of the 20s and 30s.

The first was the founder of the House of Lanvin, *Jeanne Lanvin.* Established in the late 1890s, the House is the oldest member of the French couture, continuing today under the direction of her grandnephew Bernard Lanvin.

The luxurious fashions and the *My Sin* and *Arpège* fragrances of Madame Lanvin brought her world-wide recognition. Her fame stimulated global interest in the Paris couture, contributing tremendously to the development of the industry during the 20s. For her enormous contribution, France awarded her its highest award—the Cross of the Legion of Honor.

Madame Lanvin died in 1946 at the age of seventy-nine.

Another important designer of the 20s was *Mainbocher.* An American and former French *Vogue* editor, Mainbocher was known for his

FIGURE 5-7. Balenciaga's "sculp-tured" shapes set the silhouette trends of the 50s and 60s

timeless and understated but totally original designs. His credits include the beaded evening sweater, the dinner suit, short evening dresses, and the sleeveless suit blouse.

His most celebrated client was the Duchess of Windsor.

After the outbreak of the war, Mainbocher came to America and continued his couture business. He became the only "name" designer in the United States whose business was devoted exclusively to making custom-made clothes, and though he greatly influenced Seventh Avenue fashion, he never produced ready-to-wear.

Mainbocher retired to France in 1971 where he died five years later at the age of eighty-five.

TERMS TO REMEMBER . . .

fashion dolls
boutique
Empire look
Rose Bertin
Beau Brummel
Charles Frederick Worth
Paul Poiret
Coco Chanel
Christian Dior
Christobal Balenciaga

HIGHLIGHTS OF THE CHAPTER

- The world's first fashion center was Paris. It was established by King Louis XIV in the middle 1600s as part of his scheme to culturally and politically dominate the Western world.
- During the following centuries, French women of the royal courts became the world's first fashion leaders. They encouraged and supported the French fashion industry, maintaining France's reputation as the fashion capital of the world.
- Rose Bertin, French dressmaker to Marie Antoinette during the late 1700s, was the first "name" designer. But it was Charles

Frederick Worth, an Englishman, who is the "Father of the French Couture." The House of Worth—opened in 1860—set the pattern for future couture houses.

- Paul Poiret and Coco Chanel, designers during the first thirty years of the 1900s, were the revolutionaries of the French couture. Both "freed the body" from restricting clothes and undergarments, reflecting the new "equality and freedom for women" of the early 1900s.
- The great designers are those who reflect the spirit of the times. Because of the simplicity and freedom of her clothes, Chanel is considered the greatest designer of the first half of the twentieth century.

QUESTIONS

1. Why did King Louis XIV develop France's fashion industry? Where was his palace located and how did it help France's fashion reputation?
2. Name the first French fashion leaders and describe their position in French history.
3. How did Rose Bertin become France's first "name" designer? What were fashion dolls and how did Bertin utilize them?
4. When and how did the Empire look originate? Who was Beau Brummel and what role did he play in fashion?
5. Describe how Charles Frederick Worth began his career and mention some Worth "firsts."
6. Who were the four French fashion revolutionists of the early 1900s? Why was each considered so?
7. Name the great post-war French designer who revolutionized fashion. Describe the look which made him famous.

6

TODAY'S EUROPEAN DESIGNERS

OBJECTIVES

After reading this chapter, you should be able to:

- Know the location of the European fashion centers.
- Understand how the French couture business operates and evaluate its relative importance in fashion.
- Identify the greatest of the European ready-to-wear and couture designers.
- Describe the rise of the European ready-to-wear designers and elaborate on their impact on the status of the European couture.

Most European designers work in Paris, helping to maintain that city's three-hundred-year-old fashion reputation. Others work in London, Italy, and Spain. Together—along with the great talent on Seventh Avenue—these designers set the pace of fashion throughout the world.

THE COUTURE

France

France has long been synonymous with the best—albeit, at times, the most outrageous—in fashion. For generations Paris has been a center of fashion creativity, providing the world with its main source of fashion inspiration.

Several factors have contributed toward shaping France into a world fashion leader, and all are related to the historic support and encouragement of the industry by the French government *and* its people. From the time of Louis XIV, the French have considered fashion a creative art as well as one of the country's important industries. The government considers designers major contributors to the economy, while the people—men and women alike—regard them as gifted artists and shower them with recognition and affection.

Because of this support, designers work under ideal conditions. Small specialized industries are part of this tradition. The finest trims, embroideries, and other materials are available to—and often developed for—the designer.

One of the first steps France took toward developing a fashion industry was to establish textile centers. Today, these centers provide designers with what are generally conceded to be the finest fabrics in the world. French textile manufacturers are both willing and able to cooperate fully with designers. They gladly develop new colors and textures to specifications, running off short lengths of cloth for experimental purposes.

All these agreeable and supportive conditions have served to develop and maintain Paris' reputation as a fashion center; one which, for over a century, has housed the world's most accomplished creator and expressionist of fashion: *the couturier.*

Operation of the Paris Couture. Literally translated, *couturier* is the French word for "dressmaker," while *haute couture* translates into "the finest sewing." In France, however, both terms have a broader meaning. They refer to the designers and firms who create and sell the finest, *high fashion, custom-made* apparel.

A *custom-made* item is one which is made to the specifications of the individual customer. The making of custom apparel is a lengthy and expensive process.

It begins with a presentation of a *collection* of original designs. The designs are sewn in workrooms by *midinettes* who are supervised by a *première.* Each design is called a *model.* The collection is displayed on *mannequins*—the French word for live models—and the presentation is called a *showing.* A house *directrice* supervises the mannequins, the showings, and the salespeople or *vendeuses.* After seeing a collection at a showing, clients have the models of their choice made to order—on a one-at-a-time basis—with each garment fitted and made to conform to individual size specifications.

Couture showings take place twice a year. The spring-summer collections are shown in the latter part of January; the fall-winter collections are presented in July. It is at these showings that the new French couture fashion trends emerge.

The collections are first presented to a mixed but, to the couture, important group. It includes the private customers who provide the couture with 75 percent of its couture business (often wealthy celebrities and socialites), the press, and customers who are part of the fashion industry. There are three types of customers in this latter group:

1. American and European ready-to-wear manufacturers who purchase models for use as a source of inspiration when designing their own lines.
2. American and European retail store buyers who purchase models for the express purpose of selling lower-priced, ready-to-wear copies, or adaptations in their own countries.
3. Paper pattern manufacturers who purchase models or models made in muslin (*toiles*) to reproduce into paper patterns for the home sewer.

Several weeks after the initial showings, private clients are invited to view the collections and make their selections.

All private clients and members of the press are admitted free, but manufacturers and retailers are charged a fee. The fee may consist of a *caution*—the French word for deposit; or it may take the form of a required *minimum* purchase.

The size of the *caution* depends on the importance of the couture house and can range anywhere between 500 and 3,000 dollars. The amount of the *caution,* however, is deductible from the cost of subsequent purchases. In the event a customer does not make a purchase, the caution is kept by the couture house as an admission fee.

When a *minimum* purchase is specified, it generally consists of a requirement to buy a certain number of models or paper patterns. In some houses, the customer is given a choice of paying his or her entrance fee through either a *caution,* a *minimum* purchase, or a combination of both.

The prices members of the industry pay for models are higher than those paid by private clients. The couture justifies the difference by pointing to the profitable, commercial use the industry makes of the models.

Chambre Syndicale de la Couture Parisienne. There are many designers and custom dressmakers in Paris, but only a few are officially recognized as *haute couturiers.* To earn that distinction, a designer must meet specific qualifications as set down by the *Chambre Syndicale de la Couture Parisienne,* the trade organization of the Paris couture.

The Chambre Syndicale de la Couture was organized in 1868 by Charles Worth when he recognized the need to coordinate the activities of the growing French industry.

Throughout the years, the members have changed and grown and the Chambre has changed accordingly. For example, in 1936, the Chambre's policy was reorganized to strengthen the professional unity of its members against threatening political conditions. During World War II that solidarity was successfully tested when Hitler began making plans to move the couture industry to Berlin; Lucien Lelong, then the president of the Chambre, succeeded in convincing German officials that the French couture could not operate outside of France. Remarkably, many couture houses continued to operate during the German occupation, serving as training grounds for such post-war greats as Christian Dior.

Today, the basic function of the organization continues to be based on its original premise of representing the couture in all labor, legal, and business matters.

The average membership of the Chambre Syndicale usually numbers between twenty and thirty couturiers. In 1977, the number of houses belonging to the organization was twenty-six. Only a handful of members, however, become world famous. Acceptance by the Chambre is considered prestigious and advantageous, but not all qualified couture houses wish to become members. The independent Chanel never joined. Nevertheless, members and non-members alike regard the guidelines set by the Syndicale as acceptable requirements for the establishment of a couture house.

FOCUS ON THE INDUSTRY

For Membership in the Syndicale:

1. A formal written request must be presented by the couture house to the organization.
2. Workrooms must be established in Paris with a minimum of twenty workers. Workmanship must be in the highest French tradition and, whenever possible, done by hand.
3. Each house must offer a collection designed by the designer or a member of his or her staff.
4. The clothes must be custom made and individually fitted to each client.

5. Sketches must be made by the house designer only.
6. A design must remain as it appeared in the original collection—it may never be changed to suit a client.
7. No work may be done by outside workrooms except for such specialized crafts as embroidery.
8. Each house must agree to show at least seventy-five models on live mannequins at the dates in January and July established by the Chambre Syndicale.
9. Three mannequins must be employed by the house year round, and collections must be presented a total of fifty times during the year.

Duties and Responsibilities of the Chambre Syndicale:

1. Schedule and coordinate dates and times of couture openings for both visiting buyers and the press.
2. Issue invitations and press cards for openings.
3. Arrange shipping dates so that all models are sent to manufacturers and retailers on the same date—about thirty days after the showing.
4. Set official release date of press photos and sketches to coincide with introduction of ready-to-wear copies in stores. Date is usually about six weeks after the showing.
5. Regulate copying conditions. Under current rules, manufacturers and retailers who purchase original models may sell copies in their own country, but they may not sell paper patterns of a model to other manufacturers or to pattern companies. Though copying rules are legally unenforceable in the United States, those who break them forfeit the privilege of attending future openings.
6. Register all new designs and enforce the French law prohibiting copying and style piracy in France.

L'Ecole de la Chambre Syndicale de la Couture. In 1930, the Syndicale founded a school to train French youth for the couture. Today, it is considered Europe's leading fashion school. One of its students was the great Yves Saint Laurent.

To accommodate foreign students, the school has an international division which has traditionally attracted many young Americans; the talented designer Geoffrey Beene is one of its best known alumni.

Business Organization of the Couture. Couture houses are usually founded by a designer and are known by the founder's name. The houses of Saint Laurent, Cardin, Chanel, and Dior are such examples. In the event of the death of the designer, the firms usually continue to function, employing a successor to fulfill the designer's responsibilties. Inevitably, the work and name of the successor becomes widely recognized but as in the case of Marc Bohan, designer for the House of Dior—the firm almost always retains the name of its celebrated founder.

Though all couture houses are founded by designers, most designers begin with outside financial help and guidance provided by entering into partnerships. A classic example is that of designer Yves Saint Laurent. When he opened his house in 1963, he was backed by an American businessman from Georgia and by the American firm Charles of the Ritz.

Once successful, some Paris couture houses also enter into conglomerates similar to those described under the business arrangements of American designers in Chapter 7. The great house of Lanvin, for instance, was established for many decades when, in 1971, it became part of a conglomerate headed by Squibb Pharmaceuticals. The move made Bernard Lanvin—the head of the Lanvin enterprises and grandnephew of its founder—a Director of Squibb.

Other Activities of the Couture. The Paris couture designs for the rich, sophisticated woman who demands the newest and the best in fashion, materials, and workmanship. Until ten years ago, the couturiers were confident that the high cost of producing this type of elaborate fashion would easily be absorbed by their rich customers—and by the revenue from the sales of their fragrances. But as many younger rich women turned away from the couture, the houses were forced to expand into other related business activities in order to maintain profits.

The first of these activities was the *boutique* shop. Introduced by Schiaparelli in the 20s, some post-war designers recognized the value of the boutique and installed them on the main floor of their couture houses. Today, all designers have boutiques which sell exquisite accessories and a limited amount of ready-to-wear. The merchandise is designed by the couturier or member of his staff and bears the designer's coveted label.

In addition to their boutique products, most designers now produce goods under extremely profitable licensing operations. The mechanics of licensing are described in the next chapter under American Designer Business Arrangements. But like their American counterparts, through licensing, French designers have lent their name to a wide variety of products ranging from sheets to children's wear. These products are sold internationally through normal retail outlets.

The final and most unusual means of expansion has been the entrance of the couturier into the designing of ready-to-wear. This step was taken during the late 60s and early 70s to meet the new and formidable competition of both American and foreign ready-to-wear designers. By 1977, all members of the couture but two produced ready-to-wear. The exceptions were Chanel and Madame Alix Grés, then president of the Chambre Syndicale. But in March of that year, Chanel's house finally introduced its first ready-to-wear collection, leaving Grés as the last holdout.

The Current Status of the Paris Couture. In the fashion industry, there are differences of opinion on the influence today's Paris couture wields over world fashion.

The controversy began in the 1960s, focusing on the merits of the *haute couture* versus American and European *ready-to-wear*. Ready-to-wear designers were producing fashion which was much more contemporary and which reflected that turbulent era's life styles. Over the years, these designers grew to be as influential as the couture and as a result of their strong competition, the couture lost much of its dictatorial punch.

Today, this situation persists. The Paris couture has not regained the power it once held. Many consider it hopelessly out of date—producing clothes which have no relationship to what's happening to women today. Others point to the fact that it is unprofitable. The initial production costs of presenting a couture collection can run as high as half a million dollars. Subsequent sales do not return this initial investment and couture houses must make up their losses from the profits of their boutique, ready-to-wear, fragrances, and licensed products.

Nevertheless, there are those who insist that the couture does serve a purpose—one which is more important than providing a monied clientele with made-to-order clothes. They list several by-products of the couture that compensate for its shortcomings and validate its existence.

First, pro-couture forces maintain that the couture is indispensable as a *laboratory for ideas.* Couture designers agree. With unlimited access to the finest materials and workmanship, the couturiers argue that they can uninhibitedly experiment on developing fashion trends.

Second, the couturiers point to the invaluable *publicity and prestige* they receive from their haute couture and credit it with spurring the sales of other products sold under their label. They insist that the losses of their couture collections are easily made up through the additional sales of the other goods.

Third, the French government is convinced that the couture helps to *stimulate all French fashion business and trade.* The collections draw members of the fashion industry from all over the world. Today, with line-for-line copying substantially reduced, not as many industry people buy. Most pay their *caution* or *minimum* and use the collections as a source of inspiration in their own business. These visits, however, add additional foreign dollars to the French economy through purchases by the foreigners of merchandise from other areas of the French fashion industry.

Though the above arguments are valid, the top French designers are not unaware of the couture's jeopardized position. They realize that their influence has dropped immensely, one reason being the persistence of some couturiers to present "costumy" or extremely formal "older" clothes—fashions which are irrelevant and are out-of-step with today's life style. After the February showings of the Spring 1977 couture collections, Marc Bohan, designer for the House of Dior, acknowledged the problem. Referring to the new "younger" direction of couture collections, Bohan said, "we have to appeal to a younger woman."[1]

Whether the couture will ever be totally replaced by ready-to-wear remains to be seen. Presently, the couture seems to be holding its own. It still draws those designers from all over the world who want to express their ideas in couture terms. In 1977 for instance, Hanae Mori, a successful Tokyo couturier, made news by moving her business to Paris—drawn by the city's continuing "mystique" as a mecca for creativity. At the same time, some retailers are showing a renewed interest in selling couture. Bergdorf Goodman, for example, a store which had dropped the couture eight years earlier, reintroduced couture fashions by presenting models from the three top Fall 1976 collections—Saint Laurent, Dior, and Givenchy—for reproduction through their custom salons.

Still, the competition to the couture from ready-to-wear continues to be formidable. In order for it to regain its leadership, the French couture will have to come up with the kind of fashion that has wider appeal and can weaken New York's stronghold on world fashion.

The Great Paris Couturiers. There are over two dozen Paris designers who are members of the Chambre Syndicale de la Couture de la Parisienne—but presently only a few produce collections which make an *international* impact.

All these designers produce ready-to-wear, accessories, and other goods, but it is their custom-made *couture* collections which serve as a showcase for their ideas.

The most famous and influential of these important few is *Yves Saint Laurent.* This great talent joined the couture in 1954 at the age of 17 when he became an assistant to Christian Dior. When Dior died in 1957, Saint Laurent, then only 21, successfully succeeded Dior. But two years later, he introduced young, "hippie" type clothes into the collections which were considered too "radical" by most—including his firm—and eventually he left.

[1]Bernadine Morris, "The Renaissance of Haute Couture," *The New York Times Magazine* (February 27, 1977), p. 77.

FIGURE 6-1. Saint Laurent's famous peasant look greatly influenced fashion in the late 70s

Backed by American capital and in partnership with an art entrepreneur, Saint Laurent finally opened his own house in 1962. From the beginning he was successful, introducing visionary styles which became part of fashion for years afterwards. The Rajah coat, the Safari look, "hippie" bottom-up fashion, and the "peasant" look (see Fig. 6-1) have been some of his most influential innovations.

Saint Laurent's youth has made him extremely sensitive to young tastes and he has never hesitated in accepting their influence. Approached on that subject, he was quoted as saying that he is always "trying to express by means of clothes the new way of life, the psychological revolution of today's youth."[2]

This sensitivity to current life styles and philosophies has influenced every facet of his work. For instance, early in his career, he saw the trend toward ready-to-wear and—a quiet, shy man—hoped it would change the pompous couture business. "I hope a new generation of designers will transform the whole fashion business and do away with the collections—all that circus."[3]

In 1966, he encouraged the trend by opening a world-wide chain of ready-to-wear boutiques. Called *Rive Gauche,* they sell expensive, but well-made, mass-produced Saint Laurent fashions. His label also appears on cosmetics and accessories for men and women; on menswear; and on home furnishings.

A second immensely successful couture house is the *House of Dior.* A huge world-wide organization, it is often called the "General Motors of the French couture." In addition to the couture house in Paris, it has branches in New York and other major cities; and sells fragrances, cosmetics, accessories, luggage, menswear, and home furnishings under its prestigious Dior label.

Dior's design director for the entire organization—couture and ready to wear—is *Marc Bohan.* Bohan was brought from the London branch and assumed the Paris designing responsibilities after Dior's death and Saint Laurent's short stay. Though he has never made as strong an impact as Saint Laurent, he has been extremely successful in designing elegant fashion that reflects and often projects the trends while satisfying the elegant customers of Dior.

One of the most diversified designers in France is *Pierre Cardin.* He began his first couture house in 1950, designing traditional fashion. By 1960, however, he was introducing design and business concepts which were to make him a fashion revolutionist and an industry tycoon.

The list of Cardin firsts is enormous. He was the first to sell ready-to-wear and custom clothes under one roof. In 1960, he became the first couturier to present men's clothes. He dressed the men in "space age" fashion—another innovation—and by designing similar jumpsuits, goggles, and other "astronaut" fashions for women, he was one of the first to present the prophetic "unisex" trend.

Today, the famous Cardin label and his recognizable monogram is on over 250 products. Half of his American dollars come from his menswear, and the famous Cardin suit has become a middle America male status symbol.

[2]Nan Robertson, "A Shy Designer Who Shocks, But Only With His Designs," *The New York Times* (July 29, 1976), p. 36.

[3]*Ibid.*, p. 36.

In addition to clothing for men, women, and children, Cardin markets everything from candy to wine. His goods are produced in Russia, Japan, Australia, India, throughout Europe, and in the United States. And to add to his impressive list of "firsts," in January 1979 Cardin was named as fashion consultant to the Government of the People's Republic of China.

For over a quarter of a century, the extraordinary accomplishments of this designer have made him one of the industry's most progressive and influential forces.

Another great couturier is *Hubert de Givenchy.* Urged by Balenciaga, Givenchy started his couture house in 1951. His clothes were classic and immaculately tailored, similar to Balenciaga's. During the "elegant fashion" period of the 50s and early 60s, he joined Balenciaga and Dior as the "trio" who dressed the most famous women of the world—including Jacqueline Kennedy Onassis.

Today, in keeping with the current spirit, Givenchy designs softer, younger clothes. He was a world-wide chain of boutiques and, like most couturiers, produces a variety of products under his label.

Probably the most unique modern "revolutionary" is designer *André Courrèges.* For eleven years he worked as an assistant to Balenciaga, learning immaculate tailoring from "the master." He struck out on his own in 1961, but continued to design Balenciaga-influenced fashion. In 1963, however, he departed radically from that traditional look to introduce a revolutionary new concept in modern clothes.

All his life Courrèges had been interested in architecture. Utilizing his tailoring talents, he designed structured, "architectural" mini-skirted dresses and pant suits using only antiseptic white, pastels, and tattersal checked fabrics. Accessorized by white helmets and short white boots, the Courrèges look became a part of the youth fashion revolution of the mid-60s. This—declared his proponents—would be the look of the future (see Fig. 6-2).

Fashion, however, moved on to other things, but Courrèges continued to give his fans variations of his 1963 look. Today, he is still successfully expressing and selling that look in three apparel divisions: Prototypes (couture), Couture Future (expensive ready-to-wear); and Hyperbole (inexpensive). In the mid-70s, he opened Courrèges retail boutiques for women in New York and other cities; and began to produce apparel for men.

Mention must be made of a last designer, who, though not easily copied and thereby unable to influence mass fashion, is nevertheless one of the truly great Paris couturiers. Her name is *Mme. Alix Grés* and she has become famous for intricately cut and draped evening dresses. She became a designer in the late 1920s, after studying sculpture and deciding to "sculpt through fabrics."

FIGURE 6-2. The Courrèges look of the mid-1960s

An independent woman, Mme. Grés opened her current couture house in 1942 during the Nazi occupation, only to have it closed by the Germans when she defiantly presented her collection in France's colors of red, white, and blue. Today she continues to be extremely independent. Convinced that mass production cannot copy her work, she remains the only couturiere who does not produce profitable ready-to-wear.

Mme. Grés has been president of the Chambre Syndicale since 1972.

Other European Couture

Although most of the world's couture designers are drawn to the legendary atmosphere of Paris, there are several couturiers of importance in other European cities.

The organization, operation, and business activities of their establishments are similar to that of the French Couture. Like the French, they also have profitable boutique, ready-to-wear, and licensing operations. Their main source of recognition, however, comes from the publicity of their couture collections.

Italy. As in France, the people and government of Italy have long supported their fashion industries and when the Italian couture was formed after World War II, it too received strong government endorsement and support. Today, the government continues this practice by generously subsidizing any financial losses of its couture. It justifies this extraordinary expenditure by pointing to the Italian couture as "the research sector of the clothing industry" and "a vital part of the economy."[4]

Rome is Italy's couture center. Most couture designers work there, although a growing number prefer Milan, Florence, and other cities of the North, especially since Milan has become, after New York and Paris, the world's third ready-to-wear fashion center.

Italy's counterpart of the French Chambre Syndicale is *Camera Nazionale della Moda*. It is organized and functions like the Chambre. The Italian collections are shown just prior to those in Paris, allowing foreign buyers to cover all the European collections in one trip.

The reputation of the Italian couture was made by producing fashion distinctively different from the French. Italian fashion was and is much more colorful and extravagant, and very sportswear oriented. As a result, many of our past sportswear trends have come from Italy including the skinny capri pants of the 50s and the wide-legged "palazzo pajamas" introduced in the 60s.

Today, the status of Italy's couture has diminished. Most of Italy's current fashion accomplishments are centered around ready-to-wear.

[4]Eleanor Lambert, *World of Fashion* (New York: R. R. Bowker Company, 1976), p. 141.

There are, however, several couture names who have been and continue to be outstanding.

Emilio Pucci introduced the printed silk jersey shift which, as a "Pucci print," became a world status symbol in the 50s. Today, he continues to design the colorful modern abstract prints which made him famous; and, in addition to clothing, applies these "works of art" on everything from rugs to needlepoint. *Irene Galitzine* became famous after Pucci when, in 1960, she showed wide-legged divided skirts for at-home wear. Her "palazzo pajamas" became a classic fashion and helped to establish the successful trend toward at-home wear.

Valentino is Italy's best-known couturier. He began his business in 1960 in Rome, producing understated, softly tailored fashions which were primarily in stark white, or brown and white. The popularity of his work with Jacqueline Kennedy Onassis, Elizabeth Taylor, and other celebrated clients has brought him international fame.

London. Prior to World War II, the British had a prestigious couture which dressed English royalty and society, but almost all of those couture houses are now gone. The only one of note remaining is that of *Norman Hartnell,* a couturier who has been established since the 1920s. He holds the honorable position of court designer and dresses all the ladies of the British court, including the Queen.

Since the English couture has virtually disappeared, the fashion impact of London is concentrated in women's ready-to-wear and in the menswear produced by England's highly talented men's fashion designers. We will discuss these designers in the next section of this chapter.

Spain. Like England, Spain's fashion impact comes from its ready-to-wear sector. There are several makers of couture clothes in Spain, but none have had a great influence on world fashion. The sole exception is *Manuel Pertegaz* who has received international notice throughout the past few decades for some of his interesting designs and tailoring techniques.

EUROPEAN READY-TO-WEAR

Since the mid-60s, the originality of ready-to-wear designers—particularly of those in America—has overshadowed the leadership of the couture. Couture influence has declined; and so has its business. Recognizing that the future of fashion is in mass production, almost all couture designers have added ready-to-wear lines to their couture businesses.

Today, all important European designers create mass-produced fashion and the present battle for fashion supremacy is no longer between the makers of ready-to-wear and the designers of the couture. Instead, it has become a battle between two cities: Paris versus New York. It is from these two sources that the world receives its major fashion trends.

The designers from each city produce a distinctive "school" of fashion. Paris designers create fashion which is new and experimental, and therefore considered impractical and radically *avant garde*. New York produces original, but *wearable* high fashion. It is these differences in the cities' fashion philosophies that provoke the controversy and stimulate the competition between the two.

Paris fashion has fans throughout the world. Many are American. Geraldine Stutz, president of Henri Bendel, the New York store that specializes in expensive high fashion, praises the daring originality of Paris. In an interview in *Women's Wear Daily*, the industry trade paper, Miss Stutz points to Paris as the place to go for originality. At the same time, she urges the industry not to confuse the function of Seventh Avenue with that of Paris. Paris, she stresses, specializes in avant-garde fashion while America specializes in producing mass fashion.

Supporters of Seventh Avenue disagree. They argue that although New York specializes in mass fashion, it does so without sacrificing originality. Furthermore, American originality is combined with *wearability*. They consider Paris fashion too extreme and "out of step." Americans are especially critical of Paris' "costumy" looks. After seeing a group of extravagant Paris collections, American designer Halston reacted with, "I don't want to go back to the 1930s, I think the costume party is over for America, maybe not for Europe."[5] Moreover, other Americans maintain, women the world over "are demanding clothes that work for them, that they can put on and forget about."[6]

Since New York is currently producing that type of wearable fashion, world fashion experts agree that Seventh Avenue is presently winning the battle for fashion supremacy over the highly creative, but rather impractical Paris.

French Ready-to-Wear

The French word for ready-to-wear is *prêt-à-porter*. Formerly, prêt-à-porter consisted of high priced, well-made, but traditionally styled goods with little fashion impact. For the most part they carried unknown man-

[5]Enid Nemy, "St. Laurent Impact Seems Certain—But How Much and When?" *The New York Times* (July 30, 1976), p. A10.

[6]Bernadine Morris, "Paris versus New York," Fashions of the Times, *The New York Times Magazine* (March 6, 1977), pp. 103–106.

ufacturer labels. The only exceptions were the snappy clothes of a few new young designers like Emmanuelle Khanh whose name had become famous during the youth movement of the 60s. One other exception was the ready-to-wear collection of André Courrèges who decided to offer the public his own ready-to-wear when he was repulsed by the atrocious adaptions American manufacturers were making of his designs.

France refers to her ready-to-wear designers as *stylists,* reserving the "designer" designation for her couturiers. As the number of young, avant-garde French stylists grew, the work of names like Kenzo, Karl Lagerfeld, and Sonia Rykiel became as important in French fashion as those of the established couturiers. When couture designers joined in the production of prêt-à-porter, women the world over discovered that they could obtain a prestigious French designer label by visiting their local department store, and the prestige and exports of the French ready-to-wear clothing industry grew.

In 1975, the fashion leadership of French prêt-à-porter designers was finally recognized by the French fashion industry. That year, the Chambre Syndicale—formerly restricted to couture—formed the Chambre Syndicale du Prêt-à-Porter de Couturiers et des Createurs de Mode. It was organized by Pierre Berge, St. Laurent's business administrator, and it represents designers in all areas of the French ready-to-wear industry.

In April and October, the French prêt-à-porter collections are presented at France's most important trade fair, the *Salon du Prêt-à-Porter Féminin,* which takes place in Porte de Versailles, a suburb of Paris. The fair has over 900 exhibitors, including those in an international section that features manufacturers from all over the world.

The following are the most famous designers of French ready-to-wear. Their talent and originality have made them as influential and brought them as much recognition as that received by the past greats of the couture.

Kenzo. This Japanese born designer is—along with Saint Laurent—Paris' most influential designer. *Kenzo Takada* is called the "idea man" of French ready-to-wear. Since the start of his career in the late 60s, he has produced exciting, provocative, and often-imitated fashion. He started with 200 dollars worth of flea market fabrics in a tiny Paris shop and parlayed it into a fashion empire. In 1970 he opened "Jap," a boutique chain which now has locations throughout Europe. Today, he manufactures his own ready-to-wear for women, including shoes and accessories; and has licensing agreements for menswear and home furnishing products with European manufacturers.

Karl Lagerfeld. This talented man creates high-priced ready-to-wear with a couture look. *Karl Lagerfeld* worked in the couture as an assistant for several years before becoming a free-lance designer. In 1964, one of his free-lance assignments led him to his present successful association with the firm Chloe where he is now a member.

His fashion philosophy is based on light, fluid clothes. To maintain that feeling he has eliminated linings and extra seaming, and will sometimes substitute overcasting for turned-up hems.

Today, Lagerfeld is involved in many enterprises including the presentation of his own "Chloe" fragrance for Elizabeth Arden.

Sonia Rykiel. At the age of thirty-one, *Sonia Rykiel* went to work in her husband's shops designing the kind of simple clothes she could not find elsewhere. In 1968 she was successful enough to establish her own business. She designs easy-flowing separates, which she layers, and which have a sportswear look about them. They are sold in her own boutiques and in fine stores throughout the world.

Emmanuelle Khanh. Known as the pioneer of French ready-to-wear, *Emmanuelle Khanh* was one of the first young designers to become famous during the youth revolution of the 60s. A former model for the couture, she went to work designing for Cacharel, the famous separates maker. In 1960, she opened her own firm.

Her clothes are extreme and avant-garde. In the 60s youthquake, Khanh was the leading revolutionary force in French fashion.

Other important names in French ready-to-wear are the couturiers *Yves Saint Laurent, Pierre Cardin,* and *Marc Bohan* of the *House of Dior.*

Saint Laurent is as innovative with his ready-to-wear collections as he is with his couture. He expresses the same trends in both lines so that each is equally important in terms of fashion influence. Saint Laurent ready-to-wear for men and women is sold throughout the world in fine retail stores and in his international chain of boutiques—*Saint Laurent Rive Gauche.*

Pierre Cardin and the House of Dior also manufacture and distribute clothing for men and women internationally. Because of their wide distribution, the unique ideas in the clothes of these designers have a tremendous impact on world fashion trends.

English Ready-to-Wear

British designers have been influencing fashion for some time, but this was not always so. Before the 60s, British ready-to-wear was like the French prêt-à-porter, traditionally styled with little fashion impact.

In the early 60s, young Londoners began to break with tradition in everything from music to fashion. Their fashion preferences consisted of clothes in outrageous colors with hand-me-down, handmade appearance. The clothes were a revolutionary departure from the elegant fash-

FIGURE 6-3. The London look of the early 60s

ion of the couture, but to the young, the "London Look" (see Fig. 6-3) had an enormous appeal.

The trend toward this avant-garde way of dressing was first expressed by a young Chelsea shopkeeper, Mary Quant. Dissatisfied with the clothes supplied by her manufacturers, she began to suggest changes to them which reflected her tastes and those of her contemporaries. Soon, other young people began to design and sell their interpretation of the London (or Chelsea) Look and, for the first time, designers who made popular priced ready-to-wear began to receive recognition in England.

The trend for young, "kicky" fashion spread to France and the United States. By the mid 60s, "young" was the magic word.

Today, the London Look is gone. The revolutionary changes it caused in the structure of the fashion business, however, remain. The young fashions that came out of London during the 60s marked the rise of the ready-to-wear designer and the diminishing influence of the couture.

There are several English designers who presently provide the fashion impact of Britain. The following are those who are most important.

Mary Quant. This pioneer of the youth movement started her extraordinary career by opening a small clothing shop called *Bazaar.* It catered to young people who wanted non-traditional young fashion. When her ideas caught on and she began to manufacture her own clothes, she opened up other Bazaar shops. Today these boutiques exist in stores throughout the world.

Mary Quant gained widespread recognition early in her career. In 1961, she was asked to produce special collections for one of the American giants of mass fashion—J. C. Penney. Afterwards, she expanded into many other areas producing apparel and accessories under world-wide licensing agreements. In 1966, she introduced her international cosmetic line, featuring cosmetics geared to the young.

Today, she is called the "Mother of Mod," and continues to enjoy enormous success.

Zandra Rhodes. At the present time, England's most influential fashion force is *Zandra Rhodes.* A textile and dress designer, she began her career by producing fabrics for the British "mod" designers.

In 1968, she established her own firm featuring apparel made from her own highly individualistic prints. An avante-garde designer, she is also known for her unusual personal tastes, streaking her hair in rainbow shades and painting her eyes with bizarre eye makeup.

Today, she continues to be famous for her beautiful dresses and hand-painted ball gowns, and has expanded her creative talents into designing luxurious lingerie and sheets.

Hardy Amies. This leading British designer became famous after World War II as one of England's top couturiers. His current fame, however, is due to his recent work designing men's clothing and accessories. In 1967, he was asked to design menswear for a Scottish firm and was so successful that he was given a contract with Genesco, an American firm, to design their internationally distributed menswear. Today, the *Hardy Amies* label is one of the most prestigious in menswear.

Italian Ready-to-Wear

In recent years, Milan, Italy's ready-to-wear center, has grown into the third most important design capital in the world, surpassed only by Paris and New York. During the late 70s, new, young designers like Giorgio Armani, Muriel Grateau, and Basile have produced the type of avant-garde fashion that has made headlines. They join an Italian "fashion elite" that has been internationally famous since the post-war years, and which includes designers of fine leather goods, especially shoes. The following are some of the famous group.

The most famous name in Italian ready-to-wear during the 70s has been *Missoni*. This husband-and-wife team produce knitted fashions which feature unusual stitches and colorings. Their multi-colored, striated or "blurred" stripes effects were widely copied by knit and print houses alike, and the "Missoni" look became part of mass fashion.

The Missoni business began in 1953 when the couple sensed the future importance of knits. They experimented with original knit effects with Rosita creating simple designs for Ottavio's unusual stitches. Today the Missoni's employ more than 200 people in a complex which houses both their knitting mills and their home.

The other famous designers of Italian ready-to-wear are the couturiers *Pucci* and *Valentino*. Pucci designs a great variety of items—from ski wear to sheets—for companies in America and elsewhere; while Valentino produces apparel, home furnishings and linens for his international chain of ready-to-wear boutiques.

There are many outstanding makers of fine leather shoes and accessories in Italy, but none has the fashion impact of the *Gucci* firm. The designing is not done by one individual, but by several family members so that no one really qualifies as *the* designer of the firm. Nevertheless, the Gucci fashion influence is so strong, that the firm merits listing with important Italian designers.

The Gucci name became world famous during the 60s when its low-heeled moccasin with a brass harness across the instep became a status symbol. Before the Gucci loafer, the expensive Gucci handbag was the item which received the attention of the fashionable and the rich. Today, the current Gucci status symbol is its red and green striped luggage. Its look is imitated by accessory makers the world over. In 1978 Gucci went into the apparel business via a line of simple sportswear separates.

Gucci is an old family firm, designing and producing high quality leather accessories for over five centuries, and selling its products in Gucci shops throughout the world. In 1972, every family member in the firm signed an agreement to keep the ownership of the business within the family for at least the next 100 years.

TERMS TO REMEMBER . . .

couturier
haute couture
caution
minimum
a model
mannequin
a *toile*
a showing
prêt-à-porter
Chambre Syndicale de la Couture Parisienne
Yves Saint Laurent
Marc Bohan
Kenzo
Mary Quant
Missoni
Gucci

HIGHLIGHTS OF THE CHAPTER

- The three most important European fashion centers are in France, Italy, and England—of which Paris and Milan are the leaders. The centuries-old support of the French fashion industry by its government and people is traditional and has helped to maintain French fashion leadership.
- The French *haute couture* is composed of designers who produce custom-made clothes. They are represented by the *Chambre Syndicale de la Couture Parisienne* in all labor, legal, and business matters. To become a member, couture houses must meet rigid guidelines set by the Chambre.
- The current status of the couture is overshadowed by the American and its own French ready-to-wear designers. Non-profitable, it is maintained through the profits of its licensing and ready-to-wear operations. Nevertheless, French designers insist that the couture serves a purpose as a laboratory for ideas and as a source of business stimulation through its publicity and prestige.
- The three most famous couture houses today are those of Yves Saint Laurent, Christian Dior, and Pierre Cardin. Their names are synonymous with French designer ready-to-wear as well.

- Italy has several couture houses, but the fashion reputation of Italy today is centered around its ready-to-wear producers. The English and Spanish couture has also dwindled and has no present fashion impact.
- European ready-to-wear has grown tremendously in the past decade and every top couturier also sells mass-produced goods. The French ready-to-wear designers are the most avante-garde, and therefore the most famous. Italy, however, has several unique designers who influence world fashion trends.

QUESTIONS

1. Describe some of the conditions which have made Paris a centuries-old fashion center.
2. Define and describe the meaning of *haute couture.* How does a couture house function? Who are its customers?
3. What is a *caution?* A *minimum?*
4. Give the background and function of the *Chambre Syndicale de la Couture Parisienne.*
5. How many members does it average and what are the requirements for membership?
6. How do most couture houses get their start? Describe the business background of two famous couture houses.
7. What other business activities do couture houses run to maintain a profitable business? Describe them.
8. The Paris couture has declined in stature and influence during the last ten years. Do you agree?
9. What arguments do pro-couture forces give for the continuation of the couture?
10. Name today's great Paris designers and describe their work and influence.
11. Name some of the most famous Italian designers and describe what they are best known for.
12. Who was the pioneer of English ready-to-wear? French ready-to-wear? When did they begin?
13. Present both sides of the "European fashion versus American fashion" argument. With which side do you agree? Why?
14. In your opinion who are the most influential French, Italian, and English ready-to-wear designers of today? Why?

7

TODAY'S AMERICAN DESIGNERS

OBJECTIVES

After reading this chapter, you should be able to:

- Trace the development of American fashion design.
- Understand how, when, and why American ready-to-wear designers became the fashion leaders of the world.
- Understand how designers create and how their businesses operate.
- Be familiar with the names and work of America's top designers.

For several centuries, when it came to fashion, Paris led—the rest of the world followed. But when, during the 1960s, designers from the United States and other countries began to make an impact on the direction of fashion, the dictatorial supremacy of the Paris couture began to wane.

American design was the strongest of the new influences, outdistancing all other countries as well as France. Seventh Avenue emerged into a new position of fashion leadership and by the mid-1970s, the American designer label—a Bill Blass or an Anne Klein—had become as desirable and as prestigious as a Saint Laurent or a Cardin.

Today, members of the world-wide fashion industry, while still admiring the *individual* talents of the French couture, look to the *collective* talents of American designers for broad fashion leadership. Many agree with designer Calvin Klein, winner of the Coty American Fashion Critics Award, who summed it up: "For a long time, the French set the pace for what people wore. Now we are setting the pace."[1]

THE RISE OF THE AMERICAN DESIGNER

The first American designers were really copyists who, during the 1920s, produced watered-down versions of Paris trends for American manufacturers. But by the 1930s, the originality of some American designers began to emerge, producing two unique and unmistakably American influences on fashion: Hollywood and Sportswear.

The Hollywood Influence

Before television, the movies were America's main source of entertainment. Its stars were admired, some even revered. The clothes worn on the screen by such idols as Garbo, Harlow, or Crawford greatly influenced the way women all over the world dressed.

There were several outstanding Hollywood designers, including Jean Louis and the still famous Edith Head. But the one credited with having made the most impact on American fashion design was *Adrian*.

For twelve years, between 1930 and 1942, Adrian designed for all the major stars. He dressed Harlow in sensual clinging evening dresses and Joan Crawford in wide shouldered suits, starting a trend that lasted until the return of the sloping shoulder in 1947 with Dior's New Look.

He left the movies in 1942 to open a successful couture and ready-to-wear business, retiring ten years later. But throughout his career he rejected Paris as a source of inspiration, choosing instead to produce fashion which had a look which was very much his own.

The Sportswear Influence

Although Adrian was the first American "name" designer to achieve international recognition, original American designs were being produced as far back as the late 1800s in the form of *sportswear*.

The first example of American sportswear is traceable to an early female rebel—*Amelia Jenkins Bloomer*. Fed up with the restrictive

[1]Bernadine Morris, "To Seventh Avenue, Two Designers Bring Sweet Smell of Success," *The New York Times* (July 1, 1975), p. 20.

FIGURE 7-1. First Western "pants," introduced by Amelia Jenkins Bloomer in 1850

crinolines of the 1850s, she devised a "walking suit" which featured harem-type pants (Fig. 7-1). The fashion and her *Rational Dress Campaign* was ridiculed and rejected but it marked the introduction of pants for Western women. Thirty years later, Amelia's "bloomers" were accepted as an alternative to skirts while cycling or participating in other sports.

By the 1930s sportswear had come to be identified exclusively as an "American" phenomenon. Paris ignored it—both its design and its manufacture. But the farsighted people in the American industry did not.

One of the first to recognize and promote sportswear and its influence on a developing American look was Dorothy Shaver, who, in 1945, became president of the New York Lord & Taylor specialty store. As early as 1932, she launched a campaign heralding American designers. It was a radical departure from the tradition that all fashion came from France. Some of those early talents were Tom Brigance, Claire Potter, Vera Maxwell, Elizabeth Hawes, and Claire McCardell. Hawes is still remembered for her then controversial book, "Fashion is Spinach"; but the most outstanding talent was McCardell.

Claire McCardell. Thought by many to be the most brilliant of American designers, Claire McCardell was the one most responsible for developing an American look. The ideas and concepts she introduced between the beginning of her career in the 30s and her death in 1958 have become fashion and marketing classics.

One of her first marketing innovations was coordinated separates. At first the stores were afraid of "left over" tops or skirts and would not adopt her coordinates concept. Today, it is the backbone of the sportswear market.

In the 40s and 50s she conceived what we now call the "total look," accessorizing her dresses with matching caps, hats, and shoes. This prompted her partner, Adolf Klein, to pioneer the concept of "designer licensing" by having accessory manufacturers make and sell the accessories under the McCardell label.

Her designs were as original as her marketing theories, and she may be compared to Chanel in terms of design philosophy. Both advocated simplicity and comfort; both respected and followed the natural lines of the body, rejecting rigid construction or padding; and both were utilitarian in their approach. A button must button and a tie must tie.

Her design innovations—some of which have become classics—include the dirndl skirt, the "monastic" bias-cut tent dress, hardware closings (grommets, rivets, and so on), shoestring ties, ballet slippers for streetwear, and unlined bathing suits. She was equally original with fabrics, and began the then-unorthodox use of wool tweeds and cotton for evening wear, and mattress ticking for a town suit. She was the first to revive colonial calico and popularize wool jersey, anticipating the later popularity of both cottons and knits.

Her clothes were totally American in character: easy to wear and easy to mass produce. They were also so timeless that they could be and are, in fact, being worn today (Fig. 7-2).

Several years later, in her book *What Shall I Wear?* McCardell verbalized what her clothes had been expressing all along.

> We [designers] specialize in what we like best, in what we do best and what satisfies us most deeply. For me its America—it looks and feels like America. Its freedom, its democracy, its casualness, its good health. Clothes can say all that.[2]

The clothes of Claire McCardell did.

[2]Claire McCardell, *What Shall I Wear?* (New York: Simon and Schuster, 1956), p. 156.

FIGURE 7-2. 1942 "diaper" bathing suit and 1946 "baby dress' are timeless McCardell designs

Another designer who contributed toward world recognition of American fashion was Norman Norell. Though his clothes were made under American mass production methods, Norell was the first to incorporate couture techniques and offer couture quality in ready-to-wear.

In keeping with his couture philosophy, he was the first to present a complete ready-to-wear collection which included day and evening clothes. His trademark was simple clothes which relied on silhouette and exquisite French fabrics for interest.

Norell's main contribution to the American fashion industry was the fact that he was the first to bring *status* to ready-to-wear American designer label. For that reason, as well as for his superb creativity, he was called the "dean of American designers."

Naturally, there are other designers who have contributed greatly to the development of American design. Many are still successful and they are discussed at the end of this chapter. But it was the work of fashion pioneers like Adrian, McCardell, and Norell which brought American fashion its first signs of recognition. After the second world war, the influence and prestige of the American designer climbed rapidly and America's position as a fashion leader is now firmly established. Directly or indirectly, several factors have contributed to this meteoric rise.

The Youth Kick of the 60s

The *youth kick,* a combination of youth-oriented, psychedelic fashions designed for and by the young, began in the early 1960s with a group of young London ready-to-wear designers. The most famous of these was Mary Quant. Since their look best expressed the life style of the turbulent sixties, it quickly spread to other parts of Europe and to America where new, young designers introduced their versions of what had become known as the look of the "London Mod" or the "London Look."

These young trends were successfully absorbed into the mainstream of fashion. For the first time since the 40s, when World War II prevented the Paris couture from functioning and Hollywood film designers briefly became the trend setters, fashion was originating outside of Paris. By the mid 1960s, the youth kick had spread to all ages. Psychedelic fashion of the young was "in." High fashion elegance was "out."

Though many of its clients remained faithful to the Paris couture during this period, many others—particularly the younger ones—did not. Instead, they turned to the high priced, better ready-to-wear labels which were featuring the newer and younger contemporary look.

Stung by its new competition, the Paris couture began to pick up the youth kick, turning out collections that were just as explosive as those of its young competitors. Some couturiers took their inspiration from the young, borrowing their pea coats, granny dresses, and jeans for translation into couture versions. These were perfect examples of "bottom-up" fashions, a term we have defined in Chapter 2. Others, including André Courrèges and Emanuel Ungaro, introduced their own revolutionary modern concepts and must be credited for their originality.

But the energetic concepts of young ready-to-wear designers continued to exert a powerful influence on fashion trends. Most of the designs revolved around unorthodox, wild looks—looks which seemed to come naturally to these designers and best expressed the turbulent times.

The younger people, both designers and customers, also developed a new nonchalant attitude concerning fashion. They refused to be dictated to. They designed and wore what they wished ignoring the disapproval of their elders and the dictates of the Paris couture. Their nonchalance caught on and soon many people developed a more casual approach toward fashion. By 1970, it was clear that the youth movement had revolutionized many aspects of the fashion business—including weakening the old, dictatorial Paris couture punch.

A Return to the Classics in the 70s

After a particularly turbulent period, fashion reacts by reverting to the other extreme. In the seventies, fashion simmered down; the classic look of *American* sportswear took over.

Both the French couture and Seventh Avenue designers projected the new quiet look (see Fig. 7-3). Unfortunately for the couture, it was competing with what America did best—classic, tailored clothes. Pants, shirts, blazers, and sweaters were part of the new trend and it was quite evident that the line of any top American designer could easily compete with the French couture.

From time to time Paris tried to introduce revolutionary trends, but their concepts were rejected by the American consumer. The most significant of these rejections was the midi or maxi skirt which Paris showed in 1970. Many American manufacturers and retailers backed the calf-length midi—hailing it as a welcome and timely change from the then-popular thigh-high mini-skirt. Unfortunately, American women refused to buy it and both manufacturers and retailers lost a tremendous amount of money that season. That financial catastrophe cost the Paris couture most of the remaining influence it had with America's fashion industry. On the other hand, the acceptance of American designers continued to grow. They were increasingly in tune with the kind of clothing contemporary men and women preferred. Their collections gained world-wide popularity, their names world-wide recognition. Customers in Europe, Japan, and the United States began to consider the American designer label as prestigious as that of the French couturier.

Paris Couturiers Endorse Ready-to-Wear

To meet the competition of American designers on equal terms, in the late 60s the Paris couture entered the ready-to-wear business. At that point, most of the better French ready-to-wear exports, its prêt-à-porter, were limited to high quality, but conservatively styled fashion. The few exceptions were the clothes of Khanh and other young revolutionary de-

FIGURE 7-3. In the early 70s, fashion turned to the classics, a look Seventh Avenue designers do best. For the first time, America—not Europe—was setting the pace

signers. The aim of the couture was to compete against Seventh Avenue for world-wide ready-to-wear dollars, but their entrance into that market *helped* rather than hurt American designers.

To begin with, the French couture stimulated interest in *all* designer labels. One of their natural selling points was their name. The prestige of the French label—a Saint Laurent or Cardin—was and is enormous. These designers took advantage of the fact by promoting their labels extensively. Their most ingenious method of publicity was to use their names or initials as a status symbol, integrating either one into the overall design of their wearing apparel in a print or as a monogram. Refer to Fig. 13-2 in Chapter 13.

American designers quickly joined the "status name" game and began to get equal publicity. The interest of the fashion customer in designer fashions was successfully and extensively stimulated.

The entrance of the French couture into ready-to-wear also served to democratize the caste system of designers. Formerly these French designers were producing the most expensive clothes in the world—the haute couture. That fact alone automatically gave them a heady status. Though they continued that part of their business, they were now into a new game. Their ready-to-wear operations automatically shifted them to the level of the top American designers. To the consumer, all designer names provided an equal amount of prestige. A Bill Blass and a Pierre Cardin necktie were equally desirable; it was taste which determined the sale.

The Current Status of the American Designer

Reporting on the acceptance of American fashion, the March 22, *Time* magazine cover story printed the following:

> After more than a century of obeisance to Europe's high priests of couture, American designers have won worldwide respect as creative interpreters of a way of life—and style. It is a rebellion and an achievement which has been building since World War II. But it has, in the eclectic fashion world of 1976, undeniably come of age and attained a new level of élan and confidence.[3]

The confidence referred to by *Time* magazine was illustrated a few months later in an ad run by the fine New York department store, B. Altman and Company. In the November 1976 collections, Paris had re-introduced the mini-skirt. The style was vehemently rejected by American designers, manufacturers, and retailers as well as by the American fashion press. To emphasize this rejection, Altman's ran a full-page ad headlining American designer Geoffrey Beene's strong statement "Mini-skirts? Never." (Fig. 7-4.)

As little as six years earlier, the industry would have followed the dictates of Paris as it did in 1970 when it accepted the disastrous midi and maxi skirts. The opinion of an American designer would have been

[3]Reprinted by permission from *Time,* The Weekly Newsmagazine; Copyright, Time Inc. (March 22, 1976), p. 62.

FIGURE 7-4. American designer Geoffrey Beene's independent fashion philosophy is applauded by one of America's leading fashion retailers
Courtesy: B. Altman & Co., New York

overridden. By 1976, that opinion carried such weight that it was chosen as the subject for an expensive full-page ad in *The New York Times.*

Today's trend for casual, free-form, *comfortable* clothes, reenforces the strong position of the American designer, since they are the type of clothes Seventh Avenue does best. Naturally most French designers disagree with this evaluation, disputing the leadership of American design. They continue to feel that Paris *creates* fashion—Seventh Avenue *interprets.* Through the great individual talents of an Yves Saint Laurent or a Kenzo are undisputable, the premise of French fashion supremacy is no longer acceptable. American designers are currently providing fashion which best suits the lifestyle of modern men and women throughout the world. Though each designer has his or her own unmistakable signature, all produce the comfortable, easy-fitting clothes which keynote today's contemporary look. All over the world, even in Paris, the influence of American design is automatically acknowledged, and much of current fashion is admiringly referred to as "The American Look."

THE RESPONSIBILITIES AND WORK OF AN AMERICAN FASHION DESIGNER

A person who conceives or interprets styles of wearing apparel for men, women, and children is called a *fashion designer.* Designers translate creative thoughts into visible forms by using the basic elements of design: silhouette, texture, color, detail, and trim. As discussed in Chapter 1, by combining these elements in various ways, designers give their unique interpretation of the styles which they feel are part of the current overall fashion trend.

To be successful as a fashion designer, one must have special artistic talents and creative abilities. It is not enough for a designer to produce aesthetically pleasing merchandise, however. The designs must contain a more practical quality—*saleability.* This factor, saleability, determines the success of the designer's work in terms of dollars and cents. It gives the all-important marketing value to the designer's name and label.

Designing Saleable Fashion Merchandise

As mentioned in the Combined-Need Theory in Chapter 2, the consumer buys apparel to satisfy several needs and desires at the same time. In order to create a *saleable* collection, designers must familiarize themselves with their customers' wants and needs, and then attempt to satisfy them.

The first two factors a designer must take into consideration are the *utilitarian function* and *fashion appeal* of an item.

Utilitarian Function. This pertains to the serviceable and practical features that a customer looks for in a garment. For example, a coat should provide *warmth,* while a tennis outfit must give the wearer *freedom of movement.* Fabrics used in sportswear and everyday clothes should be *durable* and *easy care.* Overall, the garment should *fit comfortably* and not constrict the wearer. Finally, the garment should be *designed for a purpose.* Very few people will buy clothes unless they have a place or reason to wear them.

Fashion Appeal. Because the majority of consumer purchasing decisions are dominated by *emotional* concerns, not rational ones, a garment may meet utilitarian requirements and still not sell simply because it does not have *fashion appeal.* Fashion appeal is that illusive ingredient in a design which makes an item desirable. It evokes positive aesthetic feelings from the consumer which say "I like that," and "that is beautiful, I want it!" Fabric, color, and silhouette are some of the ingredients contributing to fashion appeal. Another is newness. The latest look or trend can cause a customer to reject last year's perfectly usable garment because it no longer "appeals," in favor of a new one which does.

As a designer plans a new season's collection, two other factors that must be considered are: *price* and *image.*

Price. To stay within a retail price range, it is mandatory for a designer to keep material and workmanship costs within price limits that are predetermined by the firm. Designers who work for high-priced houses have greater leeway, but most who work in medium and low-priced firms give primary consideration to production costs. *Fabric, trimming,* and *labor* are the three elements which determine cost. If a better fabric is chosen, then design must be kept simple to cut back on trimming and labor costs. Should a style call for complicated workmanship, then fabric costs must be kept to a minimum.

Image. Though styles change each season to reflect the newest fashion trends, every successful designer and firm must maintain a distinct image or "look." It should pervade every collection produced by the firm so that (ideally) customers will recognize the manufacturer or designer of the garment without seeing the label. By keeping a consistent image a designer or firm can continually appeal to a specific segment of loyal customers. For example, if the past success of a designer has been built around attractive but conservatively styled clothes aimed at career women, it would be disastrous for that designer to introduce avante-garde revolutionary styling into a new collection. On the other hand, the designer who has earned a reputation for innovative, trend-setting designs is expected to continually introduce new ideas in order to preserve an image and satisfy high fashion customers.

Creating a Design

Because of its creative aspects, an aura of mystery and eccentricity often—and erroneously—surrounds the profession of fashion design. In truth there is little mystery in how designers perform their jobs. Whether seeking sources of design inspiration or performing the highly skilled techniques of sketching, cutting, or draping, most designers develop a methodic, almost scientific, approach to the art of fashion design.

Inspiration. In order to continuously develop and create new designs, a designer requires a great deal of stimulation or inspiration. There are various sources to draw from and one of the most obvious is a designer's own work. Past styles which were successful are updated; past trends which are still important are repeated. Designers also review the work of other designers and keep tabs on what's happening in the industry by reviewing domestic and foreign publications, such as *Women's Wear Daily* and *L'Officiel,* and by visiting trade shows and international fairs.

Movies, television and the music industry are other good idea-provoking sources. Each mirrors contemporary trends and can inspire and influence designers toward new directions. The distinctive dress of rock and country music groups, for example, is often copied by their young audience. Designers who create for that audience keep an eye on the clothing choices of these performers so they can design accordingly. Period and old films can also be inspirational by instigating a revival of past trends. For instance, many designers admit that the revival of the 30s look which occurred during the 70s was partly inspired by the old films they saw on late night TV.

Other sources of stimulation from the past are featured museum costume collections. In 1976, a strong trend toward a "peasant-gypsy look" developed, especially for evening wear. Between December '76 and August '77 New York's Metropolitan Museum of Art exhibited "The Glory of Russian Costume." It featured the clothes of Russian peasants and aristocrats dating from the 17th to the early 20th centuries. Certainly the show must have been at least partially responsible for strengthening the development of the 1976 "peasant-look."

Another recent museum collection that made an imprint on fashion was the famous King Tut Exhibition. Its sensational tour of the country between 1977 and 1979 inspired designers and manufacturers to present consumers with a broad assortment of Egyptian flavored merchandise.

The textile industry can also help to stimulate creativity. Well before creating a collection, designers familiarize themselves with the new fabrics of the season, choosing those they find most exciting. They not only look for new colors and textures but new technological developments as well. For instance, several years ago the introduction of vinyls with suede and patent finishes inspired designers to experiment with them for rainwear, sportswear, accessories, even evening wear. The success of these fabrics was immediate, with one—ultrasuede—becoming a status symbol. Permanent press properties in fabrics also influenced designers, particularly in children's wear. Ruffles, frills, and other "difficult-to-iron" touches could be freely incorporated into a design without fear of rejection by "anti-ironing" mothers.

Designers also draw from the events which surround them. In Part I we learned how such things as political, social, and economic events, as well as changing life styles, influence fashion. A good designer watches these developments, understands how these forces can govern fashion changes, and then designs accordingly.

For example, Americans traditionally have been sports minded. Initially, spectator sports such as baseball and basketball enjoyed a high degree of popularity. Now, as life styles change, active sports such as tennis and jogging are in vogue. These activities have inspired a look of casual sportswear for everyday use. Sweatshirts, rugby shirts, culottes, knickers, tennis sweaters, and baseball jackets and caps are just some of the items that are seen more often off the playing fields and courts than on. Figure 7-5 is a typical example of how sports uniforms can inspire a line of junior sportswear.

In 1977, this trend expanded into the "gear look" which endorsed wearing rugged sports clothes for casual wear. The business of L. L. Bean, the Maine mail order house that produces camping and sports equipment and apparel, multiplied enormously during the late 70s as this trend grew. At the same time, designers were inspired by this trend and the utilitarian appearance of the "gear look" was evident in their collections.

A final source of inspiration for a designer is his customer. Top designers like Halston and Calvin Klein freely admit that they are inspired by their clients. Calvin Klein, whose forte is designing understated "with-it" clothes which are typically American in look, remarked that he was mainly "interested in the young American woman and I *watch her*."[4]

Designers who create for the mass market also watch their customers. The majority of these customers have classic, almost conservative tastes. The designers carefully gauge the reaction of their cautious clients to the introduction of new trends and design their future lines accordingly.

Producing a Design

Designers must create three to five collections a year, depending upon the firm they work with. The work on each collection begins at

[4]Reprinted by permission from *Time*, The Weekly Newsmagazine; Copyright, Time Inc. (March 22, 1976), p. 67.

FIGURE 7-5. Active sportswear influences fashion
Courtesy: Macy's, New York

least three months before the collection is presented to store buyers, and six to eighteen months before it is bought by the consumer. For example, a fall collection, which is shown to buyers at the end of May and shipped sometime between July and September, is begun no later than February. In many cases, collections are prepared even earlier. For example, sportswear firms start to plan and order fabric requirements as much as one-and-a-half years before the merchandise is presented to the consumer.

Once designers have availed themselves of all the information which contributes toward the creating of a design—fabrics, trends, prior failures and successes—they then proceed to the job of designing a collection or line.

Designers who produce original work, the innovators of the business, begin by draping or sketching a design from scratch. Those that work with fabric drape and cut on a dressmaker dummy until their ideas are formalized. Those that prefer to set their ideas down on paper make many rough sketches before settling on a final choice. Designers may design by either method, many prefer to use both.

When an idea is finalized, the designer passes a swatched rough sketch to a sketcher for a final drawing. The sketch is then given to the assistant designer who cuts a muslin pattern of the design. Once the muslin pattern is approved by the designer, the assistant uses the pattern to cut out the fabric chosen for the design. The final garment is then made by a sample hand who returns it to the designer and the heads of the firm for approval.

Firms which produce styles which are not totally original, eliminate some of the steps in the above procedure. Designers for those firms often up-date last season's best sellers by using new fabrics and incorporating new trends into the proven designs.

Once a sample is completed and approved by the heads of the firm, it is passed on to the production department and becomes part of the new line.

TYPES OF DESIGNERS

There are four types of designers in the American fashion industry. The "couture" or high fashion designer; the moderate or popular price market designer; the stylist; and the free-lance designer.

"Couture" or High Fashion Designer

Couture is a French word referring to the business of designing, making, and selling fashionable *custom-made/custom-fitted* clothes for individual clients. This type of operation has been the backbone of the French fashion industry for over one hundred years, but in America there is no cutom-made clothing industry to speak of and therefore no true "couture." All American designers are in the business of creating ready-to-wear. There are those, however, who produce strictly high fashion merchandise and whose originality has raised their status to the level of the French couture. To emphasize their distinctive position of leadership within the industry, these designers have formed an association known as the *New York Couture Business Council;* their wearing apparel is referred to as "*couture* ready-to-wear." The quality of the clothes is so good and the prices so high that designers don't hesitate to call their work "couture." The meaning of the term, therefore, has been broadened to include all those designers who produce *top quality, trendsetting, high fashion*—regardless of whether it is custom or ready-made.

This type of designing makes extraordinary demands on the individual. It requires top talent, originality, and an inborn "sixth sense" for spotting and creating trends. It also requires an ability to cope with the many pressures of a fast-paced business and a willingness to devote practically all one's time, energy, and creative talents to one's work. The designers who have all these qualities develop into the Halstons and Trigères of the fashion business.

The Moderate and Popular Priced Market "Designer"

Most designers work in the moderately priced apparel markets. The majority of the firms in these markets produce new but "safe" fashion apparel rather than trend-setting high fashion. Though couture designers gain wider recognition and fame, designers at this level receive much satisfaction from their work. Their job is constantly challenging, as they try to produce new fashion with mass appeal.

Stylists

Many firms which produce popular priced or low priced apparel base their collections on styles which have met with success during the previous season. To choose and adapt these proven styles for the new season, they use the talents of a stylist instead of a designer. Chapters 8 and 9 describe the function of stylists in the textile and accessory markets. As in those markets, stylists for apparel firms are also thoroughly familiar with current and future trends. These fashion experts look inside and outside their firms for "runners" or "fords"—styles which catch on immediately with the public and sell in great quantity—and incorporate new versions of these styles into their lines.

Free-Lance Designer

Free-lance designers sell sketches of their designs to manufacturers. They are free to design either high fashion originals or adaptations of current styles. The choice depends entirely upon their ability and the requirements of their manufacturer clients. Once a free-lance designer sells a sketch to a manufacturer, the designer's responsibility for that particular design is complete.

FOCUS ON A CAREER

FASHION DESIGN

The four basic types of *designers* have been described on the previous pages. There are, however, other career opportunities available in fashion design. The following positions often serve as an apprenticeship for beginning designers, but in many firms they are important enough to merit consideration as ultimate career goals.

Assistant Designer

This position requires top technical knowledge and skill. An assistant interprets the ideas of the designer by making the first muslin pattern of the design and then cutting out the original fabric sample.

Patternmaker

When a sample of a design is acceptable in terms of appearance and fit, a patternmaker "grades" the pattern, making a separate pattern for each of the sizes in which the design is to be manufactured.

Sample Maker

The sample maker is the top dressmaker of a firm. He or she constructs the first sample of a design. Coat and suit houses employ tailors instead of dressmakers, while firms producing a wide range of apparel employ both.

Sketcher

Working from the rough sketches of the designer, the sketcher makes the final drawing of a design. These drawings are used for reference by the assistant designer and the sample maker during the process of making the sample. The swatched drawings are then placed in a binder for a showroom book, providing the firm and its clients with a complete record of each style in the designer's current collection.

Training

When entering the field, it is essential to choose firms which produce the type of fashion you are interested in. This initial choice is most important since experience usually dictates future jobs. For example, a young assistant who has held a few jobs with a popular priced sportswear firm might find it difficult to enter a coat and suit house; and that same assistant might find it equally difficult to "trade up" to a job with a better (or designer) sportswear firm.

Training for any of these jobs is available at both the secondary and college levels. Not all high schools, of course, offer vocational training in patternmaking, draping, and similar subjects, but there are quite a few that do. Those schools often equip students with enough training and knowledge to make it possible for them to enter the industry directly from high school. But for those whose ultimate goal is a career in design, we recommend the marvelous education and training offered by many specialized college courses throughout the United States.

BUSINESS ARRANGEMENTS OF AMERICAN DESIGNERS

There are several business arrangements under which designers work. Name designers are usually in a position to be able to choose from any of these varied arrangements. Unknown designers are not in the same position. They have limited options open to them and therefore usually begin by working for a manufacturer.

Employer–Employee Relationship

The simplest business arrangement under which designers can operate is the *employer–employee relationship.* A majority of designers in the industry work as employees who remain in the background getting little or no publicity. The name on the garment label is that of the firm. If the line is successful the firm, not the designer, gains recognition. In this way, a manufacturer protects his business. If a designer leaves the firm he can be replaced without affecting the firm's label and fashion image.

A few firms, however, do include designer names on their labels. By doing so, both the designer and manufacturer gain the prestige valued by those customers who are interested in designer labels. One such successful arrangement exists between Donna Karan and the Anne Klein Company.

Partnerships

Designer Partnerships. This business arrangement usually takes place between a manufacturer and a recognized name designer. Sometimes the designer is an employee who is offered the partnership by the manufacturer to preserve a successful relationship. Other times the partnership is formed when a designer strikes out independently and needs experienced partners to help organize, finance, and manage the production and marketing aspects of the business. An example of this type of partnership is the one existing between designer Calvin Klein and business partner Barry Schwartz.

Another example is the unique partnership between Stuart Kreisler and four top Seventh Avenue designers—Bill Tice, Clovis Ruffin, Ralph Lauren, and John Kloss. Each designer has his own firm and for a percentage of their business, Kreisler supplies them with his financial backbone and advice.

And one of the best-known business backers in the industry is Ben Shaw who was responsible for putting Oscar de la Renta, Halston, and Geoffrey Beene in business and who is often referred to as the "Angel of Seventh Avenue."

Designer–Conglomerate Arrangements

Some designers get the hard-nosed business backing they need by becoming part of a *conglomerate.* A *conglomerate* is a company which gains control over firms in various unrelated industries by acquisition or merger. The conglomerate provides financial backing, legal and managerial advice, and marketing information to the designer. For instance, the parent company may conduct consumer research projects and surveys which might be too expensive for the designer house to undertake.

The conglomerates, meanwhile, have found that acquiring designer firms is profitable. Most of that profit comes from licensing agreements and franchising operations which are based on marketing the designer's name. Two examples of profitable designer–conglomerate arrangements are the Halston company, owned by Norton Simon; and the Anne Klein firm, owned by the Japanese firm Takihyo.

Licensing Agreements

Both the independent and conglomerate designer houses have taken advantage of the sales appeal of their names and have gone into the big business of *licensing*. *Licensing* is an agreement between a designer and a manufacturer whereby the manufacturer pays the designer a fee or royalties for the use of his or her name on a product. The amount of money paid the designer varies according to the input of the designer and the merchandise, but a typical fee is 10 percent of the retail price. The design of a product is usually created by, but sometimes merely approved of by the designer. However, actual production and distribution of the merchandise is the responsibility of the manufacturer. In these licensing agreements the designer is called the *licenser* and the manufacturer the *licensee*.

The licensing of names has long been successfully practiced by European designers. For example, Pierre Cardin has his name on as many as 285 products "ranging from sausage machines to chocolate."[5] Some of the American designers who have followed suit include Bill Blass, Donald Brooks, Oscar de la Renta, Geoffrey Beene, Halston, and Anne Klein.

Licensing arrangements ring up millions of sales dollars each year for designers and manufacturers alike. For example, Halston's twenty licensed products generate about 75 million dollars in sales annually. Bill Blass, whose fifteen products range from sheets to eyeglasses, gets between 5 and 10 percent of the nearly 100 million dollars his products earn each year. Anne Klein and Company, by far the most licensed

[5]Sandra Salmans, "Turnaround on Seventh Avenue," Fashions of the Times, *The New York Times Magazine* (August 29, 1976), p. 115.

designer name, sells well over 100 million dollars worth of lingerie, active sportswear, linens and towels, children's wear, fragrances, accessories, and menswear.

The types of products which seem to be the most successfully franchised are the last three items listed above, particularly fragrances. For instance, it is well known that the perfume sales of *Chanel No. 5* made Coco Chanel a millionaire; and that the *Joy* fragrances bring in the main revenues of the French couture house, Jean Patou, Inc. Today, American designers have joined the profitable fragrance market with perfumes such as *Geoffrey Beene* and *Red* by Geoffrey Beene, Anne Klein's *Blazer, Norell* by Norman Norell, and *Halston* by Halston. Some have also introduced *men's* fragrances and *Grey Flannel* by Beene and Blass' *Bill Blass* are two of these earliest entries.

Encouraged by their success with fragrances, some designers—Diane von Furstenberg for instance—have added women's cosmetics to their label while others are expanding to include men's cosmetics and other toiletries to their line of products for men.

In the late 60s, many designers entered into licensing via the accessory market when fashion's "total look" became the dominant trend and designers decided to create their own accessories for their clothes. By the early 70s, accessories with designer names and initials had become status symbols.

Today designer-labeled accessories are a big business. Accessories manufacturers produce a wide array of designer merchandise through a substantial and ever-increasing number of licensing agreements.

The 60s also saw designer names become important in menswear. Up until that time, manufacturers such as Hart, Schaffner and Marx, and Brooks Brothers were the prestigious labels.

Three designers are credited with starting the trend of designer licensing in menswear. The first was the innovative women's designer, Frenchman Pierre Cardin who, in 1964, successfully introduced a highly styled collection for men. In 1965, John Weitz, an American designer of women's sportswear and maternity clothes, became the second as he successfully opened a designer shop for men in a New York department store. The third was another American, Ralph Lauren, who began designing menswear under his own label in 1968.

Today, these designers are joined by such people as Bill Blass, Halston, Donald Brooks, Oleg Cassini, Geoffrey Beene, and Adolfo. All began as women's wear designers and today design and license products for both sexes. The one exception is Ralph Lauren. He began his career designing menswear and then expanded successfully into women's apparel.

FOCUS ON THE INDUSTRY

INTERNATIONAL BUSINESS ARRANGEMENTS THE WAY OF THE FUTURE

As distances between lands and people decrease—opportunities for designers to become multinational in their business arrangements increase. Licensing agreements of American designers are no longer exclusively with American manufacturers. The ever-improving status of American designers abroad has made agreements with manufacturers in Europe and Japan profitable ventures. Likewise, designers from other countries have found it worthwhile to license in the United States.

One example of this international approach to licensing is between Burton—an English chain of 460 menswear shops—and American designer John Weitz. The stores feature English-made, Weitz-designed menswear and furnishings under the Weitz label. This arrangement seemed most unlikely to succeed in a country which is known as the center of the world's quality menswear. However, Weitz's styling is classic and the merchandise moderately priced, suiting the young middle-class Burton customer perfectly.

Another type of business venture is one recently made by designer Geoffrey Beene. He is the first American to both produce and sell a designer line in Europe. By manufacturing in Milan, Italy, Beene is able to lower his prices to European retailers who would normally pay three times as much for his New York-made merchandise. Beene showrooms exist in various European cities so that the retailers can purchase items from the Italian-made collection at their convenience.

These are but two of some of the emerging trends in international business arrangements which are now being made by American designers. Many more are certain to follow in places like Tokyo, London and other major cities in the world as the demand for American-designed merchandise continues to rise spectacularly.

TODAY'S TOP AMERICAN DESIGNERS

When Hattie Carnegie manufactured her first line of ready-to-wear in 1928, she also became the first *American* designer to have her name on a fashion label. Fifty years ago, she was one of the few *authentic* designers

FIGURE 7-6. Courtesy: Featured designers

in the country. Most of the others were really copyists, people who interpreted French fashions. *Today, there are more professional designers in the United States than in any other country*—and their originality equals, and sometimes surpasses that of any designer in the world.

The designers in the following pages are those currently in the limelight as *major business and creative forces* in the American fashion industry. Though the work of each is highly individual, the designers seem to share several characteristics. Based on these characteristics, they have been divided into three groups: *The Young Innovators, The Tycoons,* and *The Established Greats.* It is important to note that opportunities in this country for succeeding in the business of fashion design are excellent. Because of this, the following lists could change overnight to include the name of a brilliant, but as yet unknown designer. To that unknown designer, congratulations and a sincere welcome is extended!

The Young Innovators

Originality and youth are the characteristics the following designers have in common. Each has his or her own design philosophy and each projects their own distinctive look. Having gained recognition within the last ten years, they represent the newest designing talent in the industry. Their prices differ greatly: a Britta top may cost 30 dollars, while a McFadden number often sells for over a thousand; but their customers are similar since they all appeal to the young and the avant-garde.

Britta. German-born designer Britta Bauer came to this country as a fashion model. Although inexperienced in designing, she felt that her concept of simple sportswear utilizing natural fibers and equally "natural" colors had market appeal. In 1972, she and a partner began a line under the label "Cinnamon Wear." Her simple designs rarely change drastically from season to season making her "look" a constant one. Her clothes are moderately priced with some garments selling for thirty dollars.

Born: 1944—Germany

Awards: Nominated twice for Coty Award—1975, 1976.

Stephen Burrows. In 1966 Stephen Burrows began his career by designing boutique fashion for manufacturers. After gaining recognition for his unusual designs, he joined the New York store Henri Bendel in 1970 as their "house designer." His dressmaking concepts are revolutionary and include machine overcasting the edges of a dress to produce a ripply effect. That effect became known as the Burrows "lettuce hem" and it—along with his uneven hemlines and abstract appliqués—was widely copied. In 1973, he established his own business and is now applying his unique techniques to sleep and loungewear.

Born: 1943—Newark, New Jersey

Awards: Special Coty Fashion Award for lingerie and loungewear—1974; Coty Fashion Award—1977.

Perry Ellis. Although in the fashion business for a very long time, Perry Ellis did not become a designer until fairly late in his career. Equipped with a master's degree in retailing, he was a strong dynamic buyer with a major retailer for several years, then a "creative person"—not designer—for a manufacturer for several years after that. In 1974, he began designing for Vera Sportswear and, two years later, "Portfolio by Perry Ellis" was born. The Ellis look consists of big shirts, handmade wool sweaters and easy, relaxed jackets in only natural fabrics—cotton, wool, linen, and silk. The result is a group of casual, extremely easy-to-wear clothes—but so attractive that they immediately propelled him into the designer spotlight as a great young innovator.

Born: 1940—Virginia

Diane von Furstenberg. This unique businesswoman began her career by selling dresses for an Italian manufacturer and decided to design, manufacture, and sell her own styles instead. She established a world-wide business which is built upon the "von Furstenberg look." That look began with sexy, but simple dresses made of a clinging lightweight fabric. Today, those dresses—manufactured in Italy—are sold by the thousands, and though priced under 100 dollars, have become a chic status symbol. Under licensing agreements, the von Furstenberg empire has added many other items, including accessories and cosmetics.

Born: 1946—Brussels, Belgium

Carol Horn. This designer is known for clothes that are "ethnic-inspired." Using national costumes of countries the world over, she interprets them into inexpensive, multipurpose, loose-fitting clothes for today. Crinkle cotton afghans and gaucho pants are some of those cross-culture interpretations. She began her career in Macy's display department and though untrained for the design field went on to work for several Seventh Avenue firms. In 1974 she opened her own business—Carol Horn's Habitat—so as to be able to design around her ethnic philosophy.

Born: 1936—New York City
Award: Coty Fashion Award—1975.

Betsey Johnson. This young designer made her mark on fashion during the mid-60s when she began designing for *Paraphernalia,* an avant-garde New York boutique. Her clothes had a quaint Western look, featuring quilting and pictorial decoration, which attracted the attention of the young and the famous of that time. Presently, she is applying her distinctive touch to several wholesale areas: dresses, maternity clothes, children's wear and Butterick designer patterns.

Born: 1942—Connecticut
Awards: Coty Fashion Award—1971.

John Kloss. After a brief fling at designing in Paris, John Kloss opened a New York custom dressmaking business in 1963. He expanded into free-lance designing for manufacturers but eventually, with the help of the New York store Henri Bendel, was able to design and manufacture under his own label. The first Kloss dresses resembled abstract painting and featured unusual shapes and vivid colors—a look which was very successful during the wild fashion period of the 60s. In the early 70s he designed the first collection of simple but sexy sleepwear for Cira. Today, he continues to produce his distinctive loungewear and dresses along with a variety of other fashion items. He is part of the Kreisler Group.

Born: 1937—Detroit, Michigan
Awards: Coty Fashion Award for lingerie and loungewear—1971, 1974.

Mary McFadden. This is another designer who is inspired by the art and culture of foreign countries, particularly those in the Near and Far East. She began her business in 1973, winning immediate recognition. She considers fashion an art form and uses only the finest hand-painted fabrics and silks from the East, insisting that they be as beautiful and as good as a fine museum painting. She favors the straight cut of an Oriental tunic and wide, flowing skirts and pants for her fine silks and often features the two together. Her designing talents are also applied to furs, wall-papers, household linens and other home furnishings under lucrative licensing arrangements.

Born: 1938—Long Island, New York
Award: Coty Fashion Award—1976 and 1978.

Dominic Rampollo. In 1964, this designer began as assistant designer to the talented Geoffrey Beene and went on to become the top designer at the Teal Traina firm. In 1971 he opened his own business, returning to Teal Traina briefly in 1975 but reopening his firm in 1976. That November, his name made the headlines when Rosalynn Carter chose one of his designs to wear for the President's inaugural ceremonies. Moderately priced, his pretty clothes are simple, uncluttered and never extreme.

Born: 1935—Detroit, Michigan

Giorgio di Sant'Angelo. Like Carol Horn, this designer began his career by creating clothes which were ethnically inspired. Talented Giorgio di Sant'Angelo has a strong art background, having studied at the Barcelona School of Architecture and—through a well-deserved scholarship—with the great Pablo Picasso. He came to America at the request of the Disney Studios in Hollywood who were eager to use his talents as a graphic artist. But eventually the multi-talented designer went East to express himself in New York's famous fashion industry. After several successful ventures designing fabrics and accessories, in 1966 he opened his dress business. His American Indian-inspired designs were works of art which brought him immediate acclaim.

Born: 1936—Spain
Awards: Coty Special Award—1968; Coty Fashion Award—1970.

The Tycoons

The following people share a *design and business philosophy* which may be characterized as purely American. Their clothes, casually elegant by day and softly romantic by night, typify the "American Look." Their enormous business success meanwhile typifies American "business savvy." Their high-priced clothes are bought by affluent high fashion customers, while their sportswear oriented, less expensive lines appeal to those looking for a young and casual approach to fashion.

Geoffrey Beene. Geoffrey Beene worked for several New York manufacturers before starting his own partnership in 1968. Today, his business has expanded and includes the original *Beene Couture,* the less expensive *Beene Bag* line priced between 12 and 200 dollars and a variety of fashion items produced under eleven licensing agreements. In 1976, Beene opened a showroom and manufacturing operation in Milan, Italy, becoming the first American designer to establish a branch outside the United States. His clothes are understated, featuring loose but lean shapes, luxury fabrics and neutral colors.

Born: 1928—Haynesville, Indiana
Awards: Coty Fashion Award—1964, 1966, 1974.

Bill Blass. During the 60s, Bill Blass became vice-president and then partner of the firm that gave him his first job in 1947. By 1970 he was a major creative force in the industry and sole owner of the firm, changing its name to *Bill Blass Ltd.* His high-priced line is produced under that label while his less expensive sportswear line is called *Blassport.* The clothes for both collections are very sophisticated, stressing soft luxurious fabrics. In 1967, Blass began to produce menswear under the *PBM* label and today, under licensing agreements, his name appears on furs, bed linens, children's wear, fragrances, accessories and other fashions.

Born: 1922—Fort Wayne, Indiana

Awards: Coty Fashion Award for Women's Fashions—1961, 1963, 1970, 1971; Coty Menswear Award—1968.

Oscar de la Renta. Oscar de la Renta began his career in Europe as an apprentice and designer for the European couture houses. In 1963 he came to America to join the design staff of Elizabeth Arden, leaving in 1965 to become a partner to designer Jane Derby. Upon her death, he took over the organization, building it into an impressive business. His designs are seductive but very elegant and his evening dresses are particularly striking. His organization is made up of four divisions; furs, couture, accessories and *Oscar de la Renta II*—his less expensive line of clothes. His name is also licensed for fashion accessories and home furnishings.

Born: 1932—Santo Domingo, Dominican Republic

Awards: Coty Fashion Award—1967, 1968, 1973.

Halston. Roy Halston Frowick began his career in millinery, and, as Bergdorf Goodman's first "name" hat designer, was responsible for Jacqueline Kennedy's famous "pillbox." In 1968, he opened his own custom-made clothing business for private clientele. Shortly thereafter he began to expand into the designing and selling of men's and women's ready-to-wear accessories, fragrances, and other fashion items. His look is extremely simple, using the finest of fabrics. He imported Ultrasuede from Japan, making it one of fashion's most wanted fabrics. Halston is considered by many to be America's most successful designer—both for his fashion philosophy and business accomplishments. He joined the Norton Simon conglomerate organization in 1973, becoming an important cog in the wheels of America's big business.

Born: 1932—Des Moines, Iowa

Awards: Coty Fashion Awards—1971, 1972, 1974.

Donna Karan for Anne Klein. This designer's first job was for the firm where she presently enjoys great success—*Anne Klein & Co.* She was a novice in 1968, but by 1971 Miss Klein had recognized her ability enough to make her co-designer. Three years later, Miss Klein died suddenly and Miss Karan took over all the major designing duties of the firm. Today, along with Louis Dell' Olio, she continues as the "name" designer of the Klein organization. In this role, she continues to project the Anne Klein philosophy which stressed interchangeable separates made up of casual but elegant sportswear.

Born: 1948—Forest Hills, New York
Award: Coty Fashion Award—1977

Calvin Klein. Though one of the new young designers, Klein has already established himself as one of Seventh Avenue's tycoons. After five years of designing for several coat and suit houses, in 1967 Klein and a boyhood friend, Barry Schwartz, set up Calvin Klein Inc. His snappy, tailored clothes clicked immediately. *Vogue* magazine points to his uncluttered look as the one historians should use as an example of the American look of the 70s. In addition to ready-to-wear, his firm has licensing agreements which produce everything from sheets to shoes.

Born: 1942—New York City
Awards: Coty Fashion Awards—1973, 1974, 1975.

Ralph Lauren. Ralph Lauren began as a menswear designer and, in 1967, he created his famous English tweedy look under the *Polo* label. A year later, he went on his own and (keeping the *Polo* label) began to produce a complete line of coordinated men's apparel and furnishings. In 1972, he successfully carried over his "tailored tweeds" fashion philosophy into women's wear. He received a tremendous amount of publicity in 1974 as the menswear designer for the film *The Great Gatsby*. He is a member of *The Kreisler Group*, a management firm for ready-to-wear designers.

Born: 1939—New York City
Awards: Coty Menswear Award—1970; Coty Fashion Award for Women's Wear—1974; Coty Hall of Fame—1977.

John Weitz. This world famous designer began designing in the early 50s forming his own studio in 1954 to design for licensees. In the mid-60s he expanded into menswear, pioneering the designer licensing movement into that field. Today, a wide range of apparel for both men and women is sold and promoted internationally under the John Weitz label.

Born: 1923—Berlin, Germany
Awards: Coty Menswear Award—1974; Coty Hall of Fame Award—1976, 1977.

The Established Greats

Most of the following designers began as "young innovators" in the post-World War II period. Like their counterparts of today, they were singled out because of their originality. They have been able to remain on top because of an extraordinary ability to interpret current fashion and retain their own unmistakable looks. Known for high prices as well as high fashion, their customers include those celebrities and other rich people who appreciate and can pay for the best in fashion.

Adolfo. Entering the fashion industry in 1949 as a millinery assistant, Adolfo gained recognition as a great hat designer before going into apparel design. In 1963, he started *Adolfo, Inc.,* a millinery firm, which expanded into custom and ready-to-wear dresses in 1968. His clothes are inspired by the past and typical are his patchwork and peasant evening skirts and hand-knit interpretations of Chanel suits. In 1975, Adolfo began to design menswear under a licensing agreement with the New York manufacturer, *Leon of Paris.*

Born: 1933—Havana, Cuba

Awards: Coty Fashion Award—1955 for Millinery; 1969 for entire collection.

Donald Brooks. Early in his career, Donald Brooks established himself as a major talent while designing for a high-priced designer house. In the 60s his interest expanded into designing for the theatre and though continuing to work on Seventh Avenue he designed the clothes for the musical *No Strings* and the film *Star.* In 1973 he established his own couture business. Today, he continues to create for theatrical ventures and designs intimate apparel, swimwear, accessories, and household linens under various licensing agreements.

Born: 1928—New Haven, Connecticut

Awards: Coty Fashion Awards—1958, 1962, 1967; New York Critics 1963 Award for *No Strings.*

Bonnie Cashin. An art major, Bonnie Cashin began her career as a film designer. Two of the 60 films she designed for were *Laura* and *Anna and the King of Siam.*

In 1949, she began to work in the New York market, opening her own studio in 1953. Cashin is the creator of the now famous "layer look," designing garments which could be worn in various layers for warmth and comfort. She is also known for her distinctive ponchos and hooded sweaters, and for her preference for leather and earthy tweeds. This artistic designer also creates handbags and other accessories.

Born: California

Awards: Coty Fashion Awards—received four between 1950 and 1972; *London Sunday Times* Fashion Award—1966.

James Galanos. The career of James Galanos began in the 40s, with top Parisian and American designers. In 1953, he opened his present business in Los Angeles, California. Today, the industry considers him the genius of all American designers. His designs are very high styled, exquisitely made and about the most expensive in the industry. It is said that it is impossible to copy a Galanos because of his couture workmanship and infinite attention to detail. They are his trademark and account for the four figure prices his clothes demand.

Born: 1929—Philadelphia
Awards: Winner of many including Coty Fashion Award—1954, 1958, 1959.

Rudi Gernreich. A former dancer, Rudi Gernreich produces modern clothes which are inspired by the tights and leotards of dancers. During the early 60s, he introduced form fitting, often revealing "shock" clothes in stretch knits and other unlined fabrics—gaining world-wide recognition for his topless bathing suit. A disciple of Claire McCardell, he believes in comfort and was upset by the trend toward corseted, petticoated "peasant" dresses in 1976. Until the free fashion spirit of the 60s returns, Gernreich is content to create simple, utilitarian "non-shock" clothes and to dabble in designing for his first love—the modern dance. Gernreich was and is an iconoclast, a rebel—but it was Gernreich and other great individualists like him who spurred the development of American design throughout the twentieth century.

Born: 1922—Vienna, Austria
Awards: Coty Fashion Awards—1963, 1966, 1967; *Sports Illustrated* 1967; *London Sunday Times* Award—1965.

Gustave Tassel. Until 1972, Gustave Tassel was an extremely successful California designer who was known for elegant clothes made in the haute-couture manner. When Norman Norell died in 1972, Tassel was asked to join the organization to take the place of the master. He has continued to design clothes in the Norell tradition, preserving the reputation the high-priced firm enjoys for beautifully tailored day clothes and—a Norell trademark—lavishly beaded evening dresses. The House of Norell produces a less expensive collection, *Norell II*, and (with *Revlon*) a successful new fragrance *Norell.*

Born: 1926—Philadelphia
Awards: Coty Fashion Award—1961; Cotton Council Award—1963.

Pauline Trigère. One of the most original designers of American high-priced clothing is Pauline Trigère. She came to this country in 1937 and after working for Hattie Carnegie, opened her own business in the early 40s. Her clothes are very dramatic and she has become famous for her beautiful capes. In addition to her "couture" collection, Trigère makes a lower-priced, but still expensive line (average garment is about 300 dollars) called *Trigère Too.* She has also licensed her name to jewelry, furs and fragrances.

Born: 1912—Paris, France
Awards: Coty Fashion Award—1949, 1951, 1959.

FOCUS ON THE INDUSTRY

THE COTY AMERICAN FASHION CRITICS' AWARDS

The "Oscar" of the fashion industry is the Coty Fashion Critics' Award.

This famous accolade for excellence in fashion design was conceived in 1942 by publicist Eleanor Lambert under the sponsorship of the international cosmetic and fragrance firm, Coty, Inc. Although publicity for the Coty name certainly must have been a consideration, the prime purpose of the awards was to encourage the development of the fashion industry during World War II by focusing upon the creativity and originality of the American designer.

Several types of Coty Awards exist. The most famous is the original *Coty Fashion Critics' Award,* which is also known as the "Winnie." It is given to the American designer of women's wear who, in the opinion of the judges, has made an extraordinary contribution to the direction of that year's contemporary fashion design. A second prize, *The Coty Special Award,* is given to those who have excelled in a specialized area of the industry. Stephen Burrows, for instance, was given a Special Award in 1974 for his creative treatment of lingerie and loungewear. Since so many specialized areas exist in the industry, very often more than one Special Award is presented. Until 1968, the awards were given exclusively to those who produced women's fashions, but the innovative changes in menswear design during the 1960s prompted the introduction of the *Coty Menswear Fashion Award*. Designers who receive any of these awards more than once are presented with *The*

Coty Repeat Award. On winning their third Repeat Award, talented designers enter the prestigious *Coty's Hall of Fame.* When a Hall of Fame winner merits even further recognition, he or she is honored with a *Hall of Fame Citation.*

All Coty Award winners are judged by members of the press. A group of fashion editors from magazines, newspapers, news services, and broadcasting form two committees representing men's and women's fashions. The committees select a slate of nominees for the "Winnie" and Menswear Awards, and choose the winners of the Special Awards. The "Winnie" and Menswear Award winners are then chosen by the American press through a national ballot. Although the winners of awards in specialized categories are announced immediately by the committees, the results of the national ballots are kept confidential until the night of the Coty Awards presentation. At this great gala event, all the winners receive their prized awards.

The famous "Winnie" is a bronze female figure designed by sculptor Malvina Hoffman. The Coty Menswear Fashion Award is an abstract steel trophy designed by Forrest Myers. The Special Award for women's wear is a bronze plaque with the Hoffman figure in bas-relief; while the award for menswear specialized categories is an aluminum free form sculpture. Those who are honored with Return or Hall of Fame Awards receive silver or gold plates attached to their "Winnies."

More than a third of a century has elapsed since the Coty Awards were founded to promote America's young fashion industry. As American designers and manufacturers succeeded in establishing themselves as the world's greatest fashion creators and producers, the awards began to lose their image of being mainly a promotional tool of the industry. Over the years, the *Coty American Fashion Critics' Awards* have gained in prestige and are now recognized as the world's top award for fashion design.

TERMS TO REMEMBER

utilitarian function
fashion appeal
inspiration
"couture" ready-to-wear
conglomerate

licenser
licensee
licensing
Coty Fashion Award
"runner"
"ford"
Claire McCardell
Anne Klein
Geoffrey Beene
Calvin Klein
Bill Blass
Ralph Lauren
Mary McFadden
Halston

HIGHLIGHTS OF THE CHAPTER

- The most brilliant American designer of all time is considered by many to be Claire McCardell; she was most responsible for developing the American sportswear look. She designed from the 1930s until her death in 1958 and was the first American designer to win international fame.
- The "youth kick" of the 60s, composed of young, psychedelic fashion, originated with young ready-to-wear designers. It revolutionized fashion and brought them important fashion influence. Though some were French, most were English and American, causing France to lose some of her dictatorial fashion leadership.
- In the early 70s, fashion simmered down and the classic look of American sportswear became dominant. The trend served to make American designers as important as the French.
- To compete with American designers, by the mid-70s, most couture designers were also producing ready-to-wear. Their entrance into mass production added prestige to ready-made clothing and helped rather than hurt the American designers.
- Today Seventh Avenue designers are considered world fashion leaders and their label is as prestigious as that of the French.
- A designer's most important responsibility is to design *saleable* merchandise, incorporating utilitarian need with fashion appeal.

- Designers draw from many sources for inspiration. The world of entertainment, museums, periodicals, the textile industry, and the work of other designers are some sources.
- The process of producing a design is a lengthy one which, in addition to the designer, involves many highly skilled people.
- There are four types of designers—high fashion; mass fashion; stylist; and free-lance.
- Designer "names" are big business. Great profit can be made through licensing agreements where designers lend their name to a product for a share of the profits.
- American designers have now expanded their business internationally, lending their name to merchandise which is produced and sold in foreign countries. Some are also establishing sales, manufacturing, and distribution branches throughout the world.
- The great American designer may be divided into three categories—the young innovators; the tycoons; and the established greats. All types are major business and creative forces in the American fashion industry of today.

QUESTIONS

1. What was the "Hollywood influence?" the "sportswear influence?" Give Claire McCardell's definition of the "American look."
2. What was the "youth kick" of the 60s and who were some of its originators? How did this fashion development affect the position of American designers in terms of fashion influence?
3. What fashion trend in the 70s helped American designers? How did the French couture hope to compete with America?
4. In your opinion, what is the current status of American designers? Do you consider them as creative as the French? Why?
5. Define a fashion designer. What are the two factors necessary to design a saleable collection? How do price and image affect the overall design?
6. There are many sources of inspiration for a designer. Describe several fashion trends and the sources that inspired them.
7. How are the clothes of the couture different from ready-to-wear? Why doesn't America have any couturiers?

8. If you had a choice, which of the careers described in the chapter would you choose? Why?
9. Under which employment arrangement do most designers work? What are conglomerates and why do designers join them?
10. Name some of the products of top designers produced under licensing agreements. Who were the pioneers of licensing in menswear?
11. How are American designers expanding internationally? Do you think this trend toward foreign expansion will spread? Why?
12. What are the three categories which most American designers fall under? Pull ads of one designer from each category.

BIBLIOGRAPHY

Beaton, Cecil, *The Glass of Fashion.* New York: Doubleday, 1954.

Bender, Marylin, *The Beautiful People.* New York: Coward-McCann, 1967.

Charles-Roux, Edmonde, *Chanel, Her Life—Her World—and the Woman Behind the Legend She Herself Created.* New York: Alfred Knopf, 1975.

Dior, Christian, *Christian Dior and I,* translated by Antonia Fraser. New York: Dutton and Company, 1957.

Dorner, Jane, *Fashion.* London: Octopus Books, 1974.

Garland, Marge, *Fashion.* Baltimore, Md.: Penguin, 1962.

Hawes, Elizabeth, *Fashion Is Spinach.* New York: Random House, 1938.

Jarnow, Jeanette A., and Beatrice Judell, *Inside the Fashion Business.* New York: John Wiley and Sons, 1974.

Kolodny, Rosalie, *Fashion Design for Moderns.* New York: Fairchild Publications, 1968.

Lambert, Eleanor, *World of Fashion.* New York and London: R. R. Bowker Company, 1976.

Latzke, Alpha, and Helen P. Hostetter, *The Wide World of Clothing.* New York: Ronald Press, 1968.

Lynam, Ruth, ed., *Couture.* New York: Doubleday and Company, 1972.

Metropolitan Museum of Art Bulletin, *Fashion, Art and Beauty.* New York: Vol. XXVI, No. 3 (November, 1967).

Roshco, Bernard, *The Rag Race.* New York: Funk and Wagnalls, 1963.

Troxell, Mary D., *Fashion Merchandising.* New York: Gregg Division, McGraw-Hill, 1976.

Vecchio, Walter, and Robert Riley, *The Fashion Makers—A Photographic Record.* New York: Crown Publishers, 1968.

White, Palmer, *Poiret.* New York: Clarkson N. Potter, Inc., 1973.

IV

PRODUCING TODAY'S FASHION

The actual production of fashion merchandise, from the raw materials to the finished goods, is the fascinating subject of Part IV.

Textiles, leather, and fur are turned into an amazing array of all types of wearing apparel by both domestic and foreign manufacturers. The who, what, when, where, and how of this transformation is described in detail since these activities are at the very heart of today's fashion business.

8

THE ROLE OF THE PRIMARY MARKETS

OBJECTIVES

After reading this chapter, you should be able to:

- Identify the three segments of the primary markets.
- Cite the products and services each primary market provides for the fashion industry.
- Discuss the role each primary market plays in deciding what kind of fashion merchandise will be produced.

In order to produce goods, one must begin with raw materials. In the fashion business those who supply the raw materials—*textiles, leather,* and *furs*—are known collectively as the *primary markets.* They are so called because their activities comprise the first steps in the production of fashion goods.

THE TEXTILE INDUSTRY

Of the three industries which comprise the primary markets, textiles is the largest. Within the realm of this vast industry are four levels, each dealing with a distinct phase of textile production. These are: *fiber production, yarn production, fabric construction,* and *fabric finishing.* Some companies specialize in only one phase while others handle as many as four phases.

Fiber Production

A fiber is a natural or synthetic hair-like filament. It provides texture and substance to yarns and fabrics, and is literally what goods are made of.

Natural fibers come from either an animal or plant. They are cotton, wool, linen, and silk. *Synthetic fibers* are man-made and are either cellulosic (by-products of wood and cotton) or non-cellulosic (made chemically).

Of the natural fibers, *cotton* is the most widely produced. In the United States it is grown in fourteen states located primarily in two regions; the southeast and the southwest. Local farmers sell their crops to wholesalers who in turn move the goods to such central markets as New Orleans, Dallas, Houston, or Memphis for national and international distribution. Egypt, Brazil, China, and the Soviet Union are other recognized world cotton producers.

The United States also produces a substantial amount of *wool.* Sheep farmers, located in the Rocky Mountain states of Colorado and Utah, are the leading wool producers. However, twenty-seven states, including Alaska, also contribute to U.S. wool production. Like cotton farmers, sheep farmers sell wool locally to wholesalers who then sell it in the central wool market in Boston. Wool is also produced in large quantities by the United Kingdom countries of Australia, New Zealand, and Scotland; and by Argentina and South Africa.

Linen is a fiber which comes from the flax plant. Since the colonial period, the United States has produced flax crops each year. Today, however, the demand for the oil of the plant is greater than the demand for the fiber. Therefore, the United States has to import nearly all the linen used in apparel production from such countries as Belgium and Ireland. Fabrics made purely of linen are consequently very expensive. Linen also has a tendency to wrinkle and crease. Because of these drawbacks, the popularity of this fiber in wearing apparel has declined over the last twenty years.

The same basic criticisms can be applied to *silk.* All the silk used in apparel is now imported into the United States, making it very expensive. Silk is also a delicate fiber and it requires considerable care—not at all practical for today's life styles.

In previous years, attempts were made to bring natural silk production to the U.S. but all efforts proved to be unsuccessful. The fiber is produced by the silkworm which needs a special diet and climatic conditions to survive. Today, China, Italy, and Japan account for the world's major production of this fiber.

Both silk and linen fibers have had a major decline in usage because of the so-called "miracle fibers," the synthetics. In fact, it was the search for "artificial silk" which prompted the research and eventual discovery of the first synthetic fiber, *rayon.* It is manufactured from a substance called cellulose which is found in plants. A second group of synthetic fibers, *acetates* and *tri-acetates* are also manufactured from cellulose.

The first fiber to be produced chemically was *nylon.* Its discovery in 1938 led to the development of an entire group of non-cellulosic synthetics known as polymers, such as *polyesters, acrylics,* and the stretch fiber *spandex.* Probably these fibers are better known by their registered trade names rather than by their generic names. For example, *Dacron* polyester, *Orlon* acrylic, *Qiana* nylon, and *Lycra* spandex, are trade names of the Du Pont corporation. *Fortrel* polyester is a Celanese corporation trade name, while *Acrilan* acrylic is owned by Monsanto.

The majority of man-made fibers used here are made in the United States. They are produced in large chemical plants located in twelve states which are primarily on the east coast. The process used to make man-made fibers is simple. It involves forcing a thick liquid substance through holes in a circular device called a spinnerette which, in turn, produces long filament or staple synthetic fibers.

The business of producing synthetic fibers in the U.S. began in 1939. By 1972 over 6 billion pounds of synthetic fibers a year were being produced; per capita consumption reached thirty-six pounds per year. During that same year only nineteen pounds of *natural* fibers were consumed per capita.[1]

Yarn Production. Once the fibers are acquired, companies must spin them into long strands called *yarn.* Many synthetic fibers emerge as long filaments and, unless they are blended with natural fibers, they do not necessarily have to be spun. Since the use of blends of natural and synthetic fibers has increased dramatically, however, most large synthetic fiber producers now produce yarn as well. Today, this is a highly automated phase of textile production.

Fabric Construction

The next phase of textile production is the actual making of the fabric. There are several methods which can be used. The yarns can

[1]Source: U.S. Department of Agriculture, Economic Research Service

either be woven, knitted, bonded, felted, laminated, crocheted, or braided. Most fabrics made today are either woven or knitted. Like the fiber producers who also make yarn, most yarn makers continue on to the next steps in the textile production process. Using any of the above fabric construction methods, yarn producing companies like J. P. Stevens and Burlington go on to make and finish fabrics as well.

Once the fabric is made, it is called *greige goods*—a term used to connote unfinished fabric. As mentioned before, some companies also go on to finish their goods. Those that don't, sell the greige goods to a *converter* who then makes them into finished goods.

Fabric Finishing

It is at this phase of production that the fabrics are transformed. The dull unfinished fabrics are treated to any of a variety of steps which beautify their appearance and improve their saleability. This procedure is called fabric finishing and a few of the many finishing processes include *bleaching, smoothing, shearing, brushing,* or *embossing.*

It is also at this stage that fabrics are *dyed* and *printed.* Although some fabrics may be *yarn dyed* (meaning the yarns are dyed before the fabric is made) most goods are *piece dyed* because it is the most economical of all the methods.

The printing of fabric is done by using one of four methods: hand printing, machine printing, heat transferring, and (the newest) jet printing. The printing techniques of each method vary, producing differing results. The choice of printing method, therefore, is often influenced by the type of pattern or design desired for a fabric.

The finishing process can also enhance the fabric's performance. For instance, cotton can be *sized* to give it body. Wool and cottons can be *preshrunk* to prevent excessive shrinking when cleaned. Other fabrics may be made *crease resistant, wash-and-wear, colorfast,* or *permanent press*—simply by applying the proper finishing techniques.

Finally, the finishing process can also provide protection to the wearer of the fabric. Such finishes as *waterproofing, flame or fire retardation,* and *mildew and rot repellency* can be applied to fabrics to make them safe and durable.

Characteristics of the Textile Industry

From the beginning of fiber production to the completion of finished goods, the textile industry plays an important part in the U.S. economy. Its products, which had a 1975 value of over $35 billion, represented 3 percent of all United States manufactured goods. Profits for 1975, not considered a banner year for textile production, totalled 410 million dollars.

Labor and Import Problems. The industry has been faced with two major problems: rising labor costs and increased competition from inexpensive imported goods.

The industry provides employment for nearly one million workers (5 percent of the total labor force) in over 6000 textile plants.[2] It is the one phase of apparel production not widely represented by organized labor. Today, less than 10 percent of the workers in this industry are unionized. Currently, however, strong organizing campaigns are being conducted in the South by the Amalgamated Clothing and Textile Workers Union. The expected success of these unionization efforts is certain to increase labor costs.

The second problem—that of cheap imported goods—deals with textiles which come mostly from Japan, Hong Kong, the Republic of China (Taiwan), and the Republic of Korea. Though it is worth noting that the United States exports billions of dollars worth of textile products primarily to Canada, Western Europe, Australia and Japan, foreign imported textiles exceed American exports.

To combat these two problems, U.S. producers have invested heavily in new equipment. Much of the equipment is designed to speed up and automate production. But other equipment is for improving health and safety standards in factories. In 1977 an estimated one billion dollars was spent for these and other capital improvements.

Location of the Industry. In the search for cheaper labor and to be closer to resources, textile production has shifted from the Northeast to the South. Currently 93 percent of all cotton fiber and fabric, and 85 percent of all synthetic fibers are produced below the Mason-Dixon line. States which are leading producers of textiles (including the few in the northeast) are North and South Carolina, Georgia, Tennessee, Alabama, Pennsylvania, New Jersey, and New York.

A Change in Raw Materials. Another important shift has been in the kind of raw materials produced. Natural fibers have been replaced by synthetics. In less than half a century the growth of synthetics has been astounding. For example, in 1930 the fiber market was divided as follows: 95 percent natural, 5 percent synthetic. By 1950 synthetics were beginning to rise. The market was approximately 80 percent natural, 20 percent synthetic. In 1970 there was a complete reversal; 56 percent of all fibers produced were synthetics. Today, synthetic fiber production accounts for a 70 percent share of the market.

[2]Figures do not include cotton growers or sheep farmers.

TABLE 8-1

The Top Ten Textile Mills

1. Burlington	6. Spring Cotton Mills
2. J. P. Stevens	7. Cone Mills
3. Deering Milliken	8. Berkshire Hathaway
4. M. Lowenstein & Sons	9. Common Mills
5. Dan River Mills	10. United Merchants and Manufacturing

Within the context of synthetic fiber production, the cellulosic fibers no longer dominate; 89 percent are now non-cellulosic and this trend is expected to continue with new discoveries in the production of polymers. Two recent successful additions have been Ultrasuede (distributed by Spring Mills), and Burlana (by Burlington), a blend of 85 percent dacron and 15 percent wool which looks like wool worsted but, like Ultrasuede, is completely washable.

The Structure of the Industry. The textile industry has also been transformed from a highly fragmented, highly specialized operation into an industry dominated by giants who are *vertically integrated.* This means that a company handles all four steps in the production of textiles within its own divisions. They: (1) process the fiber, (2) spin the yarn, (3) make the cloth, and (4) finish the cloth.

Today the bulk of the 6000–7000 textile firms are small, doing less than 50 million dollars each in sales a year. However, the top ten mills (Table 8-1) generate nearly 30 percent of the industry's sales and most of these are vertically integrated.

Fiber production sales are also dominated by giants. Chemical companies such as Du Pont, Celanese, Monsanto, Eastman Kodak, and Phillips Petroleum are the leaders.

FOCUS ON THE INDUSTRY

PROFILE OF A GIANT: BURLINGTON INDUSTRIES

With sales in excess of 2.4 billion dollars in 1978, Burlington Industries is the world's largest producer of textiles and related products. The company does everything from researching and developing new fibers, to producing fabric for apparel and industrial use, to making finished products such as hosiery, carpets, and sheets.

Burlington was founded in 1923 by J. Spencer Love in Burlington, North Carolina. Corporate headquarters are still in North Carolina, but this huge firm now also operates 135 plants in fourteen states and abroad and maintains over thirty research divisions. The company's merchandising and marketing activities are centered in New York City at "Burlington House."

Listed below are Burlington's domestic divisions.

Apparel Products Divisions

Burlington Knit Fabrics
Burlington Men's Wear
Burlington Retail Fabrics Company
Burlington Winmoor
Burlington Woolens
Burlington Worsted
Galey and Lord
Klopman Mills
Burlington Greige Sales Company

Hosiery Divisions

Burlington Hosiery Company
Burlington Socks

Yarns Divisions

Atwater Throwing Company
Burlington Yarn Company
Madison Throwing Company

Home Products Divisions

Burlington Domestics
Burlington House Consumer products
Burlington House Fabrics
Catlin Farish Company
Hess, Goldsmith & Company
Charm Tred Mills
Lees Carpets
Monticello Carpet Mills
United Furniture (Renamed Burlington Furniture in 1978
Globe Furniture

Industry Products Divisions

Burlington Glass Fabrics Company
Burlington Industrial Fabrics Company
Burlington Ribbon Mills
Goodall Vinyl Fabrics

Other

Burlington Management Services Company
Burlington Export Company
Burlington Trading Company

Finally, the entire structure of the textile industry has moved from being production oriented to becoming more marketing oriented, with an increased emphasis on the ultimate consumer via *derived demand* advertising and stimulation. In previous years, the prime target for promotion and sales was those middlemen who directly bought fibers, yarns, unfinished and finished goods. Fiber producers and mills were concerned with their immediate customers, not their ultimate users. This meant that, prior to the 1960s, Mr. and Mrs. Consumer did not know one brand name of fiber from another, nor were they familiar with the names of firms responsible for producing the goods used in their clothing.

In order to gain consumer confidence and acceptance of new fibers and fabrics, as well as to establish recognition and loyalty to brand names, large chemical companies began to sponsor aggressive ad campaigns aimed at the ultimate consumer. They sponsored cooperative ads with apparel manufacturers, exposing the consumer to the virtues of the fiber and fabric as well as those of the garment. The consumer would then look for garments made of a particular fiber or fabric, thereby increasing the demand for either one in a secondary or derived manner (see Fig. 8-1).

Thus, those in the textile business are more than just weavers, knitters, chemists, or finishers. Companies in this industry have incorporated the entire marketing concept of expanding old markets and creating new markets for goods into their textile business.

Marketing Activities of the Textile Industry

Consumer Advertising and Promotion. As previously mentioned, one successful marketing activity carried on by the textile industry has been consumer advertising and promotion. Not only is the promotion if fibers done on an individual basis (as in "Dacron by Du Pont," for example), but fiber promotion is often done collectively as well.

One such co-operative group is the Man-Made Fiber Producers Association. This organization seeks to inform consumers about the virtues of all man-made fibers, regardless of which company makes them.

Among the natural fiber growers and producers, trade associations also exist. They help all members of the industry by compiling and disseminating fiber and fabric information to their members and consumers alike. Two such associations are the American Wool Council in Colorado, and the National Cotton Council of America in Tennessee.

In addition to these trade groups, advertising and promotional activities are conducted by special organizations for their producers. One such group, Cotton Incorporated, is headquartered in New York and specializes in promoting cotton to all members of the industry, as well as directly to the consumer. Monies to run Cotton Incorporated come from a one dollar a bale assessment fee collected by the Cotton Board, a division of the U.S. Department of Agriculture. Another group which functions in basically the same manner for its fiber producers is The Wool Bureau, Inc. Both these organizations have identifying symbols or trademarks (see Fig. 8-2). Both these groups also work closely with apparel manufacturers, retailers, educational institutions, and consumer groups to promote their respective fibers.

FIGURE 8-1. Courtesy: Du Pont Co.

Services for the Trade. Besides advertising, textile producers perform various other marketing services, especially for the trade. Most large companies and trade organizations maintain extensive *fabric libraries.* These libraries do not contain any books. Instead they display swatches of fabrics which are currently in production or are slated for production in the upcoming seasons. Designers, manufacturers, retailers, fashion

PURE WOOL

The sewn-in Woolmark label is your assurance of quality-tested fabrics made of the world's best...Pure Wool.

FIGURE 8-2. Courtesy: The Wool Bureau

editors, and consultants use these libraries as sources of inspiration and to gather information about future fabric and color trends.

Textile companies and associations also sponsor fashion shows for the trade. Garments used in the shows are usually described in terms of fiber, fabric, and apparel manufacturer. Probably the most lavish of these shows is put on by Deering-Milliken. The "Milliken Breakfast Show" is held annually in New York City to coincide with the most important market weeks of the year, late May to early June. This is the time out-of-town buyers visit New York to make their back-to-school and fall-winter purchases. The show provides a means of introducing the firm's new fibers, fabrics, and colors as they appear in trends. Fabric companies are an important first place to look for future fashion influences because textile firms work 18–24 months ahead of the apparel trade when planning their upcoming lines.

In the last few decades, the textile industry has assumed a much larger role in steering the direction of fashion. The introduction of so many new and innovative fibers and fabrics have often resulted in the development of a major fashion trend. Knits are an excellent case in point. The first knits of the late 50s mushroomed into a success story of unforeseen dimensions; by the 70s, most men, women, and children were clothed in knits.

The trend toward the "natural" fabrics of cotton, wool, linen or silk—in real or cheaper, synthetic versions—is a more recent example of how fabric can provide the major fashion interest in apparel while silhouette and detail remain secondary. Today, as the inventiveness and influence of the textile industry grows, it becomes even more impossible to separate the fashion direction of the apparel industry from the developments and decisions of the textile producers. Both factions—the textile producers and the apparel makers—have become completely integrated, working extremely close in order to continue prospering from the talents of each other.

Research and Planning. Because fashion and textiles are so vital to each other, the textile producers keenly recognize the importance of extensive marketing research. Though research is naturally conducted for the development of new fibers, fabrics, and methods of fabric construction and finishing, it also encompasses areas of consumer research, the development of new outlets for distribution, introducing cheaper and better methods of production, and increasing the effectiveness of promotion and advertising.

Research also helps solve fiber and fabric problems. For apparel producers as well as consumers, it provides the answers to questions pertaining to fiber and fabric strengths and weaknesses.

The long-range planning of the textile industry also involves color development. The Color Association of the United States, located in New York, researches and promotes new colors for the industry, disseminating important color trends to all members of the trade.

Consumer Information and Protection. The textile industry is beginning to take the initiative in the areas of consumer information and protection. In previous years, this aspect of consumerism pertained mainly to the fiber content and finish of fabrics, and was government imposed. For example, in 1939 the Wool Products and Labeling Act was passed requiring disclosure of fiber content. Then, in 1954, the Flammable Fabrics Act was passed, banning certain fabrics from U.S. markets. In 1973, the Federal Trade Commission amended this act. Fabrics used in certain types of wearing apparel such as children's sleepwear and home furnishings had to meet U.S. government standards regarding flammability.

Another type of federal act, the Care Labeling of Textile Wearing Apparel, was also put into effect by the FTC. Under this law, manufacturers must provide specific details regarding the washing and/or dry cleaning methods to be used by the consumer in caring for the garment or accessory.

Today, the industry itself is constantly testing and improving the safety and quality of its products. Some companies have gone far beyond merely meeting minimum government standards. For example, in 1962 Monsanto introduced its "wear-dated" guarantee. In addition to covering its fiber and fabric for one year, Monsanto also guarantees zippers, seams, color fastness, shrink resistance—in fact, everything pertaining to an item. If the customer is not satisfied, he or she may write to Monsanto for a refund or replacement.

Many companies in the industry maintain full-time customer relations staffs to handle inquiries and complaints and most take a strong position, guaranteeing the performance standards of their products.

Another offshoot of consumerism has been the concern for environmental protection. Spurred by government action, the textile industry is now researching and developing new methods of operation which are non-polluting, conserve energy and reduce waste.

Since most synthetic fibers are petroleum by-products, those engaged in this aspect of the business are also trying to develop new sources of fibers in case future petro-chemicals continue to become scarce and prohibitive in cost.

Overall, the public's concern for the environment and resource allocation has become an important concern of the entire textile industry.

THE LEATHER INDUSTRY

Another vital part of the primary markets is the leather industry. Like textile production, producing leather has long been a part of the American heritage, dating back to the first Americans—the Indians.

In recent years the leather industry has become more fashion oriented. Though leather has always been used for fashion accessories, today it is also very important in apparel. This increasing use of leather has strengthened even further the bond of cooperation which has long existed between leather producers and the fashion industry.

The Product

Leather is a natural by-product of slaughtered animals. Around the world, animals such as cattle and sheep are raised for multipurposes. In addition to providing a source of food, they supply a variety of by-products, including leather. No one raises animals for the sole purpose of obtaining skins or hides.

The raw materials termed *hides* come from large animals—mainly cows, steers, or horses. *Skins* come from smaller animals such as sheep, goats, calves, and pigs.

Leather has distinct pattern characteristics which differentiate one leather from another. These differences are found in its *grain*. The leather also has unique physical properties which are associated with individual types of leathers. For example, calfskin and sheepskin are soft and supple, and preferred for items requiring those qualities such as shoe uppers and gloves. On the other hand, leather from steers is thicker, more durable, and therefore extremely suitable for shoe soles or luggage. The dominant type of raw material used by the leather industry comes from cattle because, with world cattle population figures over 1 billion head, it is in abundant supply.

Cattle are found in great numbers in Asia (490 million), South America (209 million), and North America (195 million). The second most available raw material used for leather making is sheepskin.

Once the skins and hides are obtained from the animals they must immediately be *cured* if they are going to become leather. This treatment, although not considered part of the tanning process, retards decomposition of the skins and is an important first step affecting the quality of the finished product. There are a variety of other steps such as soaking and unhairing which the skins and hides go through before they are ready for the *tanning* step, the actual converting of skins and hides into leather. Once this complex tanning process is complete the leather is ready for *coloring*. Today, leathers can be dyed in a wide array of colors thanks to the modern technology developed by the industry.

Next, the leather is further treated, finished, measured to determine the area size of the irregular shaped piece and, finally, graded in terms of quality. All in all, there are nineteen steps—of which tanning is only one—in the process of making leather.

The entire process is usually completed in four weeks time, making leather production slow in comparison to textile production. It is for this reason that those producing leather begin eighteen to twenty-four months in advance of the sale of the finished product. Because they must work so far in advance, fashion researchers and coordinators who are affiliated with tanneries must also be able to forecast far into the fashion future. Since leather houses are then the first to project color and texture trends, those in other fields of the fashion industry use the leather fashion experts as a primary source of information for future fashion trends.

Characteristics of the Leather Industry

In the United States, the production of leather is primarily done in the northeastern and north central states. There are approximately 500 tanneries and finishing plants, employing 32,000 people. Industry shipments total over one billion dollars annually, and production statistics include the tanning of over 18 million hides and 17 million skins a year.

Since leather is used in the production of wearing apparel (coats, skirts, pants and jackets) as well as accessories, Americans consumed over ten square feet of leather per capita in 1977 with total consumption better than 2.5 billion square feet.[3] A portion of this leather also goes into the industrial sector for use in furniture and car interiors.

Labor and Import Problems. Like the textile industry, the leather industry is facing increased labor costs and the competition of imported goods. Today, nearly 13 percent of all skins and hides are imported.

Finished goods containing leather are also being imported at ever increasing rates, further decreasing the demand for U.S. leather. In 1978 nearly 50 percent of manufactured leather items were imports.

In part, this is due to a shifting of production facilities from the United States and Europe to the developing nations of Asia and South America. Traditionally, these areas have simply been suppliers of raw hides; now, they are establishing tanning and finishing facilities at a rapid pace.

One possible solution to this problem is for American tanneries to aggressively export *high quality* goods and thus capture a share of a market which is increasing in terms of world demand.

Competition has also come from those engaged in producing leather look-alikes. Vinyls, plastics, and even textiles which simulate leather have been used in increasing amounts, especially in mass-merchandised apparel and accessories.

One innovator, Allied Leather Company of New York City, sought to solve this problem by broadening its product line to include man-made leathers and textiles along with its natural leathers.

Structure of the Leather Industry. Basically, tanneries are small, with most employing under one hundred workers. They are generally located in close proximity to slaughtering houses; in some instances, they are even subsidiaries of them. For example, the largest tanner, the A. C. Lawrence Leather Company, is a division of Swift's and Company. Most companies maintain marketing operations in New York City to better service the fashion industry and, at the same time, to feel its pulse.

There are three kinds of tanning operations existing today. The first type is the *regular tannery* which buys skins and hides and sells finished leather. These operations dominate the industry. The second type of operation is the *converter.* Hides and skins are bought by these companies, but they do not engage in the actual tanning process. Instead, a converter uses a *contract tannery* which does the tanning to the converter's specifications. The converter then sells the finished goods to his customers.

[3]Source: The Tanner's Council of America, Inc.

The industry is also highly specialized. That is, tanneries work on only one type of hide. If they tan sheepskin they probably do not handle cowhide.

Marketing Activities of the Leather Industry

Like textile producers, tanners are becoming more and more marketing oriented in their operations. They have discovered the importance of advertising and promotion and, in combination with leather product manufacturers, spend millions of dollars each year advertising their products.

Marketing research naturally includes better and faster ways of completing the curing and tanning processes. But it has also been expanded to include research on consumers all over the world. Innovative uses for natural leather products, as in wearing apparel, has been and continues to be researched and promoted by individual companies as well as by the industry trade association—The Tanners Council of America, located in New York.

Efforts are being made by this association and its members to enlist public support for the leather products of the United States through educating the consumer in the virtues of American-made leather and its qualities. Those efforts include pressuring the federal government for help in resolving many of the industry's foreign trade problems.

The leather industry, in turn, has been affected by public pressure and government regulations as far as the types of hides and skins it processes. Under the Endangered Species Conservation Act of 1969, the sale and use of such heretofore popular skins as alligator and crocodile are prohibited.

Though the past few years have shown a marked decrease in the size of America's leather industry and an increase in its many problems, many within the industry feel that effective marketing decisions, the help of the federal government, and consumer support can minimize if not completely solve these problems.

THE FUR INDUSTRY

No sector of the primary markets has undergone such redirection as the fur industry. Years ago, its principal contribution to fashion was singular: *Mink.* Women, mainly those over forty, considered this fur the prized status symbol of the upper and upper-middle-class elite; the fur for those who had "made it" financially.

FIGURE 8-3. Finally, equal rights for men. Courtesy: The American Fur Industry.

Then, during the early 60s, the fur market began to undergo tremendous change. It was the time of the "young revolution" in fashion and young styling concepts were introduced into furs. Off-beat, less expensive, unusual pelts were worked into coats and all types of apparel—even pants. Heavy promotion of the new "fun" and "sport" furs by the fur industry and retailers succeeded in making customers "fur-conscious" rather than "mink-conscious."

Today, the fur industry continues to reflect those changes. The present fur market target is a much younger, more casual—though still financially secure—individual. Men are included in that target and "furs for the man" also are heavily promoted (see Fig. 8-3). All manner of fur is now accepted and demanded by the consumer so that mink constitutes only 50 percent of all fur sales. The old, staid, stuffy "mink stole" industry is gone. In its place stands an industry of fur producers who, even when they "think mink," present original and exciting fashion concepts.

It is this market re-orientation and strong fashion image which are pushing fur sales toward the billion dollar mark, even in today's competitive fashion environment.

The Product

Basically, there are about 100 different kinds of furs on the market today. These include such domestic ones as beaver, muskrat, rabbit, raccoon, fox, and seal; and imported ones like sable, marten, Persian lamb, and lynx.

Furs are differentiated from hides and skins by the fact that hair, fleece, fur fibers, or guard hairs are not removed from the animal skins. These unshorn skins are referred to as *pelts.*

Pelts are obtained either by *trapping* or by *breeding* the animals. Today the ratio is approximately 60 percent breeding (fur farming) to 40 percent trapping. Future percentile projections include an equalizing 50–50 split between the two methods. Once the pelts are removed from the animals, they are brought to central locations to be sorted in terms of size and quality. The furs are then bundled and sold at auctions to processors.

The fur *processors* then *dress* and *color* the pelts. Dressing is a process which, like the curing done in the leather industry, prevents the decomposition of the pelts. Coloring is optional, but may include bleaching, darkening, or altering the natural color of the fur completely. Finally, the pelts are *glazed*—adding beauty, luster, and shine to the fur.

At this point, the pelts are ready to be made into garments or used as trim. The *fur goods manufacturer* takes over this role. It is a highly specialized skill and nearly all the steps used in the construction of a fur garment are intricately performed by hand.

It is because of the intricate, time-consuming nature of all these processes, from breeding to sewing, that the retail prices of fur items are always relatively high and their methods of production relatively slow.

Characteristics of the Industry

The fur industry is world-wide in scope. Among the many major fur-producing countries are the U.S.S.R., Canada, France, West Germany, Scandinavia, and, of course, the United States.

Fur trapping and trading is credited with opening up and developing this country from the early days of New World colonization. In fact, cities such as Detroit, Chicago, and St. Louis had their start as major fur trading centers. Even the Seal of the state of New York contains two beavers—indicating the animal's importance in the development of the state.

Today, America's fur trapping is done in virtually every state, but most pelts are obtained from the northwestern and northeastern sections of the country. Fur farming is also principally located in these two areas.

Since the industry is an international one, fur auction centers exist in countries throughout the world, with each country specializing in selling its native pelts. New York, Seattle, St. Louis, and several Canadian cities handle pelts native to North America. Other auction centers are located in the U.S.S.R., Scandinavia, England, and West Germany.

The United States bought nearly 80 million dollars' worth of undressed pelts from these centers in 1974. However, American exports for each year during the 70s have exceeded our imports, ranging between 125 and 150 million dollars.

New York is the heart of this country's fur processing and manufacturing; it does over 90 percent of the country's business. In early June of each year, New York City's fur district hosts "fur week"—presenting the new fur collections to the retail trade over a period of about three weeks.

Nationwide, there are approximately 800 small establishments employing nearly 5000 workers in the fur industry. Many of their craftsmen are represented by the Fur Department of the Amalgamated Meat Cutters and Butchers Workers of the United States and Canada Union.

The retail distribution of the fur is varied. Fur manufacturers can sell their products to small, independent fur salons; to leased departments in retail stores; or directly to the store-owned department of a retail store.

In the past, most furs were given to the retailer on a *consignment* basis. The term consignment applies to an arrangement between manufacturer and retailer whereby unsold furs can be returned to the manufacturer along with payment for sold ones.

Because of the tremendous rise in demand for furs, consignment selling is rarely available to retailers nowadays. Most retailers must pay for deliveries from fur manufacturers as they pay the other producers of the fashion industry.

Since 1972, retail sales have skyrocketed from $250 million to $650 million in 1976, and sales were projected to reach the one billion dollar mark before the end of the 1970s.

Like the textile and leather industries, the fur industry is confronted by several major problems. The most pressing is its need to maintain an abundant supply of high quality pelts. The industry is a strong advocate of conservation and tries to keep a proper ecological balance between supply and demand. To do so, it encourages only prudent and selective methods for the trapping and breeding of fur supplying animals.

As in other industries who use highly skilled craftsmen, the industry also faces the problem of a decrease in its skilled labor supply. Traditionally, the fur industry's labor was supplied by immigrants who arrived equipped with skills obtained in their native countries. Today, with the decline in immigration, this supply is fast dwindling. However, with the help of federal funds and industry contributions, a program has been launched to attract career students into fur manufacturing. Working with schools like the High School of Fashion Industries in New York City, the fur manufacturers hope to obtain the necessary suply of highly skilled crafstmen.

The Marketing Activities of the Fur Industry

The major marketing thrust for the fur industry has not come from individual trappers, processors, or manufacturing firms. Most of these enterprises are too small to undertake specialized marketing activities. Therefore, this job has been left to the various trade associations and organizations which represent all or a segment of the fur industry.

The Fur Information and Industry Council acts on behalf of all its members to research and develop new markets, stimulate consumer interest, assist other members of the fashion industry, research new production methods, and collect and disseminate fur information. It is this organization which is most responsible for the fur industry's exciting new fashion image, picking up on young fashion trends in the early 60s and re-orienting the fur industry toward a new crop of younger customers.

Furs are also promoted on an individual basis by several industry groups. One which heavily promotes mink to both the industry and the consumers is EMBA—Eastern Mink Breeders Association. The GLMA—Great Lakes Mink Association, and ECBC—Empress Chinchilla Breeders Cooperative, are two groups which perform the same functions, promoting their respective furs.

Efforts to unite the many segmented fur groups for the purpose of coping with the major industry problems have been made by the Council of American Fur Organizations. One priority of this group is to maintain and, if necessary, upgrade a positive fur industry image among conservationists, the federal government and the general public. In doing so it hopes to counter the rising amount of imported furs and, at the same time, promote the sale of U.S. fur products to countries throughout the world.

The industry must and does strictly adhere to various federal laws which govern it in terms of consumer protection. For instance, the Fur Products and Labeling Act, enacted in 1952 and amended in 1961 and

1969, prevents false advertising and mis-labeling practices by insisting that the label include (in English) the name of the animal from which the fur was obtained and the country of its origin. Furthermore, if an item contains fur which has been used before or is made from leftover pieces (waste fur) it must be so labeled.

The Endangered Species Act of 1969, aimed at the preservation of rare animals, also applies to the fur industry. Domestic pelts from the Texas red wolf, Eastern timber wolf, and Florida panther—to name a few—cannot be used or sold. Foreign pelts from the jaguar, leopard, tiger, and cheetah—once highly valued by the industry—are also on the list of endangered species and cannot be imported into the United States in any form.

The reduction in the variety of furs and the introduction of synthetic "fake furs" could have very easily hurt American fur producers. However, due to the foresight and marketing efforts of the various trade associations, both these threats were successfully overcome.

Finally, for added consumer appeal and status, designer labels are fast being added to fur garments. Via licensing agreements, names like Halston, Givenchy, and Yves Saint Laurent are now found on prestige furs.

Although owning fur is not inexpensive, the use of new non-mink furs has helped to make fur more affordable. The fashion consciousness of the fur industry—which, for instance, is designing jackets to fit over bulky sweaters in its determination to reflect fashion trends—has combined with fur's increasingly affordable prices to make today's fur industry one of the most profitable sectors of the fashion industry.

FOCUS ON A CAREER

THE PRIMARY MARKETS

Most career opportunities in textiles, leather, and fur require specific technical skill as well as general fashion knowledge. However, opportunities do exist in these industries for those who have basic marketing or business backgrounds and who are willing to learn the specific aspects of a particular company's product line. These positions would most likely be in the sales, advertising, public relations, marketing research, personnel, and accounting areas.

The fashion careers in the primary markets would include:

Textile Designer. This job requires artistic ability as well as a thorough knowledge of textiles and their properties. It requires an educational or business background in fashion, which the textile designer needs to correctly evaluate overall fashion trends.

Fabric Stylist. Working closely with the textile designer, the fabric stylist revises or adapts existing fabric designs for a new seasonal line. The same basic knowledge and skills of a textile designer are required of the stylist. In some companies, this position serves as an apprenticeship to the job of designer. Other companies, however, consider the position of fabric stylist equally important, especially if they deal in mass fashion goods.

Fabric Librarian. This individual is responsible for preparing and maintaining the fabric library. He or she enters the fiber and fabric descriptions which accompany each swatch. The job also involves communicating with those in the trade who seek information on the properties and colors of the firm's fabrics.

Color Stylist. Generally employed by fiber or yarn producers, the color stylist needs a knowledge of textiles and chemistry. He or she is responsible for obtaining the best method of dyeing fillers or yarns and must help in selecting the tints, tones, and shades of color that are being used that season.

Fashion Director or Researcher. Most leather and textile firms have a position which requires an ability to scout the fashion markets and spot uncoming fashion and marketing trends. Sometimes, the individuals holding this position must travel to and report on trends in the United States, Europe, and the Far East. Their findings and their recommendations guide the company in its decisions concerning its future fashion and marketing trends. This job may also involve fashion coordination, staging fashion shows and exhibits for the trade, and working with members of the industry as well as consumer or educational groups.

Usually, if the company is large, this work is carried on by more than one individual. In that case, there are several staff or supportive positions which provide excellent training and exposure to the overall business of fashion.

FOCUS ON THE INDUSTRY

SOURCES OF MARKET INFORMATION

Listed below are some trade associations, groups, and representative companies which may be contacted for specific information on their particular area of the primary markets.

Trade Associations

American Printed Fabrics Council
1440 Broadway, New York, N.Y. 10018
American Wool Council
200 Clayton Street, Denver, Colo. 80206
The Color Association of the United States
200 Madison Avenue, New York, N.Y. 10016
Cotton Incorporated
1370 Avenue of Americas, New York, N.Y. 10019
Fur Information and Fashion Council
101 West 30 Street, New York, N.Y. 10001
National Cotton Council of America, Market Research Service
1918 N. Parkway, P.O. Box 12285, Memphis, Tenn. 38112
Tanners Council of America Inc.
411 Fifth Avenue, New York, N.Y. 10016
The Wool Bureau, Inc.
360 Lexington Avenue, New York, N.Y. 10017

Textile, Fiber, and Fabric Manufacturers

Allied Chemical Corporation
P.O. Box 1087, Morristown, N.J. 07960
Burlington Industries
1345 Avenue of the Americas, New York, N.Y. 10021
Celanese Incorporated, Consumer Education Department
522 Fifth Avenue, New York, N.Y. 10036

Chemstrand Company, Public Relations Department
350 Fifth Avenue, New York, N.Y. 10001

Dan River Incorporated
111 West 40 Street, New York, N.Y. 10036

Deering Milliken Incorporated
1045 Avenue of the Americas, New York, N.Y. 10018

Eastman Kodak Chemicals Products Incorporated, Education Department
Fiber Division, 260 Madison Avenue, New York, N.Y. 10016

E. I. Du Pont de Nemours & Co., Textile Fibers Department Production Information Section
Centre Road Building, Wilmington, Del. 19898

Firestone Tire and Rubber Company
45 Rockefeller Plaza, New York, N.Y. 10036

Monsanto Company
1114 Avenue of the Americas, New York, N.Y. 10036

Springmaid Fabrics
104 West 40 Street, New York, N.Y. 10018

J. P. Stevens And Company, Inc.
1185 Avenue of the Americas, New York, N.Y. 10036

Union Carbide Chemicals, Textile Fibers Department Advertising Manager
270 Park Avenue, New York, N.Y. 10017

TERMS TO REMEMBER

primary markets
natural fibers
synthetic fibers
greige goods
converter
vertical integration
derived demand
fabric library

HIGHLIGHTS OF THE CHAPTER

- The primary markets of the fashion business include textile, leather, and fur producers.
- The largest segment, the textile industry, is composed of four sectors: fiber production, yarn production, fabric construction, and fabric finishing.
- There are two types of fibers, natural and synthetic. Today, synthetic fiber production dominates U.S. output.
- Major problems facing the textile industry include rising costs of labor and competition from imported goods.
- The Industry has become increasingly vertically integrated and is dependent on derived demand for its production output.
- Leather production is a slow process that takes about four weeks to complete. Therefore leather producers work far in advance of the rest of the fashion industry.
- A major problem for the U.S. industry is the rapid increase in imports of hides and skins as well as finished products made from leather.
- There are three kinds of leather producing operations: tanneries, converters, and contract tanneries.
- The fur industry has undergone a change in emphasis from being mink oriented to being fur oriented.
- Fur pelts are obtained worldwide via trapping and breeding.
- Over 90 percent of the fur processors and fur product manufacturers are located in New York City.
- Because the industry has many small enterprises, major trade associations like the Fur Information and Industry Council carry out most marketing activities for the industry.

QUESTIONS

1. Name the four natural fibers. Which ones are produced by the United States?
2. What are the two types of synthetic fibers? Which fiber was the first to be produced synthetically?
3. Define greige goods.

4. What kinds of qualities are given to fabrics in the finishing process?
5. What geographic changes have occurred in the location of U.S. textile production?
6. Describe the growth of the synthetic fiber industry since 1930.
7. Define vertical integration.
8. What is derived demand? How does it affect the production of textiles?
9. What is the principal hide used by U.S. leather producers?
10. What are the major competitive sources for the U.S. leather industry?
11. Explain the role of the converter in the textile industry. In the leather industry.
12. Expalin the change in customer focus undertaken by the fur industry.
13. What is the difference between a hide, a skin, and a pelt.
14. How does the Endangered Species Act affect the fur and leather industries.
15. Even with competition from abroad and from fake fur producers the fur industry has been able to grow extensively in the last five years. Why?

9

TODAY'S AMERICAN PRODUCERS

OBJECTIVES

After reading this chapter, you should be able to:

- Describe the characteristics, methods of operation, and marketing activities of women's wear, menswear, and children's wear manufacturers.
- Discuss the problems facing New York's Garment Center and locate other centers of production and sales.
- Identify the five fashion seasons; define market weeks, and cite when they occur.
- Outline the steps used in the production of clothing.
- Discuss the characteristics of various kinds of accessories.

In America, the business of producing fashion merchandise is big business. The fashion industry ranks among the top ten industries in the United States. It manufactures a vast array of women's wear, children's wear, meanswear, and accessory products, generating annual sales of over 80 billion dollars.

It is an industry made up of more than 22,000 firms. Located throughout all fifty states, these operations provide jobs for nearly 1.3 million workers. There is an unusual mix of giant and small firms, with huge corporations and conglomerates existing alongside small father-and-son operations and partnerships. The industry is highly volatile—sudden style changes and customer fashion whims occur overnight, and success or failure is governed by the ability of a producer to accurately predict those changes and whims, and to satisfy them.

In all four areas—men's, women's, children's wear, and accessories—the nature of the industry is changing. Most of the changes can be observed in its largest and most influential sector: women's wear.

WOMEN'S WEAR

Characteristics of the Industry

The women's garment industry—a 32 billion dollar a year venture—is the very heart of U.S. apparel production.

Location. There are over 4,000 firms engaged in the production of women's wear; most of them are located in the middle Atlantic region, with New York, Pennsylvania, and New Jersey as the leading states.

New York City is considered the "fashion capital" of the United States. New York's metropolitan area is responsible for 60 to 70 percent of the country's annual production of women's wear, and the apparel industry is the city's primary private employer.

The "Garment Center" and world-famous Seventh Avenue are located in midtown Manhattan (Fig. 9-1). Although it is a relatively small geographic area, it contains the headquarters and/or showrooms for nearly every fashion manufacturer of women's apparel.

FOCUS ON THE INDUSTRY

NEW YORK'S FASHION MARKETS

To an unfamiliar visitor, New York City seems chaotic, unorganized, and unmaneuverable. This is not so for those who are visiting New York's garment center and related fashion markets. When buyers come to town, they discover that all of their particular resources may be found within a few short blocks of each other, or even within a few clustered buildings. Below is a partial listing of the most representative locations for each of the specialized areas of New York's fashion markets

Women's and Children's Apparel	
Couture and Higher-Priced Lines	498, 500, 512, 530, and 550 Seventh Avenue
Moderate and Budget-Priced Lines	Located in Chinatown district of the Garment Center, mostly in 1400, 1407, 1411 Broadway
Sportswear	1407 Broadway
Bridal	499 Seventh Avenue
Furs	Seventh Avenue, mostly between 30–34 Streets
Underwear and Intimate Apparel	Madison Avenue between 28–34th Streets
Children's Wear	8th Avenue between 35–39th Streets
Men's and Boys' Apparel	
Men's Clothing and Outerwear	Seventh Avenue, mostly between 14–24th Streets
Men's Furnishings	The Empire State Building
Boy's Clothing and Outerwear	Madison to 8th Avenue between 14–34th Streets.
Fashion Accessories	
Shoes	34th Street and Broadway; also the Empire State Building
Handbags	Madison Avenue and Broadway between 30–34th Streets
Costume Jewelry	Fifth Avenue between 30–40th Streets
Fine Jewelry	Fifth and Sixth Avenues between 48–53rd Streets; also Nassau and Fulton Streets in downtown Manhattan
Gloves	Madison and Fifth Avenues between 34–42nd Streets
Millinery	Fifth and Sixth Avenue between 38–39th Streets; also upper 50s.

New York City is also endowed with a heavy concentration of allied industries which are essential to apparel manufacturing. These allied trades are primarily located in and around the garment center, and include producers of belts, buttons, needles, pins, hooks and eyes, and other notions; and also embroidery, tucking, pleating and trimming firms.

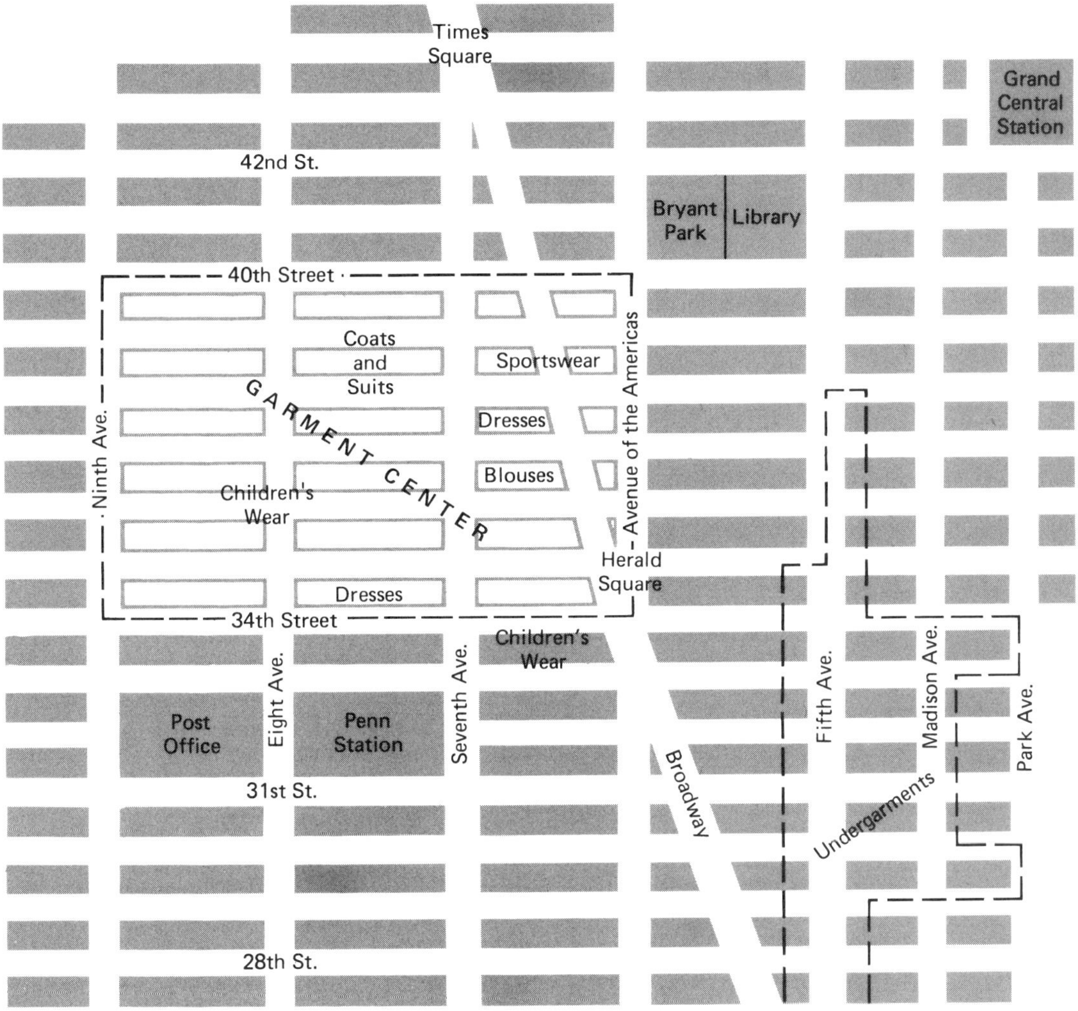

FIGURE 9-1. New York City's Garment Center

Although, in terms of fashion, New York City is "where it's at," there has been an ever increasing number of firms who are shifting part of their operations—primarily that of garment construction—outside of the New York area.

Apparel production has shifted to other areas of New York State as well as to locations in Pennsylvania, Massachusetts, New Jersey, and Connecticut. The most recent trend, however, has been to leave the northeastern region completely. Many firms have gone to the South or the West while others, because of the savings involved, have moved their production operations entirely out of the United States.

Some New York firms have also moved or expanded their *sales* and/or *distribution* operations. Most have gone to Los Angeles, Chicago, Dallas, St. Louis, Cleveland, Kansas City, or Miami; cities long established as secondary apparel centers, housing many of the nation's leading manufacturers. Los Angeles, for instance, serves as the home of all the top swimwear makers. Although they do not have as great a concentration of resources as New York, these centers draw an impressive number of buyers who welcome the "close to home" accessibility of these regional markets.

The increasing acceptance of these markets by retailers is but one of many reasons given by New York firms for shifting all or part of their operations. Here are some others:

First and foremost is *cost.* Labor, overhead, taxes, and plant construction costs are all cheaper out of town.

New York space is both expensive and severely limited. That which is available is old and in need of renovation. Construction of new facilities is virtually non-existent.

New York's readily available supply of skilled and semi-skilled immigrant labor—traditionally attracted to the needle trades—is dwindling. The simple styling of many of today's garments—especially moderate and budget priced goods—can be handled adequately by the less skilled, cheaper labor found outside of New York. And, should detailed work be necessary, it can often be done less expensively by foreign labor.

Improved *transportation,* particularly trucking, makes it easier and more reasonable to distribute from out-of-town production locations. The garment center is not designed to accommodate the easy loading and unloading of trucks; and furthermore, shipping costs within the metropolitan area are exorbitant.

Finally, since the garment industry has traditionally separated the design, marketing, and production aspects of the business, geographic separation is plausible and in many ways facilitates rather than hinders the garment making process.

Although New York remains the country's unquestioned design center and nearly two-thirds of all women's apparel is still produced there—these reasons make it apparent that New York may some day have to share the title of "America's Apparel Center" with other geographic locations.

Structure. Today, the bulk of the 4000 firms producing women's wear are small, privately owned corporations or partnerships employing under 60 workers. This fact, however, is rapidly changing. In the 1950s and 60s, large publicly owned corporations began to emerge until today there are over 100 such firms. One of the largest is Jonathan Logan, Inc. This huge corporation employs 11,500 people in 66 plants which are located in 44 cities throughout the United States. It also maintains agreements with 140 contractors who sew exclusively for Jonathan Logan.

The firm is headquartered in North Bergen, New Jersey, and is highly diversified. Its products include double-knit fabric, dresses, double-knit dresses, blouses, sportswear, girl's lingerie, girl's sleepwear, rainwear, beachwear, handbags, and shoes. This wide assortment of goods is sold under about a dozen well known labels. In 1977, the sale of those goods brought the Jonathan Logan corporation over $381 million in sales—an impressive sum for apparel sales.

But unlike other industries, no one firm enjoys a large enough share of the market to dominate or monopolize the industry. The combined volume of the eight largest firms represents only 17 percent of the total sales of the industry.

The majority of the women's wear producers have comparatively small sales volumes, ranging from $5 to 30 million annually. The industry is still fertile territory for the aspiring entrepreneur with limited capital; easy entry has long been a characteristic of this industry.

Unfortunately, because of the fickleness of fashion, so is an unusually high bankruptcy rate. It averages at about 18 percent a year; especially vulnerable are the very small firms—those with under 20 employees. The recent increase in imports has added to the industry's high mortality rate; and each year there are fewer firms in operation than there were the year before.

The industry is also undergoing a change in its method of production—shifting from "inside" to "outside" shops. The concept of separating the various manufacturing processes is not new and, as discussed in Chapter 4, these trade terms refer to firms which are specifically classified as *manufacturers, jobbers,* or *contractors.* Manufacturers who handle all phases of production are known as "inside" shops. In recent years, the number of these firms has declined, to be replaced by jobbers—firms that handle all activities but the actual sewing, and by "outside shops"—contractors hired to do the sewing.

The reasons for these changes are simple: First, the jobber and contractor are specialists—each handling the aspects of apparel production they know best. Because their operations are separate, they are naturally smaller, requiring less capital and labor to operate. Their smaller labor force minimizes personnel training, expenses and problems. Second, the jobber makes use of the services of the contractor only when those services are needed—increasing his efficiency. The contractor, meanwhile, is free to receive work from more than one jobber—fully utilizing his capacities. All these features turn into advantages which reduce the operating and labor costs of all concerned. These reduced costs result in higher profits and lower retail prices, benefiting producer and consumer alike.

In both inside and outside shops, either the *task* or *piece work* systems of operations are used. Under the task system a team of workers—a baster, sewing machine operator, finisher, and presser—are responsible for one complete garment. This system is generally used for higher priced merchandise. Under the piece work system, also known as specialization, an operator works on just one part of the garment. For instance, one operator makes buttonholes, one sews on collars, and another sets in sleeves.

Although the primary advantage of the piece work method is its low cost and simple training requirements, critics charge it causes a decline in quality and craftsmanship resulting in inferior merchandise. Still, the pressure to reduce costs in order to remain competitive make this method an attractive alternative and the one most widely used today.

Labor. Finding good inexpensive labor is difficult in any business. For the garment industry this is a special concern because labor costs can and do run as high as 50 to 55 percent of the final cost of a garment. The industry has relied heavily on women and on immigrant labor; these groups represent nearly 80 percent of the employees in the industry. But this labor pool is shrinking and both the scarcity and the rising cost of good labor has spurred research into new and faster production techniques—particularly among the giants in the field. Such devices as laser beam cutting instruments and computer assisted machines to grade patterns are already in use. Unfortunately, in spite of intense research, apparel production is still a mechanized but non-automated industry.

Efficient, affordable labor is not only a concern of management—it is a concern of the industry's union as well. The International Ladies' Garment Workers' Union, which represents nearly 90 percent of the workers in both women's and children's wear, has long recognized the importance of working with—rather than against—management for industry growth.

The following example is typical of legendary union-management cooperation. Traditionally, the ILGWU has bargained with employers for increases in the *piece rate* paid to operators. Under this system, a worker was paid on the basis of the number of units or pieces he produced. The rate paid for each piece was determined by the time it took the operator to complete each unit, the difficulty of the operation, and the skills it required. Today, in determining the piece rate, the efficiency of the plant and the total wages paid to the workers are also taken into consideration. These additional considerations benefit the employees because a modernized plant allows for greater worker productivity and thus, higher pay. But employers also benefit since the union will agree to share the fruits of plant modernization with management by lowering its piece rate. As the employer improves conditions, the piece rate is adjusted accordingly.

In addition to this example of union-management cooperation, both groups have established learning programs and scholarships to encourage young people to enter the field of fashion. Working through apprenticeship programs and with various educational institutions on the secondary and post-secondary levels, both are hoping to increase and improve the supply of labor the industry needs to survive.

Method of Operation

In the "rag" business, the start of every season represents a new challenge—a new beginning. To manufacturers, most of the styles, fabrics, and colors which sold well a few short months, weeks, or even days ago are ancient history. They are well aware that—to stay in business—at least two, but more often four or five separate times a year they must produce something new and exciting. These times correspond to the industry's five fashion seasons.

Fashion Seasons. In essence, fashion seasons are selling seasons. Each season brings some change in the styling details of fashion merchandise, and by having so many seasons, both manufacturers and retailers hope to profitably entice consumers into increasing the frequency of their fashion purchases.

Although manufacturers are constantly updating their collections or lines and retailers may receive new merchandise weekly or even daily, the fanfare of "out with the old-in with the new" corresponds basically to the following demarcations:

Fall-Back to School	Most important—possibly longest—fashion season. Most major style innovations and a major transformation in color and fabric occur at this time.
Holiday	Generally, a minor season. The most successful of the fall fashion trends are refined and interpreted in dressier, more formal wear.
Cruise—Resort	Also a minor season. Primarily a preview for summer lines and especially important to certain sportswear manufacturers such as swimwear. Some high priced manufacturers present their Holiday and Resort lines together.
Spring	Second most important fashion season. Of particular importance to designer houses and dress manufacturers. Many volume and medium priced manufacturers combine their spring and summer lines.
Summer	Designer, dress, and sportswear manufacurers—especially swimwear—are usually those presenting separate summer lines. Silhouette trends are often tested at this time and successful ones are carried into fall merchandise.

Specialization of Product. All apparel manufacturers specialize according to *size, type of apparel,* and *price.* Even the giants follow this formula, maintaining separate divisions for each type of merchandise they produce. By maintaining these divisions or—as in the case of the small firm—by concentrating on a narrow product line, producers can more effectively service and cater to their immediate and primary customer: the retailer.

Retailers have organized their operations *departmentally.* They have done so to meet the special needs of a wide array of people. For instance, a woman who is looking for a medium priced dress in a junior size will go to the department featuring moderately priced junior dresses—bypassing higher priced junior departments or those with misses' sizes.

In terms of *size specialization* for women's wear, the following three categories are used by manufacturers. Unfortunately, there is no industry-wide standardization of sizes. This means that the dimensions of a size vary from one manufacturer to another and it explains why a customer may have to buy a size larger or smaller, depending on which manufacturer made the garment.

Women's (Sizes 36–52) and Half Sizes—(12½ to 26½). This size range offers apparel for the larger woman. The half sizes are for those who are also short waisted.

Misses (Sizes 4–20). These sizes represent the majority of women—most of whom have mature, fuller figures.

Juniors (Sizes 5–15) and Petite (Sizes 3–15). These sizes are for the shorter, small-framed woman.

These distinctions generally refer to physical differences in the size of the wearer. There are also, however, styling connotations which, although less prevalent than they once were, continue to exist.

Traditionally, women's sizes have been thought of as outsized merchandise designed to cover figure flaws and with little fashion appeal. Fortunately, the manufacturers of those sizes are now paying attention to current fashion trends and are tastefully incorporating them in the fashions they produce for the larger woman.

Those producing junior sizes have also reconsidered their styling philosophy. Originally, junior sized clothing was introduced for young teenagers who were unable to go directly from children's wear to women's wear. Styling characteristics of goods produced in this size range were naturally youth oriented. When older women with junior figures discovered junior sizing, they asked for more sophisticated styling. As a result, many misses' manufacturers began to produce junior sizes under a separate division, incorporating the same fashion styling of their misses' sizes into their junior lines.

Specialization by *type of apparel* refers to the classification of goods in terms of their appearance and/or function. There are eight categories, each representing a manufacturing specialty:

Dresses—Either one or two piece. Dress manufacturers also make two and three piece ensembles which include a dress with a jacket or coat.

Sportswear—Besides pants, shorts, tops, jackets, sweaters, swimwear, and active sportswear, this group has literally mushroomed to include dresses, jumpsuits, pantsuits, coordinated separates, and also evening wear.

Outerwear—Includes coats, suits, pantsuits, jackets, and rainwear.

Evening Wear—Consisting mostly of formal evening attire.

Bridal—Also includes bridesmaids, and mother-of-the bride dresses.

Blouses and Shirts—Though most blouse and shirt makers are now also producing coordinates, a few are still specializing solely in this category.

Uniforms—For workers in medicine, dentistry, airlines, restaurants, and other commercial sectors.

Lingerie and At-Home Wear—All types of women's undergarments, including bras, panties, girdles—as well as loungewear, pajamas, robes, swimwear, and some apparel which may be worn as evening wear.

Finally, manufacturers specialize by *price lines,* producing merchandise which is expected to retail to the consumer in one of three price ranges:

Better and Designer—The industry's most expensive apparel, this category features prestige name manufacturers and designer labels. For instance, a designer such as Carol Horn may charge under 100 dollars for an item, while Halston may charge thousands.

Moderate—Refers to medium priced goods and it includes boutique merchandise and well known manufacturer brands.

Budget—The least expensively priced, but most widely offered merchandise. No major designer or manufacturer brand name identification. Includes private label and houses brand items.

Specializing in a *type,* a *size* or a *price* range of apparel offers a manufacturer several advantages. To begin with, it gives him and his product fast and easy recognition from store buyers and consumers alike. The firm of Levi Strauss, for instance, became famous for specializing in blue denim jeans—a *type* of merchandise. Other manufacturers like White Stag (makers of good but well *priced* sportswear) and Junior Sophisticates (known for their specially *sized* junior clothes) made their reputation by being "priced right" or because they "fit right."

Specialization also helps a manufacturer service his customer. By specializing and concentrating solely on the needs of a particular market, he can more effectively service that market.

The Production Process. There are two distinct phases in manufacturing a garment: the designing process and the production process.

The designing of a garment was described in Chapter Seven. Some firms nearly eliminate or at least reduce the number of steps involved in the designing process. Instead, they copy or *knock off* the styles of other designers and manufacturers. For some manufacturers, particularly those producing inexpensive merchandise, this *style piracy* is the most effective, least costly way of handling the designing process.

In most cases, the manufacturing process does not begin until prospective buyers have seen a line and have placed orders for specific styles. Only the *"hot numbers"*—those styles which receive enough orders—go into production.

In this respect, the garment industry is different from most others. Very little, if any, inventory is stockpiled. The rule of thumb for most firms is "don't cut the goods until you have the paper." Which simply means that you don't begin the production of any style until a written order has been received from a buyer. This rule gives the manufacturer tremendous flexibility, allowing him to produce only those styles which he intends to sell. On the other hand, this policy makes the production period very short: goods have to be produced and shipped within three to eight weeks time.

The actual production process begins with the patternmaker. He takes the paper pattern pieces which were used in construction of the sample and *grades* them into other sizes, meaning that the sample pattern (usually an average size) is mathematically reduced and enlarged into each of the sizes that the style will be made in.

The pattern pieces are then arranged on a large piece of paper called a *marker.* This is a very important step because it determines fabric costs. The closer the pieces are fitted together the less fabric the garment takes. The pieces, however, must follow a careful arrangement. The arrangement must take the fabric grain (the lengthwise thread of the fabric), the matching of stripes, plaids, and other pattern characteristics of the fabric into consideration.

Several copies of each original marker are made and then each is placed on top of fabric which has been *layed up.*

Laying up the fabric is also a critical step. It involves rolling out the fabric on long cutting tables—one layer on top of another. The fabric must be perfectly straight, directly in line with the piece underneath and—in the case of patterned fabrics such as plaids—each layer must be identical to the one below.

After laying up anywhere from 50 to 150 layers of fabric, the marker is placed on top and the *cutting* begins. This step is done by skilled craftspeople using an electric cutting knife. Cutters who work quickly and accurately mean a great deal to the manufacturer and are often the highest paid of the firm's production staff.

The next step involves *assembling* the necessary pieces of the garment. The cut pieces are *bundled* according to size and shipped to sewing operators. After the garment is sewn together it is *finished,* meaning that all of the small and final construction details such as hems and buttonholes are completed. Then it is *pressed, inspected,* and *bagged* (placed on hangers and covered in plastic). The completed garments are then sent to the firm's shipping facilities where orders are *packed* and made ready for shipping.

The entire process is repeated for styles which become *"runners"*— the term applied to reordered goods.

Marketing Activities

Producing saleable merchandise is only part of a manufacturer's job. The other part is marketing it profitably. Because this activity is required of all manufacturers, regardless of the type of product involved, many marketing procedures are standard. But certain marketing techniques used by apparel producers are unique. These include their methods of selling goods to retailers, their financial arrangements, and certain aspects of their advertising and promotion.

Selling Goods to Retailers. One of the sales methods manufacturers employ to sell their products to retailers is road or territorial sales personnel who visit retail establishments showing the manufacturer's line. This method is quite expensive and, more important, time consuming. Its use, therefore, is limited to very large firms who desire and can afford national distribution and to manufacturers of "basic" merchandise, such as undergarments and hosiery which do not experience fast fashion changes.

The majority of garment manufacturers find it easier and decidedly less expensive to maintain showrooms in New York or in the various regional merchandise marts and have the retailers send buyers to them. This method has several advantages. It gives the manufacturer the flexibility to add and delete styles from a collection because of instant and direct buyer feedback; and it maintains the tradition of presenting the new lines to all retailers at the same time during certain specified periods of the year called *market weeks.*

Market weeks are held for each of the five fashion seasons and are timed for the convenience of both the manufacturers and retailers. Table 9-1 lists the approximate times of the market weeks held in New York.

Buyers whose operations are located some distance from the markets visit manufacturers only during market weeks. Buyers who are located close to the market can visit their resources on a monthly or even weekly basis. Very large retailers such as Sears or J. C. Penney, whose orders are in the thousands of units, plan their upcoming market week purchases by working with their resources much earlier than the scheduled market weeks.

Traditionally, sending the buyers "to the market" meant going to New York City. But since apparel markets with permanent manufac-

TABLE 9-1

New York Market Weeks

Fashion Season	Market Weeks
Fall-Back to School	End of May-Early June
Holiday	End of July-Early August
Resort	August
Spring	Early November
Summer	Late January-Early February

turer showrooms have emerged in other parts of the country, buyers may now opt to go to more than one market (see Table 9-1).

Visiting manufacturer showrooms, particularly those of designer and high priced lines, may mean seeing an elaborate fashion show complete with music, models, and much fanfare. The more typical buyer's visit, however, involves a private "off the rack" (on hangers) presentation of a line by a specialist—the showroom salesperson.

Usually, a salesperson is assigned to a buyer and after several seasons, the salesperson develops a knowledge of the type of merchandise and services that buyer needs. Specifically, a salesperson's job consists of "showing the line," providing buyers with information on trends, and helping to plan and coordinate any joint advertising and promotional ventures.

Good salespeople are essential to the manufacturer. In addition to their important selling role, they also provide invaluable feedback. From the reaction of the buyers, a salesperson can project the acceptance of a

TABLE 9-2

Some Regional Markets and Their Market Weeks for Women's Wear

Location	Important Market Weeks
Los Angeles—*The California Mart* (1500 showrooms)	Mid-January for summer lines Mid-August for holiday lines Mid-October for spring lines
Chicago—*The Apparel Center* (3500 showrooms)	Early June for fall lines October for spring lines
Dallas—*The Dallas Apparel Mart* (1550 showrooms)	Late January for summer lines April and May for fall lines August for holiday lines October for spring lines
Miami—*Miami Merchandise Mart* (300 showrooms)	Mid-October for spring lines June for fall lines January for summer lines

trend or style. This information can help a manufacturer refine a line and anticipate the future demand of a style or a trend. Showroom personnel, therefore, are usually well paid, working on a salary plus commission basis.

Financial Arrangements. Garment manufacturers rely heavily on a technique known as *factoring* to obtain the necessary cash for operational expenses.

Factoring involves a third party—a factor—who enters into the sales agreement between a retail buyer and a manufacturer. It may be simply described as follows: When a buyer writes up an order for merchandise and gives it to the manufacturer, the manufacturer needs cash for materials and labor to begin production. The manufacturer obtains the cash by "selling" the order to a factor who pays the manufacturer a *discounted* amount of the total sum of the order. When payment is due, the retailer sends the full amount to the factor.

This system is most suitable for the garment industry. It gives maximum flexibility to the manufacturer and reduces his investment requirements, allowing him to produce up-to-the-minute styles at reasonable prices.

Advertising and Promotion. Until several years ago, the advertising and promotional activities of manufacturers were minimal. These activities were primarily the responsibility of the retailers. Now, large and small manufacturers alike engage in several kinds of advertising and promotion.

There has been a considerable increase in *direct* advertising to the consumer; some manufacturer brand names such as Jonathan Logan and Bobbie Brooks have become as famous as those of leading designers.

As a result consumers place less importance on store labels. But the de-emphasis of the store label does not imply that manufacturers and retailers do not work together to promote fashion. *Cooperative* advertising, where each shares the limelight and the advertising costs, remains especially important for both.

A manufacturer may also supply *promotional aids* to the retailer. These include display materials and fixtures, mailing pieces for charge customers, hang tags for garments, photographs and mats for newspaper advertising, and selling aids such as training sessions for salespeople on current fashion trends. Finally, some manufacturers provide merchandise, props, scripts, and, in some cases, even a commentator for presenting in-store fashion shows.

Some of the larger firms also maintain aggressive public relations departments. These publicists use many techniques to bring a firm's name to the attention of the consumer; probably one of the most familiar is that of supplying television personalities with a wardrobe in exchange for an airwave mention or "plug" of the firm's name.

MENSWEAR

Less than twenty years ago, a discussion on the subject of fashion would have most likely excluded any reference to menswear. Except for "the man in the grey flannel suit"—the male uniform of the 50s—there just wasn't much to say about menswear. Men's styles changed ever so slowly. Designer names were unimportant and consumer interest in such things as color, coordination, and the fashion direction of menswear was minimal.

Today, menswear is an integral part of the fashion picture. Granted, its pace of change remains rather slow in comparison to that of women's wear. But since the conservative fifties, there have been very obvious, sometimes revolutionary changes in the designing, production, and marketing of menswear. These changes have altered the attitudes of Middle America and increased its interest in what men wear.

Characteristics of the Industry

The industry classifies firms by the following garment categories:

Clothing (suits, sportcoats, separate trousers, overcoats and topcoats; all are also referred to as "tailored clothing")
Work Clothes (overalls, jeans, work shirts and pants)
Heavy Outerwear (jackets, parkas, snow suits, ski wear)
Furnishings (shirts, socks, pajamas, neckwear, underwear)
Miscellaneous (rainwear, uniforms, hats, etc)

Because of the manner in which the industry is organized, separate statistical facts about menswear are usually not given. Instead, they are combined with those of boyswear. For example, there are nearly 3,000 firms employing approximately 290,000 workers that produce men's and boys' apparel. Some make clothing for men, others make clothing for boys; while still others make apparel for both.

Location. The production of menswear is carried on in all sections of the country. However, the heaviest concentration of manufacturers is found in the Middle Atlantic region. Three states—New York, New Jersey, and Pennsylvania are responsible for over 48 percent of the entire industry's output. In the rest of the country, California, Georgia, Texas, and Missouri are the top menswear and boyswear producing states.

New York City serves as the design and marketing headquarters for the nation's industry. The New York metropolitan area also houses a very large share of the industry's present production facilities. But, as in women's wear, the number of manufacturing operations doing business in the metropolitan area continues to decline as firms move to other areas of the country.

In the men's and boys' industries, manufacturers tend to congregate together according to the type of apparel they produce, and there seem to be several very definite geographical distinctions. For instance, tailored clothing (with the exception of separate trousers) is produced almost exclusively in the Middle Atlantic region where highly skilled labor is available. Trousers, work clothes, and furnishings are made in the South and Southwest. There, less expensive—although less skilled—labor is found. Several manufacturers have found ideal plant locations outside of the continental United States in Puerto Rico, Mexico, some South American countries, and the Far East.

FOCUS ON THE INDUSTRY

IMPORTANT MENSWEAR MARKETS

The following cities and their apparel specialties are established production and marketing centers for meanswear:

New York. Largest and most important menswear center. All grades of apparel are produced and sold. Important for formalwear. Leader in terms of high fashion, and trendsetter for industry.

Philadelphia. Known principally for medium to medium-better priced tailored clothing and formalwear.

Chicago. Home of several very large manufacturers of separates and medium to better priced, excellent quality tailored clothing.

Rochester. Recognized for its high quality tailored clothing.

Baltimore. Noted for rainwear. Important also for medium and better priced tailored clothing and specialized summer merchandise.

Cincinnati. Center for medium to better priced tailored clothing and separates. Also produces summer merchandise.

Boston. Primarily noted for outerwear and rainwear.

Los Angeles. Dominates in sportswear production. Becoming increasingly important as a trend-setting center for all of menswear—especially medium to top-grade high fashion garments.

Structure. The majority of the 3000 firms which produce men's and boys' apparel are small, none employs more than 250 workers.

Each firm specializes in some particular type or category of merchandise such as tailored suits or shirts. These categories correspond to the various departmental divisions used by retailers.

Of the five types of garment categories, more than half the firms (over 1500) produce tailored clothing. Within this category, those producing separate trousers have recently enjoyed a tremendous increase in business because of the trend toward more casual dress. As might be expected, the trend also caused a similar sales increase in the work clothes classification as jeans, flannel shirts, and work shirts became extremely popular.

There is one important difference between the nature of the women's wear and menswear industries. In menswear, a few large firms dominate the market in terms of sales volume. For example, firms whose annual sales volume is in excess of 25 million dollars number only 39 or 1.3 percent of the total industry. But they control nearly 35 percent of the industry's sales. The emergence of these giant menswear firms is primarily a result of the acquisitions and mergers which have taken place within the industry.

Several firms have gone one step further and have become publicly owned corporations or part of major conglomerates. Some of these larger and better known companies include Phillips-Van Heusen (Van Heusen Shirts); Cluett Peabody (Arrow Shirts and Van Raalte); McGregor-Doniger (sportswear producers); Hart Schaffner & Marx (retailers as well as manufacturers); and Manhattan Industries (Manhattan Shirts).

Labor. Contributing greatly to the nature of the men's and boy's wear industry is its union: The Amalgamated Clothing and Textile Workers of America. Known simply as "The Amalgamated," this union—with over 400,000 members—has long been regarded as one of the most progressive and successful trade unions in the country.

Since its inception in 1914, the Amalgamated has consistently sought to meet the needs of its members by bargaining for decent wages and extensive fringe benefits. It is considered a "pioneer" in America's labor movement for its introduction and operation of a broad range of services for its union members. These innovative features include: housing facilities, a bank, a life insurance company, health and day care centers, and college tuition assistance programs for members' children.

The Amalgamated has also helped to strengthen the industry through its willingness to cooperate with management. Union-management relations are so remarkable that for 53 years, until 1974, the union had not struck the industry. (The 1974 strike lasted one week before a settlement was reached.)

The Amalgamated does not only represent workers who produce men's and boys' wear; its membership also includes workers from retail stores, laundries, and those who produce cotton garments. Formerly known as the Amalgamated Clothing Workers, the union recently changed to its present name to accurately reflect its latest undertakings: the organization of workers in the country's textile mills.

Well over 95 percent of the workers who produce tailored clothing—suits, sportcoats and overcoats—are represented by the Amalgamated. However, certain segments of the industry, including producers of separate trousers and many operations located in the South and Southwest, remain unorganized.

As in women's wear, the composition of the labor force in menswear has changed. Immigrant tailors, mostly male, have all but been replaced by women who now hold jobs as sewing machine operators and finishers. In fact, the custom tailor once so indispensible to the production of menswear is but a tiny minority of the menswear work force of today. Tailors who operate their own retail stores number a scant 1000 or so; and tailors to-the-trade—those who work in firms which specialize in individual made-to-measure garments—produce less than 5 percent of the industry's output. Meanwhile, the majority of men presently entering the menswear field prefer to fill positions as cutters and shippers, causing a further decrease of tailors in the menswear labor force.

Ethnically, there is a large percentage of black and Hispanic workers in low and unskilled positions in today's industry. There is also a disproportionate number of older workers who, upon reaching retirement age, will leave without the industry finding qualified replacements. These facts indicate that a sufficient amount of well-trained labor may be at a premium in the very near future unless both the industry and the Amalgamated take quick action to remedy the situation.

Methods of Operation

The steps used in producing a line of menswear are basically the same as those used for women's wear, with two notable differences. First, most menswear is produced by "inside" shops. The use of "outside" contractors and jobbers is limited to inexpensive lines and to some sportswear items. The extreme flexibility needed by women's wear producers to keep up with style changes is not essential in most menswear. Furthermore, menswear producers must maintain direct control over production to maintain quality.

Secondly, the construction of men's clothing is more difficult and complicated than that of women's clothing—requiring a great deal of hand sewing and tailoring. For example, a man's jacket is a "structured" (firmly shaped) garment. To achieve its shape, portions of its interfacings, facings, and lining must be applied and sewn by hand—slowing down the entire manufacturing process. Of course, when the styles of garments change to a more casual unstructured look, the production process time is reduced. But today, the majority of men's clothing continues to be "structured," requiring some type of time-consuming handwork.

Fashion Seasons. Traditionally, menswear manufacturers showed only two collections a year: the fall-winter line presented to buyers in late February through early March and the spring-summer line shown late August through mid-September. As production methods have been speeded up, and as more and more fashion interest in menswear is shown by the consumer, an ever-increasing number of menswear manufacturers are beginning to show four lines a year. The four collections more or less correspond to the "fashion seasons" in women's wear and are presented and delivered to retailers as shown in Table 9-3.

Like women's wear, the two most important collections in terms of fashion direction are the fall and spring lines. Both the winter and the late spring-summer collections follow the styling trends of the previous season, making modifications in the weight and in the colors of the fabrics.

In spite of the constantly increasing speed in modern production methods, fashion evolves rather slowly in menswear. Silhouette changes take about twenty years to complete their fashion life cycle. Style changes such as the widening of a lapel or trouser leg generally change ever so slightly each year, so that a jacket or a pair of pants may not appear "outdated" until two to four years after the change is introduced.

TABLE 9-3

Timetable of Fashion Production

Season	*Shown to Buyers*	*Delivered to Stores*
Back to School-Fall	January-February	June-August
Winter	March-April	August-October
Holiday-Spring	July-August	November-January
Late Spring-Summer	September-October	January-April

In the 1960s, menswear manufacturers and those in the social sciences described the newly emerging fashion consciousness among men as the "Peacock Revolution." They foresaw men wearing a rainbow of colors and a variety of styles which changed as quickly and as dramatically as women's wear. Although there was a great proliferation of new styles such as the Nehru Jacket and the safari suit, and although there has been a great deal of color added to most men's wardrobes, it does not appear as if a fashion *revolution* has taken place. Rather, most change has turned out to be *evolutionary,* proceeding at a quicker but nevertheless orderly, systematic pace.

Specialization of Product. As mentioned earlier, the menswear industry is divided into five categories for statistical and reporting purposes. Individual manufacturers within each category either limit their lines to one specific type of garment within a category such as suits; or they produce a variety of items within a classification. An example of the latter is world-famous Levi Strauss and Company, which manufactures all types of clothes, not just jeans.

Clothing within the tailored category is classified even further. It is graded from 1 through 6+: the higher the number, the more hand-tailored operations, and the more expensive the item. Some companies build their reputations on this grading system, boasting of a high amount of hand-tailored operations in their production process to sell their product. They also use the grade of their product to determine its price and, subsequently, these firms are classified by price.

At the top of the 6+ list are firms like Hickey Freeman and Oxxford. These companies specialize in "hand-tailored" clothing, meaning that a man's suit must have a minimum of 25 separate hand operations in its manufacturing process. For example, in an Oxxford suit, the majority of the 160 construction steps of the jacket and 65 steps of the trousers are done by hand—bringing the minimum cost of any of the firm's suits to at least $450. At the other end of the spectrum are firms which produce suits to retail for $50 and under with obviously few if any hand-done manufacturing operations.

Generally speaking, there are four distinct price lines in tailored clothing. Low—suits which retail for $50 and under; popular—suits which sell for $55-$100; better—suits which sell for $80-$150; and high priced—suits which sell for above $150.

Sizing. Compared to women's wear, the number of sizes used in menswear is mind-boggling. First, five basic figure types are used by suit manufacturers for sizing purposes. These include:

Regular	for men with average proportions with a height of 5′7″ to 5′10″
Short	for men with shorter arms and legs with a height of 5′5″ to 5'7"

Long	for taller men with longer arms and legs with a height of 5′11″ to 6′3″
Portly	for men of average height but heavy in stomach and waist areas with a height of 5′8″ to 5′10″
Stout	for heavier men with a height of 5′7″ to 5′10″

Additionally, there are various combinations of these sizes—such as portly long or portly short—which may be included in a manufacturer's size offerings.

Within each of these figure type classifications are numerical sizes. Some examples are as follows:

Regular sizes	35 - 48
Short sizes	36 - 44
Long sizes	37 - 48

In sportswear and separate trousers, sizing is doubly defined. For instance, men's pants are cut in waist sizes 27–42 and, if hemmed, inseam lengths of 29–36 inches.

Shirt manufacturers also use two measurements. They cut a shirt with neck sizes ranging from 14–17 1/2 inches; and sleeve lengths between 30–36 inches. Sport shirts have the least number of size offerings. These are sized small, medium, large, and extra large, and have short or long sleeves which are average for each particular size.

With so many variations in sizes, manufacturers must acquire large numbers of orders before going into production. Only then is it profitable to cut a particular size and style.

Marketing Activities

Menswear manufacturers hold market weeks, use cooperative advertising, rely heavily on factoring, and in fact, use many of the same marketing techniques found in the rest of the apparel industry. However, there are two aspects to marketing menswear which are unusual and therefore worth mentioning. The first involves its methods of distribution and the second its fashion promotion.

Distribution. Although an overwhelming majority of today's menswear manufacturers sell their merchandise to independent retailers, some still sell their goods exclusively through their own retail outlets. This *exclusive method of distribution* is a holdover from the "slop shop" days when retail tailors found it profitable to manufacture an inventory of menswear, thus performing both the manufacturing and retailing functions themselves. These "vertically integrated" manufacturer-retailer operations reached their peak in menswear during the late 1920s. Names such as

Robert Hall, Crawford Clothes, Richman Brothers, Rogers Kent, and Bonds gained national recognition—not only as famous brand names in menswear, but as retailers as well.

Unfortunately, the success of this type of operation has diminished. When economic times are good, the business of these firms is doubly good—benefiting both the manufacturing and the retailing ends of the operation. But when times are bad, losses are doubled, making a firm's recovery doubly difficult to achieve. The latest firm to fall victim to these circumstances was Robert Hall. Owned by the conglomerate United Merchants and Manufacturing, its 447 retail outlets were closed in 1977.

Another method of distribution which originated in earlier days is a process known as *dual distribution.* Through this method, a manufacturer sells goods directly to the consumer through his own manufacturer-owned retail outlets. He also sells merchandise wholesale to independent retailers. In a sense this makes the manufacturer supplier *and* competitor to the independent retailer. This unusual relationship has been successfully maintained only by an exceptional few of the very large and very well known manufacturers in the industry. Some of these dual distributors include Botany Industries, Eagle Clothes, Phillips-Van Heusen, Cluett Peabody, Genesco, and the king of dual distribution in menswear—Hart Schaffner and Marx. Each of these firms operates its own retail stores—usually under different names. The stores primarily sell the goods of their manufacturer owners. However, since most of the stores try to offer a well rounded, full line of apparel and furnishings for men, whatever merchandise the parent manufacturer does not produce is bought from other manufacturers.

Although this distribution method has been highly successful for some firms, it is not a widespread industry practice. In fact, the federal government has attempted to curtail the growth of dual distribution, aware that its use could lead to price manipulation and other unfavorable conditions for the consumer.

FOCUS ON THE INDUSTRY

HART SCHAFFNER AND MARX

The name Hart Schaffner and Marx has been associated with high quality menswear since it was founded in 1881. Today its name continues to stand for quality, but within the menswear industry it also stands for much more.

Hart Schaffner and Marx is a huge, complex, manufacturing-retailing conglomerate. Besides the suits, sportcoats, and topcoats it makes under its original Hart Schaffner and Marx label, the firm produces many other lines of tailored clothing. The most prestigious of these is Hickey Freeman, but its other brand names include Society Brand, Sterling and Hunt, Graham and Gunn, Walter Morton, and Austin Reed.

In addition to tailored clothing, this highly diversified firm produces several specialized lines. Two of the best known are Jaymar-Ruby trousers and Gleneagles rainwear. Within this group of specialized lines exists the company's sole item for women—a collection of uniforms marketed under the Fashionaire label.

Besides running a manufacturing empire, Hart, Schaffner and Marx also leads in the men's retail field, owning and operating nearly 200 men's specialty stores.

The retail operations of the company date back to 1926 when Hart acquired the floundering Wallach's chain. These New York-New Jersey stores were soon joined by the Baskins chain of Chicago, the Silverwood group of Los Angeles, and the Hastings and Moore outlets of San Francisco and Sacramento—with each group retaining its original name.

Although these retail operations contribute greatly to the company's profits, Hart Schaffner and Marx distributes about 70 percent of its merchandise to independent retailers. Nearly 2000 accounts handle H. S. and M. goods and these stores receive the same kinds of services that are given company-owned operations. These services include: conducting seminars in inventory control, providing bookkeeping assistance, supplying promotional materials for display and advertising and, of course, giving advice on fashion coordination and fashion trends.

Fashion Promotion. Traditionally, menswear manufacturers have been a conservative group—hesitating to introduce unusual or extreme fashion and building their lines around quality and price. When exciting fashion changes began to occur in menswear during the 60s, progressive industry members welcomed the opportunity to generate increased interest in menswear. Every leading trade group and organization began to place a stronger emphasis on fashion, hoping to encourage all members of the industry to move in that direction.

There are several trade associations in the menswear industry and, in one way or another, all help to develop, stimulate, and promote menswear fashion.

One of the oldest is the Clothing Manufacturers Association—the CMA—which represents manufacturers of tailored clothing. It was initially formed to bargain for manufacturers with "the Amalgamated." But as the importance of fashion grew and style changes increased, manufacturers also began to turn to the CMA for fashion direction. The association then expanded its activities, developing a very successful fashion program which coordinates and presents styling and fashion trends to its members.

Another trade association is NAMSB—The National Association of Men's Sportswear Buyers. As its name implies, the NAMSB is made up of retailers, and one of its purposes is to keep its membership informed of the industry's fashion trends.

The menswear industry also has a trade group which is responsible for establishing an industry image to the public. Called the MFA—Men's Fashion Association—it promotes menswear fashion to consumers through the press and other media.

One of the most valuable tools for improving the fashion image of menswear has been the use of the designer label. Designer names have long been a source of excitement, prestige, and drama in women's wear, but in menswear they are a relatively new phenomenon.

The designer first credited with offering menswear under his label was Pierre Cardin. The time was the late 1950s—a period in which his type of European continental styling became important in men's clothing. Cardin's success inspired other well known women's wear designers to successfully enter the menswear field:

Hardy Amies of London	Bill Blass
John Weitz	Halston
Oleg Cassini	Geoffrey Beene

One important menswear designer who did not come from the ranks of women's wear is Coty award winner Ralph Lauren. He began his career in menswear, designing for women well after he became successful designing for men.

Today, interest in menswear designer name merchandise—which runs the gamut from tailored clothing to cosmetics—continues to increase. Manufacturers believe in the fashion impact of designer labels and are eager to enter into licensing agreements with well known names, as discussed in chapter 7.

Through its own concerted efforts, the menswear industry has been able to radically change its fashion attitude and image. This industry, once rigidly conservative, has—in less than twenty years—transformed itself into one of the most creative contributors to the fashion business.

CHILDREN'S WEAR

Characteristics of the Industry

Up to and including the Victorian era, children were dressed in clothes which were miniature replicas of those worn by their elders. Although that custom no longer exists, fashion for the young set still takes its cue from the adult world. Each season, it echoes the colors, fabrics, and other fashion trends that are being promoted for the grownups.

Adapted versions of adult fashions are particularly prevalent in higher priced children's clothes. Joseph Love, Kate Greenaway, and designer Helen Lee are some well known names who have a prestigious reputation for high fashion children's wear. To capitalize upon the mother who wants "my kind of clothes for my children," several well known designers and firms of expensive *adult* high fashion have expanded into children's wear. Yves St. Laurent, Geoffrey Beene, Jean Muir of England, Dominic Rampollo (designer of Rosalynn Carter's 1977 Inauguration Day outfit), and French manufacturer Cacharel are successfully selling little versions of their designer clothes for children.

As boys and girls grow into the pre-teen and teen stage, they look to their peers and to the fashions of their older brothers and sisters—the "young adult" group—for fashion direction. Manufacturers for this category (youngsters at the junior and early senior high school level) are aware of this change. They make clothes that appeal to the tastes of their young customers—rather than the parents. To do so, they keep tabs on the fashions of the young adults as well as on the trends and fads of their own teen customers—styling their lines accordingly.

Location. The majority of the children's wear firms are located in the Middle Atlantic region, most notably in New York City. But each year an increasing number of manufacturers have been moving their production facilities South. The distribution, design, and sales operations of these firms, however, has remained at their original locations in New York City, which continues to be the headquarters for the children's wear industry.

Structure. There are over 600 firms in the children's wear industry and, with the notable exception of giants like Carter's and Health-Tex, the majority of these firms are small. Collectively however, they are able to employ over 100,000 workers and produce over $1.5 billion worth of goods annually.[1]

[1]These children's wear statistics do not include boys' wear, which is traditionally combined into the menswear industry.

Methods of Operation

The design and production methods used by children's wear manufacturers are basically the same as those used in the women's wear industry—only less elaborate.

Most manufacturers simply produce two collections a year: fall and spring. However, some of the higher priced and high fashion firms find it profitable to cater to their more affluent customers by showing four lines a year—adding winter and summer collections.

Specialization by *price, size* and *type of merchandise* is also similar to women's wear. In terms of *price,* most manufacturers produce either moderate or better priced goods. The less expensive goods sold on the American market are usually from foreign sources.

The *sizes* within the children's wear industry are divided into six groups and manufacturers generally specialize in one of the following:

Sizes *Newborn-18 Months and 1-4* are classified as Infants' and Toddlers' of both sexes.

These sizes are followed by four separate categories—two for boys and two for girls. Young *girls'* sizes begin with *2-6X* range and continue with *7-14. Boys'* are similarly divided, beginning with the *2-6X* size range and continuing with *8-20.* To accommodate the changing figure and sophisticated stylings required by the pre-teen and teen-age girl, *girls' teen* or *"young junior"* sizes in *6T-14T* make up the final classification.

Each of these size groups corresponds to a department within a retail store. For instance, infants' and toddlers' sizes are usually found in a separate "Infants and Toddlers World," while the teen sizes are almost always housed in a "Young Junior" or "Young Teen" department.

Finally, manufacturers also specialize in producing a *type* of merchandise. For instance, Danskin is known for its children's knit sportswear, Mighty Mac for its quality boys' parkas, and the Rainbow Girl Coat Company for its fashionable girls' coats.

Marketing Activities

Some of the marketing activities of the children's wear firms are identical to those of the women's wear industry. Children's firms use the same methods and techniques to sell their goods to retailers (e.g., the showroom and showroom salesperson), and they use the same type of financial arrangements to operate their businesses (e.g., the factor). But in advertising and sales promotion, their activities are limited. With the exception of several giant firms and a few high fashion companies—most children's manufacturers leave consumer advertising to the retailer. The larger firms that do advertise, however, do it rather aggressively; Health-Tex, Carter's, and Danskin are some of the giants who have become well known to the consumer through their constant direct advertising. Because of cost, the advertising done by high fashion and designer name firms is not as aggressive, but these smaller firms often reduce their advertising costs through cooperative advertising arrangements with the larger fiber and textile firms.

WOMEN'S INTIMATE APPAREL, WOMEN'S ACCESSORIES, AND MEN'S FURNISHINGS

There has been a virtual fashion explosion in the intimate apparel, accessory, and men's furnishings industries. Manufacturers have recognized the importance of coordinating their products with the rest of ready-to-wear, and now offer a wide assortment of goods in an array of styles and colors keyed to current fashion. Intimate apparel, accessories, and men's furnishings have all become indispensible additions to the wardrobe of a consumer who wants a "total look."

For the purposes of our discussion, manufacturers have been grouped into the following classifications: women's intimate apparel; hosiery; cosmetics; footwear; handbags; jewelry; millinery; and an assortment of other special accessories. With the exception of intimate apparel, each classification is discussed as it relates to both men and women. Although these items may be sold in different retail departments, they play the same role in the fashion picture of both sexes and, in most cases, have experienced the same changes, problems, and consumer reactions.

Women's Intimate Apparel

Technically, there are three distinct kinds of intimate apparel: *foundations* (bras, girdles, garter belts); *lingerie* (slips, panties, petticoats); and *loungewear* (robes, nightgowns, at-home wear).

Until the late 50s, the industry was highly specialized, with one firm manufacturing bras and girdles while another produced lingerie. However, fashion soon dictated an industry-wide organizational change. Consumers wanted color coordination between foundation garments and lingerie as well as intimate apparel whose colors, fabrics, and styling followed outerwear fashion trends. As a result, many companies found it advantageous to expand into other classifications or to join forces through merging. Although there are now 1300 firms in operation, these organizational changes produced an industry dominated by large companies and conglomerates, where the bulk of the sales are generated by nationally known giants.

Another major change in the intimate apparel industry occurred in the 60s when, due to lagging sales, the industry expanded into other areas of wearing apparel. Customers can now shop in lingerie departments for swimwear, beachwear, playwear, leotards, body suits and—the most striking innovation of all—at-home wear.

The at-home classification in intimate apparel began in the early 60s with long robes and palazzo pajamas designed for at-home entertaining. Today, lingerie houses produce fashions which are equally appropriate in bedroom, living room, or restaurant. Using colors, fabrics, and style trends of the outerwear market, intimate apparel manufacturers now have a reputation as very sophisticated fashion producers. It is therefore not surprising that they have been joined by fashion designers—Halston, Rudi Gernreich, John Kloss, and Stan Herman, to name a few—who, under licensing agreements, market intimate apparel lines.

Although these designer names carry a great deal of fashion impact, manufacturer brand names also enjoy national and international recognition. Vanity Fair, Warner, Maidenform, and Lily of France are labels which are recognized throughout the world.

Traditionally, intimate apparel manufacturers have provided retailers with extensive marketing services. The help—in the form of generous cooperative advertising agreements—is usually financial, but a great deal of it is advisory. These producers have comprehensive fashion display and advertising promotional programs which are extremely helpful to retailers.

New York is the industry's market center. Two market weeks are held, one in January and the other in June. The city also serves as the home of over half the industry's manufacturing plants. Nationally, the intimate apparel industry employs over 100,000 people; its output has an astounding annual retail value of over 5 billion dollars.

Hosiery

The hosiery industry manufactures more than 3 billion pairs of socks, stockings, and pantyhose for males and females of all ages. It too has experienced the same type of organizational and fashion styling changes which revolutionized the intimate apparel industry. For instance, the hosiery industry is now composed predominantly of large companies. These are either divisions of textile giants like J. P. Stevens and Burlington, or members of apparel conglomerates such as Warnaco and Kayser-Roth.

This tie-in with mills and conglomerates is a natural one, resulting from the hosiery industry's tremendous dependence on synthetics. Almost all stockings and pantyhose produced today are made of 100 percent nylon. Most socks are either 100 percent nylon, or a wool-synthetic or cotton-synthetic blend.

Manufacturers of women's hosiery make up 45 percent of the industry. Influenced by the fashions in women's outerwear, hosiery is categorized into stockings; knee highs; mid-calfs; anklets; footsocks, and pantyhose. Of these products, pantyhose is the newest and most popular, representing nearly 75 percent of all the women's hosiery sold today.

Pantyhose were created in the 1960s for the mini and micro-mini skirts, but they also came to symbolize a physical aspect of women's liberation: freedom from the girdle and garter belt.

The introduction of pantyhose in the 60s and the later introduction of pantyhose with panties are just two examples of how the hosiery industry coordinates its styling to respond to consumer needs. Another example is knee-high hosiery. This item had been around prior to the 1970s, but it was unimportant until slacks became popular. Responding to the consumer's need, manufacturers quickly improved and aggressively marketed "knee-hi's."

Coordination between hosiery and outerwear is not limited to styling trends. For decades, the women's hosiery industry has worked very closely with the fabric industry, coordinating its subtle shades, bright colors, and interesting patterns and textures to outerwear color trends.

Men's hosiery is divided into three categories: dress, casual and work. Manufacturers have also increased the fashion impact of these items, introducing texture, patterns, and colors which compliment current menswear fashion trends.

In recent years, the hosiery industry has experienced several changes in its marketing methods. The most revolutionary of these has been the introduction of self-service hosiery displays. Because it minimizes the need for sales help, this innovative selling technique has made it possible to sell hosiery in other than the traditional retail outlets. Many manufacturers now sell through supermarkets, drugstores, discounters, and even vending machines. This development has made packaging and retail display much more important, since manufacturers rely on these features to "sell" their product.

These marketing changes have affected the position of brand names within the industry. Traditionally, Hanes and other nationally advertised manufacturer names were of primary importance in women's hosiery. Today, hosiery is produced under many labels, and most of it is inexpensive. As a result, the consumer is now price rather than label-oriented.

To compete effectively with low priced brands, Hanes, Round-the-Clock, Christian Dior, and other high fashion, high priced brands, offer color and fashion coordinated hosiery in the country's leading stores and emphatically refuse to sell in supermarkets or any other non-traditional retail outlet.

To compete even further for a portion of the low priced market, some of the better brand manufacturers have introduced their own nationally advertised low priced brands. Hanes, for instance, produces "L'Eggs" hosiery, which is imaginatively packaged in egg-shaped containers. Hanes sells L'Eggs directly to supermarkets and drugstores, providing them with attractive self-service features and displays.

Cosmetics and Toiletries

Today's beauty business produces one of fashion's most valuable accessories: *cosmetics*. The "right" look and appearance for hair, face, hands, legs, feet, and in fact, for just about every part of the body is as important as the right apparel accessory.

More than 20,000 different products for both men and women are sold as cosmetics and are categorized as follows: makeup; fragrances; shampoos; hair care products; dentifrices and mouthwashes; deodorants; and a final category of creams and lotions which includes suntan oils, after-shave, hand and body preparations, astringents, and various beautifying and cleansing creams. Each and every one of these comes under the scrutiny of the Food and Drug Administration and the Federal Trade Commission. The FDA tests every product for potentially harmful ingredients. It also monitors accuracy in labeling. The FTC, meanwhile, enforces the Food, Drug and Cosmetic Act of 1938 which forbids false and exaggerated claims in advertising about product performance.

The industry is made up of approximately 1,000 firms, employs nearly 51,000 workers, and (in 1977) had retail sales well over $6 billion—with estimates of a 9 percent increase in volume by 1985.

Half the industry's sales volume is generated by its ten largest companies which include Avon, Revlon, Estée Lauder, Helena Rubinstein, and Elizabeth Arden.

Small firms have the nearly impossible task of competing with these giants. To begin with, they simply do not have as much money for advertising as the big ten. (Total industry outlays for advertising amounted to over 500 million dollars in 1975.) Nor—with the average cost of developing a product estimated at $10 million—do these small firms have the resources to research, develop, and introduce competitive new products.

Among the leading firms, however, viable competition does exist—and it is fierce. Through extensive advertising and sales promotion campaigns, each aggressively tries to maintain its national brand reputation. Each also competes for the other's market by constantly introducing a never-ending array of new colors, new items and, in many instances, entirely new cosmetic lines.

Cosmetics are also developed to coordinate with fashion trends. Stylists in cosmetic houses work closely with the ready-to-wear markets, developing cosmetics which complement the colors and trends in fashion apparel. For instance, fashion's preference for soft colors and "natural" fabrics and silhouettes during the 70s, was interpreted by the cosmetic industry in a number of ways. Cosmetic colors were softened to natural tones. Fragrances emphasized earthy, fresh scents. Skin preparations and shampoos were introduced as having "nature's own" ingredients.

Since the cosmetic industry is so closely tied to the apparel trade, it has long been a practice for famous name designers to sell cosmetics under licensing arrangements. Although fragrances remain as the traditional product choice, some designers like Christian Dior, Halston and Mary Quant sell an entire line of cosmetics under their label.

Traditionally, men's shampoos, deodorants, and other toiletries have sold well. During the 60s, however, men's interest in after-shave lotion and cologne fragrances increased and Canoe—a French fragrance for men—became very popular. American cosmetic manufacturers soon began to compete with fragrances like Aramis by Arden and Braggi by Revlon. Designers such as Bill Blass also added their names to fragrances for men and by 1976, sales revenues of these products exceeded a huge $400 million.

But the latest excitement in this category has been generated by the introduction of full lines of men's cosmetics—lines which include blushers, moisturizers, and other makeup and skin preparations. The acceptance of these products has so far been excellent—and cosmetic firms anticipate that these "beautifiers" will become as important for men as they have been for women.

Footwear

The American footwear industry produces shoes, boots, slippers, and galoshes for men, women and children.

Footwear is a major fashion business in this country, generating retail sales in excess of $10 billion annually. Of the 800 million pairs sold, 50 percent are for women.

With such a large share of the country's footwear market, American manufacturers of women's shoes have become a highly organized group. Their trade organization is the American Footwear Manufacturers Association—the AFMA. It is extremely fashion oriented and—through strong dynamic programs—aggressively promotes fashion in footwear.

The shoe industry's market weeks are held twice a year in New York City. Because shoe production is a slow process, manufacturers show their lines far in advance of ready-to-wear. Fall-winter footwear is presented in February while resort-spring-summer lines are shown in August. The AFMA schedules and organizes the many events which take place during National Footwear Market Weeks, their official name. One of its most exciting presentations is the National Shoe Fair which gives retailers and the press an opportunity to see new trends.

Although it works far in advance, the shoe industry successfully coordinates its colors and styling to future ready-to-wear. The AFMA is responsible for this success, serving as a liaison between the footwear and garment industries. The AFMA also directs its attention to the consumer, keeping the public informed on footwear through educational materials and press releases.

The imaginative fashion treatment of footwear by the industry has made it an exciting accessory. Perfectly coordinated to apparel, it is very much a part of the total look. Several dress designers have confirmed the fashion importance of footwear by producing their own signature shoe collections. The names of Halston, Geoffrey Beene, Anne Klein, Bill Blass, and Diane Von Furstenberg may now be found printed on the inside or embroidered on the outside of footwear.

National brand names are also important in the industry. I. Miller, Golo, Adler, Chandler, and Red Cross are just a few of the name footwear manufacturers sold in shoe and department stores.

Many of the manufacturers who sold footwear exclusively through footwear stores are finding it more sensible and profitable to also sell in department stores. To accommodate them, retailers have expanded the floor space allocated to footwear and today it is not uncommon to find two or more footwear departments in one store—each catering to a particular type of customer.

There are about 700 firms in the American shoe industry, providing jobs for 165,000 workers. Most of the industry is located in the northeastern states of Pennsylvania, Massachusetts, and New York, mainly dominated by large corporations and conglomerates. Eight firms account for 35 percent of all industry sales. But it is also an industry where automation and technology has lagged and where the cost of labor and raw materials has increased, making domestic shoe production expensive. As a result, American manufacturers have lost a great share of the country's footwear market and imports account for nearly 50 percent of all footwear sold in this country. For example, in 1976, of the 799 million pairs of footwear sold, only 460 million were domestically produced.

Individual manufacturers are trying to compete with imports by decreasing costs and improving manufacturing techniques. They are replacing leather with vinyls, plastics, canvas and other less expensive materials; in their plants, they are replacing old machinery with modern equipment.

Collectively, the industry has asked for and received the help of the federal government in its fight to stem imports. In 1977, the government negotiated agreements with several foreign countries for their voluntary reduction of shoe exports to the United States.

The federal government is also providing assistance to the industry through research grants. These grants are used to study ways to get a larger share of the domestic and foreign markets; improve production methods; find cheaper raw materials; and attract new capital to the shoe industry.

Some of the government money has also gone to the industry's AFMA. The association received $225,000 to create a computerized "Advance Fashion Information System" which provides manufacturers with accurate and specific fashion trends.

The industry hopes these efforts will help to eliminate at least some of the major problems which plague American footwear manufacturers. Meanwhile, this dynamic industry continues to provide outstanding fashion leadership to the rest of the fashion industry.

Handbags

For centuries, both men and women have carried a bag or pouch—some sort of handbag. Its initial purpose was functional: to hold money and personal items which were too heavy or big for pockets.

Over the years, a sufficient number of pockets were added to men's suits and jackets and the use of handbags by men disappeared. During the mid-70s, however, handbags were reintroduced in Italy and France by men who favored a slim silhouette minus pocket bulges. Although the fashion has not spread among the majority of American men, manufacturers now produce satchels, shoulder bags, and bags that double as small hand luggage for a select group of American and European fashion conscious men.

Women, on the other hand, have uninterruptedly considered a handbag indispensible. It has developed into a useful fashion item. Most women have a "handbag wardrobe"—one which is coordinated with their other clothes and accessories. To provide this coordination, the industry works very closely with all other areas of the apparel industry. It uses the same leathers and fabrics as the shoe and apparel industry; and it creates handbag styles and shapes which compliment and coordinate with the silhouettes and looks in dresses, coats, and all other wearing apparel.

Yearly, handbag sales in this country increase. But because of imports the size of the American handbag industry has declined. Only 55 percent of the handbags sold in this country are American made. Of the 545 firms operating in 1963, only 400 are in existence today.

To date, there has not been any concerted effort on the part of manufacturers of the industry's trade association—The National Authority for the Ladies' Handbag Industry—to effectively compete against the import problem. Most American producers have individually tried to cope with the problem by turning to synthetic materials to reduce production costs and keep retail prices down. More than 80 percent of the bags produced here are from other than leather materials.

Domestic handbag production is heavily concentrated in the New York City metropolitan area. The city is also the handbag industry's market center—housing the majority of its sales offices and showrooms. Handbag manufacturers hold market weeks twice a year, presenting their spring-summer lines in June and fall-winter lines in January.

Most handbag firms are very small and unable to conduct the type of marketing activities which are necessary to establish well known, nationally recognized brand names. There are, however, several large firms that do make a country-wide impact. One of these, Etienne Aigner, has also introduced some new merchandising concepts to the industry.

FIGURE 9-2. Courtesy: Etienne Aigner, New York

As one of the industry's largest firms, Etienne Aigner employs over 400 workers. It produces handbags of high quality leather which retail between $40 and $120 each. The firm has diversified into other merchandise—belts, shoes, hats, coats, and small leather goods—all of which are manufactured abroad.

Aigner is a division of the women's wear producer, Jonathan Logan, and, as such, has the mighty promotion and marketing expertise of its large parent firm at its disposal. This expertise has helped Aigner develop a unique retailing concept for its products. All the items the firm produces are grouped together in the handbag or accessory department of leading retailers and presented as an Etienne Aigner boutique. Each item is color and texture coordinated and each carries an identifiable gold "A" set inside a horseshoe emblem. These boutique and designer initial treatments (see Fig. 9-2) have added status and sales appeal to the merchandise and in the late 70s, Aigner accessory sales averaged at over $28 million—a healthy share of the accessory industry's business.

Jewelry

Jewelry is divided into two categories: fine jewelry and costume jewelry. The division is based on the type of materials and production methods used.

Fine jewelry is made from precious metals and gemstones. Gold is the most popular metal, followed by platinum, then silver. The gems are natural, precious, and semi-precious stones. These include diamonds, rubies, cultured pearls, opals, and jade.

It requires a great deal of skill, handiwork and careful design planning to produce fine jewelry and, although the cost of precious materials is extremely expensive, the cost of expert craftsmanship adds greatly to the price of fine jewelry.

Costume jewelry was made popular by designer Coco Chanel during the 1920s. Until then, "nice" women never wore "fake" jewelry. Chanel placed ropes of fake pearls and long metal chains around the necklines of her expensive clothes and made costume jewelry socially acceptable.

Costume jewelry makes use of a variety of materials such as plastic, glass, wood, cord, and plated metals. It is mass produced using simple procedures in an assembly-line fashion. Most manufacturers use stylists who "knock-off" the design of fine or better costume jewelry. The materials and production methods of costume jewelry make it relatively inexpensive.

Like the other accessory industries, the makers of both fine and costume jewelry have most of their showrooms in New York City. The industry has a permanent exhibition center which supplements the seasonal showings held during the January and June market weeks.

Most fine jewelry is made in New York City; while costume jewelry is produced in Providence, Rhode Island—the capital of costume jewelry—and in other cities in the Northeast. Together, 22,000 fine and costume jewelers produced an astronomical $2.6 billion worth of jewelry in 1977. One of the factors contributing to this huge figure is that the American jewelry industry is not threatened by imports. Only about 20 percent of the jewelry, including watches, sold in this country is imported.

With the exception of Timex and other watch firms, there are very few jewelry companies with recognizable brand names. The few include Coro and Swank—makers of women's and men's jewelry respectively; and Cartier, Bulgari, and Tiffany—the status names in fine jewelry. There are also relatively few designer names in jewelry with Elsa Perretti of Tiffany's and David Webb rare exceptions.

Among fine jewelry producers—vertical integration is common. This means the firm designs, manufactures, and retails its products. Tiffany and Cartier have this type of business and perhaps their names have become famous for their magnificent retail operations as much as for their fine jewelry.

The Jewelry Industry Council is the industry trade association; their projection for industry growth is favorable, especially in fine jewelry. Many consumers looking for a good investment buy fine jewelry, both for fashion and financial reasons. Men, too, have increased their demand for fine jewelry—particularly neck chains, bracelets, and pendants.

Millinery

From the beginning of the 60s, the use of headgear for men, women, and children declined. So, unfortunately, did its status as an important fashion accessory. As a result, the American millinery industry has shrunk to fewer than 500 firms employing 14,000 people. Industry sales were $350 million dollars in 1974.

Unlike other fashion accessories, this industry's problems cannot be attributed to a rise in imports. The bouffant hairdos of the early 60s, longer hair styles, and the trend toward casual dress in the 70s were the factors which most hurt the millinery industry. Fashion, it seemed, emphatically rejected hats.

Since the mid-70s, a mild interest in hats has returned. Most are understated, complementing the casual themes of ready-to-wear. Hats for men and women have become simpler, easy to wear. Many are functional, providing protection from the elements.

To help sales, retailers have eliminated the pompous millinery departments of the past and display hats informally throughout the store. Hats are now found next to gloves and scarves; in casual boutique settings; or scattered throughout all types of ready-to-wear departments.

Designer and brand names are not as significant to the industry as they once were. Designers like Adolfo and Halston—both of whom received initial recognition for their hats—have expanded into ready-to-wear and today there are no millinery "stars" to speak of. In fact, most firms are small and their promotional activities are handled collectively by the National Millinery Institute, the industry's trade organization.

Perhaps if fashion trends continue to change so that they emphasize formality and elegance, the hat industry of old may be revitalized. If, however, casualness and comfort in fashion continues, millinery producers will remain an important but not necessarily a major part of the fashion scene.

Other Special Accessories

Although, in terms of output and size, each of the following accessories may be considered a minor fashion industry—all play a vitally important role in the total fashion picture.

The makers of gloves, small leather goods, neckwear, umbrellas, and sunglasses run businesses which are similar and which have much in common. For instance, all use New York City as their marketing center; all have had to cope with competition from imports; designer and brand names play a significant role in their sales; and all have increased their assortment of styles and colors to stimulate consumer interest in their merchandise.

Gloves. Twenty years ago, gloves were mandatory: an indispensable accessory of the well-dressed man or woman. Like millinery, however, gloves are no longer a fashion essential. Today, most gloves are worn for utilitarian purposes.

Gloves are made from kidskin, pigskin, and suede leathers; and from wool, synthetics, vinyl, and cotton fabrics. These materials are often combined with each other or accented with fur.

Because the sales of all but casual gloves have been on the decline, both manufacturers and retailers have introduced new glove merchandising techniques. To stimulate sales, manufacturers coordinate gloves and mittens with hats and scarves, selling them separately or in sets. Meanwhile, retailers have combined gloves with other fashion accessories in sales-provoking displays.

Small Leather Goods. This accessory category includes such items as wallets, belts, small purses, glass cases, key cases, cigarette and travelling cases, and any other item which may be carried in pockets or handbags.

It is a small, highly specialized industry, comprised of only 244 firms and with an industry output of $360 million. The top five firms of the industry—of which Buxton is the current leader—do approximately 40 percent of the industry's business.

Except for women's belts, all the items in this category are usually in constant demand. The belt industry often suffers from the changes and whims of fashion. When fashion emphasizes the waist, the sales of belts soar; but when fashion raises, lowers, or eliminates the waist, the demand for belts understandably diminishes.

Neckwear. Neckwear has always been an important fashion accessory for both men and women. Neckwear manufacturers are highly diversified, creating a great variety of items. They produce long ties, bow ties, ascots, and scarves for men; and varied assortments of merchandise for women. They include scarves of all shapes, sizes, and fabrics; separate collars and dickies; and, more recently, shawls, stoles, halters, ponchos, and unblocked hats.

Umbrellas. Although the primary purpose of the umbrella is to provide protection from the rain or snow, today's umbrellas have become a fashion accessory. They are signed by designers, printed in the latest fabric patterns, and coordinated to fashion raincoats and rainwear.

This fashion concept has been the only noticeable change in the design and construction of umbrellas in recent years. The canopy is made primarily from nylon, cotton, or plastic. The shank and ribs are often metal, and the handle is either wood or plastic. Two basic styles of umbrellas are sold: regular and folding. Prices vary widely depending on materials, methods of construction, and, of course, fashion impact.

Sunglasses. Like umbrellas, the original and primary function of sunglasses is to offer protection. Before the 60s, the indoor use of sunglasses was considered a fad. Then sunglasses changed from a fad to a fashion, becoming a status accessory.

Today, sunglasses come in a tremendous variety of styles and colors. Most are designed for fashion impact and many dress designers have added this accessory to their lists of licensed products. Dior, Halston, and St. Laurent are some who make prestigious and expensive sunglasses, selling them for $35 and up.

The majority of sunglasses however, are produced by national brand manufacturers and are moderately priced, retailing for under ten dollars. The sales figures of this unique industry are impressive, totalling over 800 million dollars annually during the late 70s.

FOCUS ON THE INDUSTRY

The following is a representative lising of trade, labor and industry associations in the apparel and accessory fields.

Amalgamated Clothing and Textile Workers of America
15 Union Square, New York, N.Y. 10003

American Apparel Manufacturers Association
Suite 800, 1611 N. Kent Street, Arlington, Va. 22209

American Footwear Manufacturers
342 Madison Avenue, New York, N.Y. 10017

American Textile Manufacturers Institute
Wachonia Center, 400 Tryon Street, Charlotte, N.C. 28285

Apparel Manufacturers Association
1440 Broadway, New York, N.Y. 10018

Boys and Young Mens Apparel Manufacturers Association
10 West 33 Street, New York, N.Y. 10001

Corset and Brassiere Association of America
220 Fifth Avenue, New York, N.Y. 10001

International Ladies' Garment Workers' Union
1710 Broadway, New York, N.Y.

Jewelry Industry Council
608 Fifth Avenue, New York, N.Y. 10020

Lingerie Manufacturers Association
41 East 42 Street, New York, N.Y. 10017

Luggage and Leather Goods Manufacturers Association, Inc.
220 Fifth Avenue, New York, N.Y. 10001

Mens Fashion Association of America Inc.
1290 Avenue of Americas, New York, N.Y. 10016

National Association of Glove Manufacturers
Gloversville, N.Y., 12078

National Handbag Association
347 Fifth Avenue, New York, N.Y. 10016

National Mens and Boyswear Council
135 West 50 Street, New York, N.Y. 10017

National Millinery Planning Board, Inc.
10 East 40 Street, New York, N.Y. 10002

National Outerwear and Sportswear Association
1 Pennsylvania Plaza, New York, N.Y. 10001

United Garment Workers of America
Room 1614, 200 Park Avenue South, New York, N.Y. 10003

United Textile Workers of America
420 Common Street, Lawrence, Mass. 01840

TERMS TO REMEMBER

fashion seasons
knock-off
style piracy
marker
hot number
runners
market weeks
factoring
dual distribution
intimate apparel

HIGHLIGHTS OF THE CHAPTER

- The majority of women's wear manufacturers are located in New York City's "Garment Center." But Los Angeles, Chicago, Dallas, St. Louis, Cleveland, Kansas City and Miami are growing secondary apparel markets.
- To service the similarly defined departments of retailers, apparel manufacturing is categorized by price, size, or type of apparel. Large firms often produce merchandise in several of these categories, but most apparel manufacturers specialize in one.
- The production process of apparel involves almost a dozen technical steps which include patternmaking, cutting, machine and hand sewing, pressing and packing operations.
- Apparel manufacturers use standard marketing procedures to sell their products, but a few of their procedures are indigenous to the apparel industry. These include the methods apparel producers use to sell to retailers; the arrangements they make to finance their business; and some of the techniques they use to promote and advertise their products.
- Buyers of fashion merchandise visit manufacturers several times a year during designated market weeks. At that time, expert showroom salespeople present the season's new lines, selling and advising buyers of the type of merchandise which will be most saleable for their stores.

- Due to an increase in the advertising and sales promotion activities of manufacturers, consumer recognition and demand of manufacturer brand names has markedly increased.
- Except for a few minor differences, the characteristics, methods of operation, and marketing activities of the menswear, children's wear, and accessory industries are similar to those of the women's wear industry.

QUESTIONS

1. Where is the "fashion capital" of the United States? How large is its "Garment Center" and what is its most famous street called?
2. Where are some of the secondary apparel centers? Why are they drawing apparel manufacturers away from New York City?
3. What are some of the industry's labor problems? How are the industry and the union trying to solve these problems?
4. Describe the type of merchandise shown during the five fashion seasons of the New York market.
5. Why do manufacturers prefer to specialize in producing a single category of merchandise? Name a well known firm which specializes in producing one type of apparel. Name another that is diversified in several types of apparel.
6. Describe how manufacturers sell their goods to retailers. How do their sales methods differ from those of other industries?
7. Describe *factoring.* What are its advantages?
8. What is the difference between an inside and outside shop? What type is most used in the production of women's wear? Menswear?
9. What significant changes have occurred in the intimate apparel industry since the late 1950s? In the cosmetic, hosiery, shoe, and millinery industries?
10. If you had your choice, in what area of apparel manufacturing would you like to work? Why? What kind of work would you like to do?

10

TODAY'S FOREIGN PRODUCERS

OBJECTIVES

After reading this chapter, you should be able to:

- Describe the ready-to-wear industries of foreign countries and identify the countries whose industries are most successful.
- Elaborate on why imports have been able to compete so effectively with American producers for the American dollar.
- Have some insight into how the United States can ultimately solve some of its fashion import problems.

As discussed in previous chapters, the technique of mass producing clothing was developed in the United States, undergoing its most rapid rate of growth and refinement in the first half of this century. Foreign mass production of clothing was minimal. Ready-to-wear was basically an American phenomenon.

After World War II, however, foreign governments began to rebuild their economies by offering financial as well as moral support to their industries, particularly those which could produce goods for export. Aware of the wide global market for fashion goods, governments gave special encouragement and subsidies to fashion firms and designers. Due to these reconstruction efforts, the second half of this century has witnessed the emergence of ready-to-wear industries on a global scale.

Almost all of these countries export Western influenced fashion. Some, encouraged by their governments to use materials from their native lands, also produce exports reflecting ethnic culture and roots. Scandinavia, for instance, exports marvelous wool ski sweaters, featuring native jacquard patterns, while India turns its cotton into soft Indian gauze for blouses and shirts. Some countries also export versions of their national dress; white "wedding dresses" from Mexico, ponchos from Guatemala, and even saris from India may be found in stores throughout the world.

EUROPEAN FASHION PRODUCERS

France

In 1947, a group of farsighted French business people came to the United States to study American expertise in sizing and production methods. The visit marked the beginning of the successful development of the now famous French prêt-à-porter (ready-to-wear) industry. By the early 60s, France was producing fashion goods for both domestic consumption and export. Most of the exports, however, were limited to expensive, conservatively styled clothes—minus "name" designer labels. They made little fashion impact; French fashion leadership came exclusively from its couture.

During the late 60s the fashion look and image of French ready-to-wear radically changed. It became youth oriented and, because of this change, exports grew. By 1971, France was exporting about $550 million worth of fashion merchandise. French prêt-à-porter designers became as well known and as influential—sometimes even more so—as the top couture names.

This transformation is discussed in *Chapter 6* under *French Ready-to-Wear* Designers.

The new fashion image of prêt-à-porter is not relegated to designer-name fashion alone. Imaginative merchandise from firms like Dorothée Bis, Cacharel, and Micmac have also brought French *manufacturers* into the limelight. It has been the *combined* efforts and talents of the French prêt-à-porter designers *and* manufacturers that has made French ready-to-wear so successful.

Twice a year, in April and in October, the French exhibit their spring-summer and fall-winter lines in Porte de Versailles, Paris—and whereas, until the 60s, fashion professionals flocked to Paris to cover the couture, today, the prêt-à-porter showings are now the main attraction.

To coordinate the showings for the convenience of visiting prospective prêt-à-porter buyers and to increase exports, various French organizations exist. The success of their efforts can be statistically documented. Prior to 1976, French goods accounted for less than 1 percent of the entire American market. Since then, fashion exports to the United States have jumped consistently, bringing them closer to their ultimate goal of nearly 2 percent of the entire American market.

The development of the French ready-to-wear industry is undoubtedly one of the top post-war success stories. In a few short decades—and in spite of having to competitively deal with the formidable French couture and America's Seventh Avenue—the talented French have been able to organize and develop one of the world's leading ready-to-wear industries.

Italy

Italy was among those countries whose government helped to create a flourishing post-war ready-to-wear industry.

Much of Italy's initial success was due to its innovative sportswear and leather accessories, notably shoes. Both caught on with American buyers and—during the 50s and 60s—very much influenced American fashion.

Today, Italy's biggest business is knitwear. The original styling of knit producers like Mirsa and the Missonis has made Italian knits highly desirable. Even so, women's sportswear, menswear, and leather goods for men and women continue to be the top categories of Italian productivity. In fact, in 1976, when the United States imported 50 percent of its women's shoes and 25 percent of its men's and boy's shoes, Italy was the country's leading shoe supplier.

Italy has two cities that serve as fashion centers for its ready-to-wear. Coordinated showings are held in Florence and Milan, where every category of women's ready-to-wear may be seen and ordered. The showings take place in April and October and are timed so they may be scheduled as the first stop in a buyer's Italy–France–England itinerary. Although both cities house important manufacturers, the latter part of the 1970s has seen Milan emerge as an extremely strong fashion center. Every important Italian firm shows in Milan and the fashion offerings of these firms have been widely acclaimed by buyers from all over the world. For these reasons, many now consider Milan—after New York and Paris—the world's third-ranking fashion capital.

Men's ready-to-wear shows are held in Florence in February and September, while the exhibitions for leather goods are given in Milan in January and June. There is also an annual shoe fair in Bologna which is held in March; this was organized to accommodate foreign buyers who are visiting the late March–April showings of ready-to-wear.

Great Britain

Great Britain is a major stop for American buyers when they shop the European markets.

In the last decade the number of trend-setting English designers and firms has dwindled, but there are still several who are important. Names like Mary Quant, Zandra Rhodes, and Hardy Amies, designers of women's wear and menswear, are labels which, though expensive, sell well in America.

In addition to London fashion, Britain also offers a wide range of goods from other parts of the British Isles. The famous Harris tweeds, Shetland woolens, and the world's softest cashmere come from Scotland. Each makes a sizeable contribution toward British trade.

Scotland, along with the Republic of Ireland, also offers a variety of unique items produced by their cottage industries. Some, like their handknit, bulky fishermen's sweaters and crocheted and knit lace sweater-dresses, have become classics.

But in spite of its great experience and productivity, Britains's current position in the international ready-to-wear market is relatively weak.

Before World War II, its woolens and tailoring made England the world's fashion center for menswear. Though the very best menswear designers continue to operate there, the post-war conversion by men to "off-the-peg" clothing has undeniably diminished England's custom-made business. Today, the English menswear industry finds itself in the ready-to-wear business, in tough competition with other countries for a piece of the world's ready-made menswear pie.

In women's apparel, London has lost the influence it held during the 60s when it was the center of that era's young fashion revolution. As the fashion of that period changed to a softer look, London did not follow the trend, and thus lost much of its fashion leadership.

Aware of these problems, and with the help of its government, Britain's fashion industry has taken several steps to improve its position. To stimulate exports, for instance, the British Export Clothing Council was formed. It sponsors trade and clothing exhibits throughout the world. And, to accommodate visiting buyers, British firms now present their merchandise in one collective London event rather than on an individual basis. Timed to dove-tail with the April and October showings of the Italians and the French, London has been made an attractively convenient third European stop for foreign buyers.

Spain

Spain's exports are primarily leather goods. Though Spain sells some moderately priced knitwear, the majority of the fashion goods she exports to the United States are made of leather and suede. Jackets and coats for men and women, handbags, gloves, small leather goods, and shoes are beautifully hand produced by Spanish craftsmen. It is these products that draw foreign buyers to Barcelona—Spain's ready-to-wear fashion center. Spanish-made shoes have a reputation for fine quality and Spain is second on the list of foreign shoe suppliers to the United States.

Spain's government has had a complicated system of export control which has hampered foreign buyers. With the recent change in political leadership, however, the Spanish fashion industries anticipate a liberalization of existing controls which should help them increase their exports.

Scandinavia

The Scandinavian countries are Finland, Sweden, Norway and Denmark. Grouped together geographically, they all work with the same basic materials of wool, fur, leather, man-made fabrics, gold and silver; and, due to its international ambience, use the city of Copenhagen in Denmark as their central fashion market.

Finland produces the most exciting and original fashions. Marimekko, a firm which makes the clothing and products for the home that are so popular in America, is in Finland. Finland's fashion industry is a major contributor to the country's economy, and textiles and clothing represent the country's third largest export.

Sweden is known for its "young" fashions. In fact, it claims to have introduced the string bikini in 1973. Favored Swedish imports are jacquard wool sweaters, knitted separates, leather and suede coats, sportswear for men and women, and rainwear—all designed in a young spirit.

Norway also produces a wide range of moderately priced clothing for men, women, and children. Outerwear is a very popular export item to the United States.

Denmark produces very highly styled, expensive clothes. Many of their designers create on a wide scale, also designing avant-garde jewelry, silverware, kitchenware, and other products for the home. Because of their high price and styling, Denmark exports fewer fashion goods to America than do the other Scandinavian countries.

Other European Countries

Austria, Portugal, and Switzerland are other European countries who export their fashion goods to the United States. The amount and type of merchandise received from each of these countries varies.

Austria's specialty is toggle-buttoned loden cloth coats for men, women, and children. Portugal excels in hand-embroidered cottons (dresses for infants and blouses for women) from her famed Madeira Island.

Switzerland—whose fabric firms like Stehli Silks have an international reputation—sends the United States the finest in textiles. And from the Bally Shoe Company comes the shoe many men and women consider to be the best in the world.

West Germany is Europe's largest clothing producer, providing about 69 percent of all the clothing sold in the European Common Market—an organization composed of nine European nations which are bound together in free trade and economic unity.

Rumania, Poland, and Yugoslavia—though they are East European communist nations and not members of the Common Market—are other countries whose clothing productivity is healthy. But West Germany and these three countries presently export very little to the United States.

MIDDLE AND FAR EAST FASHION PRODUCERS

Israel

Israel is one of the most exciting of the new post-war fashion centers. This small country has been able to develop an internationally recognized apparel industry worth nearly 240 million export dollars in 1977. During the 70s, the industry has grown as much as 20 percent in gross sales each year. Today, the manufacture of apparel is Israel's second largest industry, with an accompanying textile industry ranking third.

Much of this success is due to the fact that the Israelis studiously patterned their industry after America's textile and ready-to-wear operations. To teach young Israelites the fashion business, Israel has even opened a school similar to New York's Fashion Institute of Technology.

Israel's initial success began with its production of knitwear and leather fashions in the early 60s. Leather makers like Begged-Or pioneered into the export market by offering men's and women's beautiful leather and suede jackets and coats, while knitwear manufacturers supplied exquisite hand knits. Both caught the eye of American store buyers and began to sell.

Today, Israeli fashion is even more imaginative, reflecting the talents of its new, young designers and manufacturers. It includes sportswear, swimwear, and rainwear as well as leather and knits.

In 1977, over 600 buyers attended the collective fashion showings held in Tel Aviv. To encourage exports, the government has offered foreign buyers a 20 percent price cut in wholesale prices. Though Israel is offering saleable, exciting fashion, this subsidy has served as an additional incentive to foreign buyers.

India

Due to internal problems, India has not been able to fully develop her apparel industry. In the past few years, however, the fashion trend toward "natural" fibers and textures stimulated a demand for soft gauzy cottons. That demand was met by India's cottage industries. Clothes for men, women and children were exported to the United States on a large scale, contributing to an enormous growth in India's textile and apparel cottage industries. By 1978, it ranked as one of the world's five biggest foreign exporters and Indian-made fashion goods were strongly promoted by major American stores.

Whether or not this growth will continue is difficult to assess. Much depends on the progress the Indian government makes in solving internal problems and industrializing the nation.

The Far East

Four of five of the world's biggest foreign exporters are in the Far East. In 1977, Hong Kong, Japan, Taiwan, and South Korea joined the fifth—India—to become responsible for "61 percent of all blouses, children's clothes, fabrics, sweaters and men's suits that [came] into the United States."[1] Although Hong Kong presently exports the greatest amount of this apparel, the first of these five nations to enter into the production of apparel for export purposes was Japan.

Japan. After World War II, a devastated and defeated Japan began to rebuild her industries and—with the help of the United States—transformed itself into the third largest producing nation in the world.

One of Japan's great industrial successes was her clothing industry. It is build around the manufacture of ready-made Western-styled clothing for men, women and children. The majority of the firms that deal with the United States serve as contractors for large American manufacturers and retailers.

The "made in Japan" label once stood for inferior, cheap goods, but, over the years, the Japanese have upgraded their standards so that

[1]Deborah Sue Yaeger, "Third World Threat," *The Wall Street Journal* (June 24, 1977), p. 32.

all their export products—from automobiles to clothing—are no longer stigmatized.

The Japanese also appreciate top quality Western fashion for themselves. Since the mid-70s, Japanese stores have been successfully selling Japanese-produced clothes of Anne Klein, Oscar de la Renta, and other American designers to Japanese fashion-conscious women.

Because of this keen appreciation for fine Western fashion, the better American firms have preferred Japanese contractors over those in other Far Eastern countries, so that, until very recently, Japan has maintained the exclusive right to call herself the "quality high fashion producer of the Far East." In the second half of the 70s, however, the Japanese producers of better ready-to-wear began to feel the strong competition of a Far Eastern neighbor: Hong Kong.

Hong Kong. The spectacular growth of Hong Kong's clothing industry has made this British colony the largest exporter of garments in the world. By the end of 1976, Hong Kong was exporting over 3 *billion* dollars worth of ready-made clothing (981 million dollars of that total came from the United States). To reach that position, Hong Kong took a cue from Japan's success story: *it traded-up.*

Hong Kong's past reputation had been built upon its cheap imitation of Western fashion. Today, the colony is concentrating on changing that reputation from one of "making knock-offs" to "making fashion."

To publicize its new image, the top clothing firms have formed the Hong Kong Development Council. As part of its sales promotion efforts, the Council stages spectacular fashion presentations in Hong Kong, Los Angeles, New York, and other cities throughout the world. Reaction to the fashions shown has been excellent.

Pierre Cardin, Givenchy, and Calvin Klein are some of the famous French and American designers who have their ready-to-wear made in Hong Kong. They, and other foreign manufacturers of high priced lines, praise the sophisticated workmanship of the current Hong Kong contractors.

In their upgrading process, many Hong Kong contractors have become manufacturers. The clothes from these manufacturers has convinced American retailers of Hong Kong's ability to produce top fashion without the direct guidance and supervision of the Western middleman. Interviewed in *The New York Times,* Irene Satz, vice president of Orbach's, complimented the new firms: "We do a tremendous business with Hong Kong styles . . . The change lately is that you can get the fashion looks there now without working them out for yourself."[2]

[2]Bernadine Morris, "Inventive Styles of Hong Kong in Four Movements," *The New York Times* (March 25, 1976), p. 44.

FOCUS ON THE INDUSTRY

The success of the Bang Bang Fashions Company of Hong Kong is typical of the change and growth of other Hong Kong firms.

In 1972, Jimmy Yip was 28 years old, and in the business of making wigs. The young owner was tuned into the rapid fashion changes of that era and—when the fashion for wigs died down—quickly converted to designing and producing Europe's latest craze: faded blue jeans.

In 1973, its first year, Bang Bang's sales were $10 million. By 1976, sales had soared to $100 million. Part of those sales dollars came from the United States where Bang Bang goods are sold under the well known *Faded Glory* label.

Bang Bang is privately owned by Mr. Yip and an American, Michael Shane. The young Chinese owner credits the youth of his executives, which helps them recognize fashion change, and large advertising campaigns with Bang Bang's past and (he hopes) future success.

Taiwan and Korea. As in Japan and Hong Kong, most of the clothing produced for export in Taiwan and Korea is for Western consumption. "Made in Korea" and "made in Taiwan" are now widely seen on labels of medium and low priced goods sold in American stores.

Most of the firms in the clothing industry of these countries function with some type of foreign help or advice. Many are either owned, co-owned, or supervised by foreigners who provide technical know-how. It is not uncommon for foreign brand name companies to maintain branch factories or to have licensing agreements with native manufacturers. American retailers also utilize the service of these native firms for their competitively low priced "store brand name" merchandise.

The spectacular success of these two countries has been due to "cheap (low-quality) goods and cheap labor." However, the world recession, over-ambitious expansion, increased labor costs, and an American consumer switch to more expensive "natural fiber" goods has cut into their sales and profits. Furthermore, other Far East neighboring countries like the Philippines, Indonesia, and Malaysia, who have lower labor costs, are now placing their competitively priced goods on the world market.

As a consequence, most Taiwan and Korean manufacturers are beginning to "trade-up." They feel the future is in the production of better goods and that they must now compete with the more sophisticated styling and workmanship of Japan and Hong Kong in order to remain in business.

OTHER IMPORTANT FOREIGN EXPORTERS TO THE UNITED STATES

Canada

In 1963, Canadian exports of fashion goods to the United States were minimal. In order to promote their goods, that year the Canadian government invited several American fashion editors and representatives from leading retail firms to Toronto for the purpose of having them become acquainted with Canadian-produced fashion goods.

As a result of that and other subsequent promotional efforts, between 1967 and 1974 Canadian fashion exports to the United States tripled. Today, Canada's unsurpassable leathers, outerwear, active sportswear, accessories, and other ready-to-wear for men, women, and children are enthusiastically purchased by American department stores.

Montreal and Toronto are Canada's two major fashion centers—with 65 percent of its over 2,000 designers and manufacturers working in Montreal.

To maintain and increase Canadian exports to the United States, the Canadian Ministry of Industry and Commerce annually sponsors a weekend in Canada for the American press, while the industry frequently shows the Canadian collections in the United States.

Latin America

Some unique ethnic items are exported to the United States from various Latin American countries, but—with the notable exception of Brazilian footwear—most of the ready-to-wear produced in Central and South America is for native consumption.

In the last decade, Brazil has been able to develop a huge leather goods industry with major emphasis on shoe production. The cattle herds of the Brazilian pampas provide an abundant supply of hides, while strong anti-strike government restrictions give the industry cheap labor. Insured of raw materials and captive labor, astute Brazilians have built a shoe industry which is the fourth largest exporter of shoes to the United States. In 1975, for example, it exported over $120 million worth of shoes to this country. Other Brazilian leather exports—handbags and belts—are also prevalent in the American retail market.

In 1979, enterprising Brazilians began an effort to enter into the production of design apparel for native consumption as well as for export to the international market.

WHY IMPORTS?

By 1977, the United States was importing more than 35 percent of all its wearing apparel. This means that one out of every three items worn by American men, women and children was made elsewhere.

Since America is the pioneer and acknowledged world expert of ready-to-wear, why have wholesalers and retailers turned away from goods made at home to purchase those of other countries? Why do people like Rudi Gernreich and Calvin Klein go to Hong Kong to have their clothes produced? The answers are simple: fresh ideas and good workmanship at a lower price.

Price

One of the prime reasons for buying foreign goods is *price.* American wholesalers and retailers have discovered that despite the need to supervise foreign production and despite extra shipping costs, most imported goods are still very much lower in cost than those made in the United States.

The low price of imports is primarily due to cheap foreign labor. In determining the price of a garment, labor is usually the most costly ingredient. When labor costs are cut, the price of goods comes down. Foreign workers get as little as one tenth the wages received by highly paid unionized American workers, giving foreign producers the ability to price their goods far below the prices set by the American industry.

In some countries, costs are brought down even further by the subsidies of their governments. Many foreign governments provide "rebates" in the form of discounts—some as high as 20 percent—to Americans and other outside buyers.

Workmanship

Fine handwork, a tradition in Europe and the Far East, is scarce in America—and that which is available is costly. Although lured by price, many of the better American manufacturers and retailers are also turning to imports because of the fine workmanship in foreign products.

This is happening in all areas of the American clothing industry but it has been particularly prevalent in shoes. Bertram Geller, vice-president of Andrew Geller, Inc., makers of expensive fine footwear, attributes the need of his firm to go to Italy for shoes to the lack of skilled American labor. Says Mr. Geller, "nobody young wants to be a shoemaker."[3] Italy, on the other hand, is pointed to by the head of I. Miller & Sons—another quality shoe firm—as making "the best shoes in the world and that's where we get most of them. There is something about the pride they have in their workmanship."[4]

Fashion

A search for new, varied merchandise and—most importantly—fashion that is fresh and quite different from our own are the final reasons small and large retailers send their buyers and executives abroad.

Europe continues to be where most foreign fashion trends originate. But as the Far East increases its skill in interpreting and directing new trends, it has begun to exert a fashion leadership of its own. Meanwhile, it continues to be unbeatable in terms of price.

IMPACT OF IMPORTS ON AMERICAN INDUSTRY

After World War II, as part of an effort to help rebuild their countries, the United States government encouraged European and Japanese businessmen to study our clothing and textile manufacturing methods. At that point, the United States was the largest and most advanced producer of ready-to-wear in the world. Unable to export American ready-to-wear to these foreign countries because of high tariffs and other foreign restrictions, American manufacturers saw no reason not to help them.

Unfortunately, once familiar with how America styled and made clothing, some of the foreign visitors made it clear that they would now try to market their exports in this country. Aware that cheap foreign labor would enable these countries to produce lower priced comparable goods, American manufacturers quickly withdrew their offers of further technical assistance. In later years, however, many American technicians were hired by foreign firms and—by the late 1950s—most countries in Europe and the Far East had developed clothing industries capable of producing apparel for themselves and for export.

[3]Toni Kosover, "Shod in Style," *The New York Times* (January 30, 1977), p. F11.

[4]*Ibid.*

Today, the exports of these countries have made a tremendous impact on America's textile and apparel industries. With one third of the nation's clothing and one half of its shoes imported, the number of manufacturers and workers in the American fashion industries has dramatically dwindled.

Unable to compete with low priced foreign goods, many manufacturers have fled from unionized Seventh Avenue to non-unionized importing operations in places like Hong Kong, Taiwan, and South Korea—while others have simply gone out of business. Shoe firms, for example, have been thinned out from 600 in 1968 to 380 in 1977. Over the same ten-year period, the shoe industry lost over 70,000 of its 233,000 workers, while all the apparel industries lost 145,000 of their 900,000 workers.

Adding to the difficulties is the anticipated increase in operating costs for America's textile industry as it meets government requirements for pollution control.

Disturbed by the decline of the American textile and apparel industries, American manufacturers and organized labor jointly stepped up their efforts to slow down the flow of imports. In full page newspaper ads, Burlington Industries—the country's largest textile producer—expressed the concern of the industry saying: "We have become increasingly alarmed over the rising tide of textile and apparel products entering this country from abroad that threatens ultimately to drown a major segment of the U.S. textile and apparel industry and all those who derive their livelihood from it."

COMPETING AGAINST IMPORTS

The United States functions under the principle of free trade. Under that principle, our total exports once considerably outnumbered our imports, producing more jobs and profits for this country than were lost through the imports from abroad.

But that situation has changed. In 1976, we imported more goods than we exported, particularly in the categories of clothing, textiles, and shoes. Although these industries have been badly hurt by imports, the government must very carefully weigh any action it may take to alleviate the situation. It is forced to look at the export-import picture *as a whole.* Should there be curbs on imports in any one given area—such as the fashion industries—its chances for regaining its former advantageous *total* export position may be jeopardized.

With this in mind, many top government officials have indicated an unwillingness to sacrifice the nation's total exports in order to give the textile, apparel, and other threatened industries the protection they want against imports.

Nevertheless, both management and labor have demanded government curbs on imports—labelling the mushrooming growth of imports as a "potential threat" to the survival of the American fashion industries.

Under the Multifiber Textile Arrangements Act there exist textile/apparel trade agreements between the United States and various countries. The agreements control the amount of apparel and textile imports entering this country. In 1977 for instance, the growth in domestic production of fashion goods was 3 percent. The amount of imports coming into our country however grew to 6 percent. That year, new agreements were being negotiated to reduce the growth rate of imports to the domestic level. As a result, some cuts were made. For instance, American and Taiwanese officials agreed to cut the amount of low priced footwear shipped to this country by more than 28 percent.

FIGURE 10-1. Courtesy: International Ladies' Garment Workers Union, New York

The government feels, however, that import curbs alone will not solve all of the industries' problems. For example, because it is one of the hardest hit fashion industries, the government is offering its full resources to the depressed shoe industry. To help it become more competitive, the assistance includes supplying technological and financial help to increase and improve production; develop new markets; and improve marketing techniques.

Meanwhile, the industry is also trying to help itself. American manufacturers are "trading-up" and turning to the production of better goods—an area offering the least amount of foreign competition. They are also looking to enlarge their fashion exports to other countries. And in a strong advertising campaign, American labor has joined the fight against imports by urging the public to "buy American." The International Ladies' Garment Workers' Union uses the media to get its message across, spending part of its multi-million dollar effort on television commercials which have popularized the union theme song, "Look for the Union Label" (see Fig. 10-1).

As discussed throughout this section, competing against foreign made goods is an especially critical problem facing all those in the textile/apparel complex of industries. In summarizing possible solutions, it seems essential for United States fashion producers to work collectively to gain increased American consumer support. More importantly, the fashion industry—with the help of the government—must not *react* to the threat of foreign imports but must *actively* increase the demand for high quality, beautifully styled, "made in the U.S.A." merchandise in the expanding consumer markets around the world.

TERMS TO REMEMBER

European Common Market
trade-up
rebates
Multifiber Textile Agreements Act

HIGHLIGHTS OF THE CHAPTER

- Before World War II, foreign countries did not have thriving ready-to-wear industries. Their mass production of clothing began as a result of the post-war reconstruction efforts of the United States and their own governments.

- France, traditionally known for its couture, developed one of the world's most important prêt-à-porter industries; its development is hailed as a major post-war success story.
- Post-war Italy also established a strong ready-to-wear industry, with Florence and Milan as its most important apparel producing cities. During the late 70s, Milan emerged as Italy's major fashion center, second only to New York and Paris.
- Great Britain, West Germany, Scandinavia, and most other European countries produce fashion products, but by comparison with those of France and Italy, the quantity of their fashion exports to the United States are small. The majority of exports from each country reflects its raw materials, culture, and technology.
- India and Israel are the two greatest producers and exporters of clothing in the Middle East; while Japan, Hong Kong, Taiwan, and Korea are the leading ready-to-wear producing nations in the Far East.
- Imports of wearing apparel have become a grave problem for the United States in recent years. Currently this country is importing about one-third of its apparel needs. Because of high labor costs and a dwindling supply of skilled workers, it is difficult for American clothing producers to compete with the cheaper imports.
- Although the United States government would like to help control the influx of foreign goods, it must look at the export-import picture as a *whole.* Should she curb fashion imports, American export of other types of products may be jeopardized. But both government and fashion industry officials are trying to find a solution to the import problem.

QUESTIONS

1. Where and when do the French prêt-à-porter showings take place?
2. Name some of Italy's top ready-to-wear items. What cities serve as centers for Italy's clothing industry? Which is most important?
3. Why haven't other European countries developed as strong an apparel industry as France and Italy?

4. What has been the basis for Israel's ready-to-wear success? How do the apparel industries of Israel and India differ?
5. What kind of ready-to-wear is produced in Japan? In Hong Kong, Taiwan, and Korea? How are these countries trying to stay competitive on the world market?
6. What is the current status of exports to this country from Canada and Latin America?
7. How do you think the American fashion industry and government can solve some of the problems caused by fashion imports?

BIBLIOGRAPHY

BENNETT-ENGLAND, RODNEY, *Dress Optional.* London, England: Dufour Editions, 1968.

COBRIN, A. HARRY, *The Men's Clothing Industry—Colonial Through Modern Times.* New York: Fairchild Publications, 1970.

HALL, MAX, ed., *Made in New York.* Cambridge, Mass.: Harvard University Press, 1959.

HAMBURGER, ESTELLE, *Fashion Business—It's All Yours.* San Francisco: Canfield Press, 1976.

KAPLAN, DAVID G., *World of Furs.* New York: Fairchild Publications, 1974.

LAMBERT, ELEANOR, *World of Fashion.* New York & London: R. R. Bowker Company, 1976.

LEVIN, PHYLLIS, *Wheels of Fashion.* New York: Doubleday and Company, 1965.

Profitable Merchandising of Men's Clothing. New York: National Retail Merchants Association, 1967.

ROSHCO, BERNARD, *The Rag Race.* New York: Funk and Wagnalls, 1963.

TALMAN, RUTH, *Guide to Fashion Merchandise Knowledge,* Vol 1. New York: Milady Publishing Corporation, 1973.

WINGATE, ISABEL B., KAREN R. GILLESPIE, AND BETTY G. MILGROM, *Know Your Merchandise: For Retailers and Consumers,* 4th ed., New York: McGraw-Hill, 1975.

V

MERCHANDISING TODAY'S FASHION

The final and most direct link between the fashion industry and the consumer is provided by fashion retailers. As middlemen, they buy an assortment of fashion merchandise from various manufacturers with the express intent of reselling that merchandise to their clientele *at a profit.* To do this successfully, retailers must be completely informed on the most effective merchandising and promotion techniques. This part describes those techniques.

11

FASHION RETAILERS—WHO THEY ARE AND HOW THEY OPERATE

OBJECTIVES

After reading this chapter, you should be able to:

- Trace the birth and growth of fashion retailing in the United States.
- Identify and give an example of the various types of retailing operations existing today.
- Explain the four types of retail organizations.
- Outline the duties and responsibilities of various retail personnel.

Like the rest of the fashion industry in the United States, fashion retailing evolved in response to the changing social and economic climate of a developing nation. As this country grew and changed, various types of retail institutions emerged to meet an ever-increasing consumer demand for goods and services.

THE DEVELOPMENT OF FASHION RETAILING

The Early American Retailers

The exact origin of "fashion" retailing in this country is obscure, but it was the desire for luxurious furs, skins, and hides for fashionable wearing apparel which promoted the European exploration of North America and the eventual establishment of America's first retail outlet: the *trading post.*

The European fur trading companies dotted the landscape of Canada and northeastern United States with these trading posts. (One of the oldest and most famous of these companies is the Hudson's Bay Company of Canada which was chartered by the Queen of England in 1670.) Settlers and trappers exchanged their fur bounty for necessary foodstuffs at the posts—making the tiny outlets the first type of retail store in the New World.

Although trading posts were generally located at convenient crossroads, most were in outlying areas. For those who came to the New World and settled in or near port cities such as Boston and New York, another type of retail establishment emerged during the 1600s: the "little" or *specialty* shop. The name came from the fact that these merchants *specialized* in a particular type of goods. These outlets were often located in the shopkeeper's home; they offered products which were made on the premises and/or imported from Europe. Basically, their merchandise was classified as either "dry goods" or foodstuffs. Wearing apparel and accessories such as capes, shoes, millinery, wigs, fabrics, thread, and trimmings fell under the "dry goods" classification. Although the little shops usually began by carrying one of these items, in time many expanded their assortments to include several or all types of dry goods. Known as *dry goods stores,* this type of retail establishment eventually gave rise to the modern day department store.

As the population of the United States grew and expanded westward, the *peddler* became an important retailer. Loading a back-pack or wagon with an assortment of goods purchased in the port cities, this enterprising merchant would travel inland, selling wares from house to house. Sometimes this original "door-to-door salesman" would decide to settle down permanently, but would continue his retail trade by opening a *general store* in a suitable location. Such was the case with Adam Gimbel, founder of Gimbel Brothers, and David May, organizer of the May Company.

The First Department Stores

By the middle of the 1800s, eastern cities were flourishing and retailers dramatically increased the quantity, quality, and variety of their fashion merchandise. During this period, several of this country's most famous dry goods stores were founded, including John Wanamaker's in Philadelphia (see Fig. 11-1), Marshall Field's in Chicago, and A. T. Stewart's Marble and Cast Iron Palaces in New York (see Table 11-1). Al-

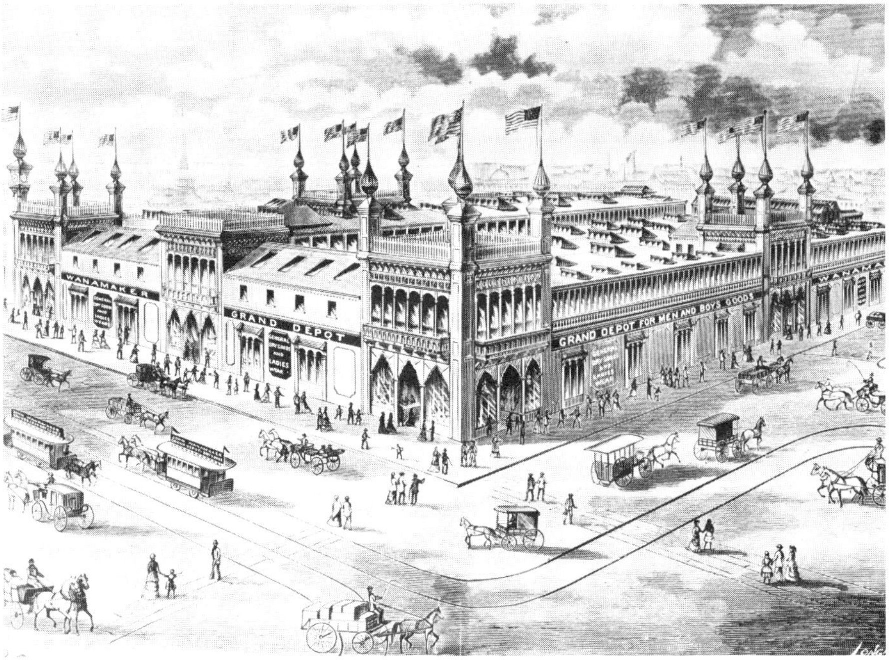

FIGURE 11-1. John Wanamaker's Grand Depot
Courtesy: John Wanamaker, Inc.

TABLE 11-1

Some Large Department Stores and Their Founding Dates

Lord and Taylor, New York	1826
Gimbel Brothers, Inc., New York	1842
D. H. Holmes, New Orleans	1842
Jordan Marsh, Boston	1851
Marshall Field, Chicago	1852
Carson, Pirie, Scott & Co., Chicago	1854
Younkers, Des Moines, Iowa	1856
Meick and Frank, Portland	1857
R. H. Macy, New York	1858
Goldwater's, Phoenix	1860
Higbee Company, Cleveland	1860
A. T. Stewart's, New York	1861
Wanamaker's, Philadelphia	1862
L. Hart and Son Company, San Diego	1866
Strawbridge and Clothier, Philadelphia	1868
Herpolsheimer Company, Grand Rapids	1870
Joske Brothers Company, San Antonio	1872
Forbes and Wallace, Inc., Springfield, Mo.	1873

FIGURE 11-2. Interior of John Wanamaker's Grand Depot
Courtesy: John Wanamaker, Inc.

though their exciting merchandise drew public praise, these stores were also magnificent structures that were hailed as architectural wonders. Appearing more like palaces than stores, these outlets were built with marble columns and facades and decorated with magnificent statues, chandeliers, and elaborate mosaic glass (see Fig. 11-2).

The great merchants of the 1800s did much to influence the retail business that exists today. From the beginning they emphasized the importance of attractive physical surroundings and tastefully planned merchandise displays. They introduced such merchandising policies as non-negotiable prices on goods; free delivery service; the training of sales personnel; and full money-back guarantees. Finally, these merchants recognized the importance of catering to the consumer—particularly the female customer. For example, the second floor of Stewart's Cast Iron Palace was exquisitely decorated with elegant furnishings and full-length mirrors and became known as the "ladies' parlor." In Marshall Field's, female clerks were used in the lingerie department and in the ladies' fitting rooms to accomodate the modesty of the ladies. And all stores maintained elaborate custom-made dress operations for those women who could afford hand-tailored apparel.

In time, the merchandise assortment of these clothing stores grew and diversified to include housewares and home furnishings. The merchandise was displayed and offered for sale departmentally—becoming known as *department stores.*

Early Mail Order Retailers

The department store, however, was basically an urban phenomenon. For those who lived in the rural areas and were unable to travel to the city, another form of retailing was devised: *mail order* selling.

In the late 1800s the U.S. postal system introduced the postal money order and rural free delivery. These two features made it possible for mail order catalog companies such as Montgomery Ward's and Sears, Roebuck and Co. to profitably service rural America with a variety of merchandise including wearing apparel. During the 1920s, the automobile improved transportation to the towns and cities, and mail order merchants added retail outlets to their operations.

The First Discounters

Until the 1950s, most fashion retailers followed the service oriented philosophy of the first retailers—providing customers with attention and atmosphere as well as fine merchandise. The cost of these extras was automatically incorporated into the retail price tags of the merchandise. But when the post-World War II buying boom began, some young enterprising "revolutionary" retailers felt it was an opportune time to introduce a different selling approach—one which had the following features: little if any customer services; outlets which were void of atmosphere but high in volume; and—most important to the customer—low, low prices. These "mass merchandisers" or *discounters* were so successful in stealing customers away from traditional retail operations, that this period is often referred to as the "retail revolution."

Most of the now-famous discounters such as Korvette's began during this period, opening small operations in the major cities and specializing in *hard goods.* "Hard goods" refers to merchandise lines such as appliances, luggage, housewares, linens, china, silverware and any other items which are not within the clothing classification. All manner of wearing apparel is classified as "soft goods."

The discount selling approach of these stores was not, however, entirely new. Wearing apparel had long been discounted by stores like Ohrbach's (which had been around since 1923), Alexander's, Loehmann's and Mays. All pre-dated the retail revolution. But the conventional retailers of the industry had been basically unaffected by the unconventional sales methods of these early fashion discounters, and it was not until lower and middle-income families began their post-war mass migration to the suburbs that the discount store become an important retailing force. The discounters followed the ex-city dwellers to suburbia and grabbed a large share of the cost-conscious new home owner's dollar by selling them *discounted* appliances and furniture for their new homes.

Eventually, the discounters sought to provide the suburban family with one-stop shopping and they began to expand into soft goods. Because most discount stores did not have the background to merchandise fashion, they *leased* their fashion apparel departments. A *leased department* is one which is run by an outside independent merchant who pays the store owner a rental fee or/and a percentage of the sales for the use of the owner's store space. Today, most discounters have acquired the staff and ability to run their own fashion apparel departments, sales from these departments now account for 25 to 40 percent of the discounter's total sales volume.

The Boutique

The large scale operations of the mass merchandisers or discounters which mushroomed in the 1950s was followed in the 1960s by a resurgence of the small specialty shop in the form of *boutiques*. Literally translated, boutique means "little shop." But their appearance on the retail scene at that time meant much more as they introduced traditional retailers to an entirely new approach to the merchandising of fashion. Emphasizing the off-beat and the unusual in both their merchandise and in their displays, the boutiques carried a complete assortment of unique wearing apparel—including outerwear and accessories. All were youth-oriented, expressing the "youth-kick" fashion philosophy of the early 60s.

The success of these first boutiques is best measured by their influence on other retailers. Overnight the "boutique concept" became an integral part of the merchandising plans of most traditional retailers. Large department and specialty stores installed small "boutiques" among their regular departments, stocking them with merchandise which was quite different from the traditional goods in the rest of the store. The in-store boutiques flourished and are now an established form of presentation in most large stores.

CURRENT TYPES OF FASHION RETAIL OUTLETS

Today's fashion retailing scene is as diverse as its history. As the discount store, the boutique, and other new types of retail outlets emerged, they supplemented rather than replaced the older established methods of retailing. At present, many types of stores exist. All, however, fall into one of these categories: (1) the *specialty store* which offers a narrow assortment; or (2) the *general merchandiser* or *department store* which offers both hard and soft goods. Under these broad headings, stores differ in terms of merchandising philosophies and organization structure.

The Specialty Stores

Specialty stores are either *single* or *limited* line operations. If the store sells only hosiery, ties, millinery, or any other single classification, it is a *single* line operation. If the store sells an assortment of items such as outerwear, suits, sportswear and accessories, then it is referred to as a *limited* line operation.

The majority of today's approximately 1.7 million retail operations are single or limited line specialty stores. Most are small, having annual sales of under $100,000, and are individually owned. They are especially important to the distribution of menswear, accounting for more than 60 percent of its sales volume.

Some limited line specialty stores such as Filene's of Boston, Neiman-Marcus of Dallas, Barney's of New York, and Bergdorf-Goodman of New York are so large that they have separate departments for each of their merchandise categories. Their size and the variety of merchandise they carry often causes them to be mistakenly identified as department stores. However, since they do not carry all types of merchandise they must still be considered specialty stores.

The General Merchandiser or Department Store

In order to be classified as a *department store,* a retailer must fit into the category of general merchandiser by carrying both hard and soft goods. It must employ twenty-five or more employees and have a physical layout which lends itself to the departmental grouping of related merchandise. Although there are some exceptions, traditionally the department store offers extensive customer services, including free delivery, store charge accounts, and gift wrapping. It derives nearly 40 percent of its sales volume from all kinds of women's apparel and accessories—selling more than one half of all the women's wear sold in this country.

The Discount Store

Discount stores may run a specialty store type of operation, or they may be general merchandisers that carry both soft and hard goods. But because of their unique discounting merchandising policies, they are grouped separately and referred to as "discount stores." Under their merchandising policies, discounters eliminate or reduce customer services and de-emphasize store decor and display, while stressing high sales volume through competitively lower prices. Some discounters promote recognized manufacturer brand names and labels while others cut out labels or promote their own private brands.

The role of the discounter in distributing fashion has been a variable one. A store like Ohrbach's became successful by distributing discounted high fashion and it is still known to carry European couture copies. On the other hand, K-Mart and other similar discounters have concentrated on offering the public mass-produced volume fashion merchandise. But in recent years, most of the mass fashion discounters have been upgrading their fashion operations, and many now offer a higher quality of fashion goods. As part of their "trading-up" campaign, these discounters are also offering store charge accounts and other "department store type" customer services.

The Branch Store. Many specialty and department stores have found it profitable to join the discounters in opening *branch stores* in suburban locations. These branches are under the control of the main store; originally they carried a modified line of merchandise, one that was particularly tailored to the suburban customer's needs. As these branches began to enjoy unprecedented business from the increasing suburban population, their size and merchandise assortments increased. Today, branch stores are major retail outlets; many are as important in terms of sales and profits as most parent stores.

The Mail Order Firm. Mail order firms today account for almost 10 percent of all retail sales. They can be either general merchandisers or specialty type operations; the three largest and most famous—Sears, Roebuck and Company, Montgomery Ward, and J. C. Penney—fall under the general merchandiser classification. Specialty mail order firms are those which offer a unique line of merchandise. A good example of this type of operation is L. L. Bean of Maine, who has become highly successful by offering the best in sporting goods and sports apparel to its mail-order customers (see Fig. 11-3).

Although they may run a successful mail order operation, many firms have found it advantageous to supplement their mail order business with retail store operations. On the other hand, many stores have discovered catalog sales to be a most viable supplement to in-store sales. The recent entry of stores into the mail order business is discussed in Chapter 13.

Selling through the mail is a unique operation. The mail order houses must rely on a catalog presentation to sell their merchandise to

FIGURE 11-3. Merchandise from L. L. Bean catalog
Courtesy: L. L. Bean, Freeport, Maine

their customers. The preparation of those catalogs is a lengthy process. To get them to the consumer at the beginning of a selling season, mail order houses must begin producing their catalogs far in advance. For instance, the planning of a Fall–Winter catalog, which is made available to customers about July, begins at least one year before its distribution. Most manufacturers do not have their regular lines ready that far in advance, but they supply the mail order houses with early samples of forthcoming styles for illustration and photographic purposes. The styles are kept simple so that they will not become outdated by the time the catalog is distributed. As a result, the catalog offerings of the large mail order houses like Sears, Montgomery Ward, and J.C. Penney are usually classic and conservatively styled. Nevertheless, these firms do a tremendous mail order business in all types of fashion apparel for men, women, and children.

Other Forms of Retailing

Three other retail institutions which distribute fashion goods to the consumer are *variety stores, military exchanges,* and *direct sales operations.* All have declined in importance over the past few years, but they still are effective fashion outlets.

The *variety store* or the "5 and 10 cent store" is defined as one which carries a wide assortment of all types of low priced merchandise in limited amounts. The assortments of low priced fashion merchandise are knock-offs of popular styles, and emphasize accessories rather than larger items of ready-to-wear. The leading retailers in the variety store business are F. W. Woolworth and S. S. Kresge.

Because of a decline in military personnel, the significance of the *PX* and the *military exchange* has also diminished. However, these government-run retail operations continue to sell a wide variety of merchandise including cosmetics, ready-to-wear, and fashion accessories. Located throughout the world, their merchandise often reflects both foreign and domestic fashion trends.

Direct sales operations include selling door-to-door and selling through at-home parties. Through these sales methods, the merchandise is brought directly to the customer's home by a sales representative. Probably the most successful direct sales company in existence today is Avon. This international firm began by selling cosmetics door-to-door, expanding into jewelry and fashion accessories in recent years.

With the exception of Avon (which is the leading cosmetic company in the country), the performance of most direct sales firms has declined. The decline has been attributed to the fact that most people now have a greater and easier access to shopping centers and all types of stores.

FOUR INNOVATIVE FASHION RETAILERS

There are many stores which have reputations as great fashion retailers. However, the four stores chosen for this section have something extra: unusual but highly succesful merchandising techniques.

Loehmann's

Frieda Loehmann transformed an automobile showroom in Brooklyn, New York into a virtual "dress palace" with elaborate furnishings and marble in 1921 (see Fig. 11-4). But it was not the decor that attracted shoppers to Loehmann's. It was the merchandise: the latest couture and designer clothes at low, low prices.

FIGURE 11-4. A Loehmann's store in Brooklyn, New York
Courtesy: Loehmann's, Brooklyn, New York

Before her name became synonymous with high fashion at bargain prices, Frieda had been a well known buyer for a Fifth Avenue store. With entré into many manufacturer showrooms, she was able to buy their samples, overstock, and closeouts. She agreed to remove the labels before selling the items at reduced prices.

This Loehmann's tradition for innovative retailing was continued by her son Charles, who established firm merchandising and advertising policies: no credit, no refunds, no exchanges, no alterations, no delivery service, and no featured merchandise in store ads. The policies were extremely successful and Charles Loehmann was able to expand the operation into what is now a forty-store Loehmann's Inc., chain.

Although samples, closeouts, and overstock still make up a great portion of the Loehmann inventory, current merchandise is now offered to the Loehmann's customer—but also at reduced prices. Loehmann's can undersell competitors on current merchandise because it obtains discounts from manufacturers by paying them within five days of delivery.

Over the years, Charles Loehmann has maintained his mother's innovative merchandising premise: *high fashion at unbelievably low prices.*

Neiman-Marcus

What store would consider it appropriate to feature a rare antique secretary and desk, fabulous furs, and original uniform buttons from the

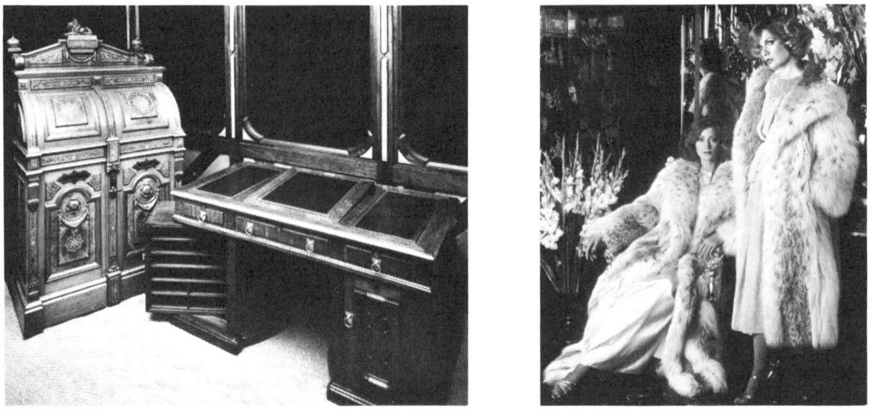

FIGURE 11-5. Merchandise featured in the 1978 Neiman-Marcus catalog
Courtesy: Neiman-Marcus, Dallas, Texas

Republic of Texas Army for sale in a mail order catalog? Only a store that bases its operation on *"complete customer satisfaction":* Neiman-Marcus.

The above named items were part of the 1978 Neiman-Marcus Christmas Catalog—a mail order catalog like no other (see Fig. 11-5). In fact the entire Neiman-Marcus operation has, from the beginning, been like no other.

Neiman-Marcus was founded in Dallas, Texas, in 1907 by Carrie Neiman and her brother, Herbert Marcus. Young and ambitious, it was their dream to bring high fashion apparel to the southwest. They attracted the patronage of the oil-rich millionaires of Texas, but word of their exquisite merchandise and extraordinary personal service soon spread nationwide.

In 1926, Stanley Marcus, Herbert's son, joined the store. Although the merchandising policies of his family were legendary, young Marcus was intensely interested in expanding upon the sales promotion activities of the store. To supplement the work of the store's advertising staff, he created a public relations department. That department was responsible for instituting many innovative promotions. One of these, the annual "Fortnight" promotion, is discussed in detail in Chapter 13.

In 1968 Neiman-Marcus became part of Carter-Hawley Hale Stores, Inc. Neiman-Marcus stores exist or are planned for in a number of major cities across the U.S. including Atlanta, St. Louis, Fort Worth, Chicago, Bal Harbour, Newport Beach, Beverly Hills, and San Francisco. Each store carries on the innovative merchandising and sales promotion techniques which originated in the famous Dallas store.

Henri Bendel

It's a small store on 57th Street in New York City, but due to its dynamic innovative president, it has a reputation for being a giant among fashion retailers.

Geraldine Stutz became President of Bendel's in 1957 when she was in her early 30s. It was a nondescript, financially troubled store, but Ms. Stutz transformed it into a very special place for a specific market. That market reflects Ms. Stutz herself: *small, thin, and very interested in sophisticated fashion.*

Upon joining Bendel's, one of Ms. Stutz's first steps was to change the interior layout of the store. She transformed the entire first floor into small selling areas, called it "The Street of Shops," and became the first retailer to incorporate the "boutique concept" into a major store.

Bendel's merchandising policies were also drastically altered. Volume priced lines of apparel from Seventh Avenue were omitted. So were European couture clothes. In their place Bendel's buyers brought back original European ready-to-wear, by then-unknown designers including Chloë, Cacharel, and Sonia Rykiel. Although three-fourths of Bendel's merchandise is still imported, American designers were also cultivated. Bendel's was responsible for introducing the work of John Kloss, Stephen Burrows, and other highly original American talents.

Over the years, Geraldine Stutz has continued her unique approach to retailing. For instance, to service her busy, highly selective customers, she's added "fashions in living" shops, consisting of a mini-delicatessen, a florist, and even a "sentiment" shop which features fragrances for every room in the home.

Although Bendel's annual sales volume is about $12 million, Ms. Stutz adamantly refuses to expand. She believes in a philosophy of "small and unique"; and that philosophy dominates the size of her store as well as the characteristics of its fashion merchandise. Fortunately, Genesco, Bendel's parent company, agrees with and encourages Ms. Stutz on her individual but most successful retailing approach.

Filene's

Opened in the late 1800's as a dry goods store, Filene's has become "The World's Largest Specialty Store," for men, women, and children. But Filene's is also known for its highly unusual and most creative retailing concept: *The Automatic Markdown Basement* (see Fig. 11-6).

When it was introduced in 1909, the Automatic Markdown Basement was considered a folly—doomed to fail. But it became the haven for smart bargain-seeking shoppers; a boon to apparel manufacturers who needed an outlet to sell their excess stock; and a place for over fifty other high fashion retailers to sell their markdowns.

To obtain merchandise for the Basement, Filene's pays other retailers and manufacturers cash for their stocks. In return, Filene's ob-

FIGURE 11-6. Shoppers hunting for Filene's high-class bargains
Courtesy: Filene's, Boston, Massachusetts

tains the lowest possible prices on this merchandise. These savings are passed on to the Basement's customers.

The Basement is called "Automatic Markdown" because of its unique price reduction concept. After 12 days on the floor, the price of the merchandise is reduced 25 percent. A second markdown of 25 percent is made after 18 days, and if the goods are still unsold after 24 days, a third 25 percent markdown is applied. Whatever stock remains at the end of thirty days, is given away to local charities.

The Basement operation has contributed greatly to the success of Filene's and its over 100 million dollar annual sales volume. But the store has other fine departments, with the newest fashion looks and designer merchandise. They have established Filene's as an authority on fashion and have made it one of the most important fashion retail operations in the Federated Stores Corporation.

TYPES OF RETAIL ORGANIZATIONS

Up to now, this chapter has concentrated on describing the various types of retail *establishments* which are used to sell fashion merchandise, but it is also important to learn of the various types of *organizations* which own and sometimes manage these establishments. All retail establishments operate under one of the following forms of ownership and management: (1) as independents, (2) as part of a franchise, (3) as part of a chain, (4) as part of a corporate group, and (5) as part of a conglomerate.

An *independent* establishment is privately owned. The majority of retailers in this country are independents; their businesses are either family run, a partnership, or a closed corporation (in a closed corporation, the public does not have the option to buy stock in the business). A ladies specialty shop in town or a department store which is operated by a local merchant is a typical example of an independent retail organization.

Some fashion retail stores operate as *franchises.* Under this arrangement, a company provides its name, merchandise, management, and marketing knowledge to a merchant in return for the merchant's capital investment, and a share of the profits. The merchant is a co-owner of the store and is responsible for its operation. The St. Laurent Rive Gauche boutiques are a good example of successfully franchised stores.

The Rive Gauche group is also a typical *chain store* operation. A chain store organization has two or more stores which are similar in physical appearance, carry the same merchandise, and are centrally owned and operated. Sears, and J. C. Penney are general merchandiser chains, while Lerner's and Bonds are specialty store chains.

Through mergers and acquisitions, the *corporate group* has become another type of retail owner-management organization. These companies are made up of large department and specialty stores which were once independently owned. Allied Stores, and Federated Stores, are two major retail corporate organizations. Each company owns a number of stores which are located throughout the country. The stores operate under their original names (see Tables 11-2 & 11-3), and—assuming their original method of operation has been successful—have continued to maintain their own merchandising policies. As a result, most stores in a corporate group are quite different from each other—with each functioning under policies which are most profitable for its store. However, corporate group headquarters maintains close contact with each store, supplying management advice and fashion direction as well as absorbing the profits and/or losses of each member store.

Federated Stores, Inc. Sales volume: over 4.4 billion dollars in 1977. Owns 205 department and discount operations, and 98 supermarkets, including:

TABLE 11-2

Abraham and Straus	Gold Triangle Stores
Bloomingdale's	Lazarus
Bullock's North	Levey's
Bullock's South	I. Magnin & Co.
Burdines	Ralph's
Filene's	Rich's
Foley's	Rikes
Gold Circle Stores	Sanger-Harris
Gold Key Stores	Shillito's
Goldsmith's	

Allied Stores, Inc. Sales volume: over 1.7 billion dollars in 1977. Owns 158 stores, 7 shopping centers, and 10 discount operations, including:

TABLE 11-3

Almart Stores	
J. M. Black Company	Levy's
Wm. Block Company	Maas Brothers
Bon Marche	Mabley & Carew
Cain Sloan Company	Missoula Mercantile
Dey Brothers	Muller Company, Ltd.
Donaldson's	The Paris Company
L. H. Field & Co.	A. Polsky Company
B. Gertz, Inc.	Pomeroy's Inc.
Hardy-Herpolsheimer	D. M. Read Co.
Heer's	Stern Brothers
Herps	Titche-Goettinger
Jordan Marsh	A. E. Troutman Co.
Joske's	Edward Wren Company

Fashion retail stores are often owned by giant *conglomerates.* These are corporations which control a variety of enterprises in addition to their retail operations. Genesco, for instance, is a huge corporation with interests in textiles, footwear, and many other manufacturing operations.

FOCUS ON THE INDUSTRY

GENESCO

Perhaps the largest conglomerate engaged in both the manufacturing and distribution of fashion goods is Genesco. The sales volume of the company was over 1.4 billion dollars in 1977. It operates 1,692 retail stores and leased departments. It also produces clothing, accessories, footwear, and hosiery for men, women, and children.

Although the name Genesco may not be familiar, its stores and the national brand names of its products are widely recognized. The company also manufactures under various private labels.

Retail Operations

Department and Specialty Stores

Bonwit Teller
Plymouth Shops
Henri Bendel
Gidding Jenny
Baron's
Whitehouse & Hardy
Frank Brothers
Burkhardt's
Burkhardt's/Davidson
McFarlin's
Gilbert's
L. Strauss & Co.
Graves-Cox
Hall-Brown
Tate-Brown
Roos/Atkins

Women's Wear labels

Rona
Dalani
Dal Knittery
Berkshire
Hobnobbers
Parkshire Original
City Scene
Plaza South
Kenrose
Sunshine Alley
Vivo
Susan Thomas
Gordon
Male for Gals

Lingerie labels

Formfit Rogers
Vera

Pucci
Leisuretown
Lady Serena
Geisha

Swimwear

Robby Len

Hosiery

Van Raalte
Berkshire
Camp d'Orsay
John Weitz

Shoe Stores

Flagg Brothers
Hardy
Jarman
I. Miller
Charles Jourdan
Agnew Surpass

Discount Stores

Elmore
S. H. Kress
Valmart

Menswear labels

Phoenix
Lanvin
Donald Brooks
Chaps by Ralph Lauren
Tom Weiskopf
Guy LaRoche
Regatta
Pleetway

Men's accessories

Dante
Don Loper
Lanvin

Footwear labels

Jarman
Johnston & Murphy
Douglas
Fortune
Frank Brothers
I. Miller
Adar Crest
Sandy McGee
John Ritchie
National Vogue
Christian Dior
Easy Street
Cover Girl
Charles Jourdan
Pierre Cardin
Charm Step
Story book

RETAIL PERSONNEL

All retailers have the same basic function: to deliver goods and services to the ultimate consumer at a profit. But the success of any retailing operation ultimately depends on the people who are charged with the various responsibilities of running the business. Although these responsibilities vary widely in retailing, they may be grouped under two broad categories: (1) activities which are *directly* related to the profitable buying and selling of merchandise, and (2) activities which *indirectly* support the profitable buying and selling of merchandise.

Although the size of a store controls the size of its personnel, all retailers—from the small "Mom and Pop" specialty store run by family members, to Sears, the world's largest retailer—have people who perform both types of activities.

Direct Buying and Selling Activities

Merchandising and *sales promotion* are the two activities which deal *directly* with the *buying and selling* of fashion goods.

Under the heading of *merchandising,* stores carefully plan the purchasing or buying of fashion merchandise, taking both fashion trends and monetary limitations into consideration. This function is performed by a store's merchandising executives who—after thorough research into market conditions—must decide what and how much merchandise to buy and how much they wish to spend. In essence, a store's method of operation is usually determined and coordinated by this merchandising staff.

Under the heading of *sales promotion,* stores advertise, display, and publicize the merchandise they have purchased in order to *sell* that merchandise to customers. The techniques employed in sales promotion are discussed fully in Chapter 13.

Indirect Retailing Activities

Finance; personnel; and *store operations* are three divisions which perform "behind the scenes," but each provides a variety of services that are indispensable for the successful operation of a store.

Bookkeeping; accounting; payroll; credit; expense control; taxes; and insurance are some of the many responsibilities of the *finance* division.

The *personnel* department handles all matters which pertain to store employees. Its primary function is to recruit, select, train, place, and evaluate employees for a store; but it is often also responsible for worker–management relations and may be called upon to handle all aspects of labor negotiations.

The main responsibility of the *store operations* division is to maintain the physical upkeep of a store—performing housekeeping, repair, maintenance, and store security tasks. The operations division will also supervise any architectural or structural changes which may be undertaken by a store.

Although the activities of these three divisions do not deal directly with the buying and selling of merchandise, they do make an important contribution to the "image" customers get of a store. For instance, an efficient and courteous credit and billing service by the finance division, or the expert maintenance by operations can greatly contribute toward a store's acceptance by the public and its continuous success.

FINDING A CAREER IN FASHION RETAILING

Many students who wish to become a part of the fashion business can do so by taking advantage of the many career opportunities which are available in all types of fashion retail stores. Those who are drawn to the excitement of buying and selling can enter into the merchandising or promotion of merchandise; while those who have an interest in finance, store operations, or personnel, can begin lucrative careers by joining those divisions of a store.

Careers in Fashion Merchandising

Many large retailers offer executive training programs which prepare qualified young people for fashion merchandising positions. In order to be accepted in these excellent programs, the applicant is usually expected to have a college background, some selling experience, and a keen fashion sense. Upon completion of the program, the career path of the trainee would probably progress in this order:

Assistant Department Manager. This position offers the novice an excellent opportunity to learn the basic day-to-day merchandising techniques of retailing. An assistant manager is required to help the manager with all phases of running a department, particularly with inventory control, sales personnel supervision, and merchandise display.

Department Manager. The key role of a department manager is to maintain an efficiently run, profitable department. The two major responsibilities of this position are (1) to supervise and train a well informed and cooperative sales staff, and (2) to supply the department's buyer with accurate, up-to-date information on the sales performance of the department's merchandise.

Assistant Buyer. As the buyer's "helping hand," an assistant buyer has the excellent opportunity to learn the intricate but exciting technique of buying fashion merchandise. Under the buyer's guidance, the assistant covers the market; does the majority of the department's "paperwork"; assists the buyer in evaluating the department manager's merchandise reports; places re-orders; and contacts manufacturers (or "follows-up") on the on-time delivery of goods. Because the assistant performs so many of the buying functions for a department (although none of the actual buying), this position usually serves as an "understudy role" for the position of buyer.

Buyer. All ultimate buying decisions on the merchandise that is purchased for a department rests with the buyer. Since these decisions determine the success of a department, all good buyers carefully analyze their customers, their market, and all current and incoming fashion trends before coming to their conclusions. Most of their information is obtained through their coverage of the market by visiting manufacturers, fabric houses, and fashion editors. But they also consult with some of the other fashion executives of their organization—particularly their merchandise manager and the store's fashion director. Other information and guidance for the buyer is available from the various auxiliary merchandising organizations most retailers subscribe to. These include buying offices and fashion consultants; their advisory role is discussed fully in the following chapter.

The position of buyer is exciting and well paying. Buyers are among a store's most highly respected executives, and buying is a challenging career goal for the talented and aggressive student. Although the backgrounds of many present-day buyers vary in terms of academic and professional experience, almost all have been assistants before moving up to their buyer's position. This type of on-the-job training as an assistant is invaluable, and is a "must" for almost all buying positions.

Careers in Promotion

For creative people who are interested in using their creativity within the fashion industry, retailers offer enormous opportunities through their sales promotion divisions. The fashion, advertising, display, and publicity departments of these divisions employ artists, writers, and other creative people to sell and publicize the merchandise and name of a store. All aspects of sales promotion, including the many exciting careers found in this field, are discussed in detail in Chapter 13.

Careers in Finance, Store Operations, and Personnel

There are many career opportunities in the finance, operations, management, and personnel divisions of a retail store. For instance, some of the country's top retail executives began in finance, rising through the ranks to become comptroller and eventually president of major retail organizations. Those who have an interest in any of these three areas will find that the retail field is a lucrative and creatively rewarding one.

TERMS TO REMEMBER

dry goods store
specialty store
department store
discounter
leased department
boutique
independent store
franchise
chain store
corporate group
conglomerate

HIGHLIGHTS OF THE CHAPTER

- The first retailers in early America were small trading posts, specialty shops, general stores, and mail order houses. These grew and evolved into the large retail institutions of today.
- Specialty stores deal in one kind or a limited line of merchandise while department stores sell all kinds of goods (hard and soft), presenting them "departmentalized."
- Post-World War II was a time for much innovation on the part of retailers and discounters; branch stores and boutiques emerged during that period.
- The discount store is identifiable by its merchandising policy which encourages cut-rate prices, large volume, and a limited amount of service. Branch stores are retail outlets which are usually built in the suburbs by inner-city stores to accommodate the growing suburban populations. The boutique is a small shop which carries unique fashion merchandise not ordinarily found in traditional stores.
- Stores are owned and managed by five types of retailers: the independent; the franchiser; the chain store operation; the corporate group; and the conglomerate.
- The activities of people who work in a retail store fall under five categories: merchandising; promotion; finance; personnel; and store operations.

- **The majority of executive positions in retailing are those in merchandising where talented people can become department managers and buyers, usually beginning as their assistants.**

QUESTIONS

1. Describe how America's first retail stores were founded and the course of their development into today's great retail institutions.
2. What is a leased department? What is the difference between a *single* and a *limited* line specialty store. Give an example of each in your home town.
3. How have discount and branch stores changed since they were introduced?
4. Describe the five types of ownership for retail establishments.
5. If you had the opportunity to open a store, what type would you choose and what kind of merchandise would you sell? Why?
6. Would you be interested in any of the careers offered in retailing? Explain why.

12

AUXILIARY MERCHANDISING OPERATIONS

OBJECTIVES

After reading this chapter, you should be able to:

- Identify the types of outside consultation firms which are available to retailers to assist them in merchandising and promoting fashion merchandise.
- Define the specific functions of some of those firms.
- Understand how these firms gather, analyze, and define fashion information for incorporation into a store's merchandising, promotion, and advertising plans.

To help retailers have the "right merchandise, in the right amount, at the right price, at the right time," the fashion industry offers many specialized services. Fashion consultants and fashion magazines; trade organizations and trade publications; textile and clothing manufacturers—are just some of the many people and operations that assist stores in the buying and selling of fashion goods. But perhaps the most valuable helping hand comes from still another source: the resident buying office.

RESIDENT BUYING OFFICES

Definition and Background

In an industry where today's "ford" (a popular style) may be tomorrow's markdown, stores must keep constant tabs on all the changes and developments occurring in the wholesale market place. Since out-of-town store buyers and executives do not have daily access to the country's wholesale market centers, stores can learn what is happening in the market by using the services of a resident buying office.

A *resident buying office* is an organization which serves as advisor and buying representative for one, several, or many non-competitive retail stores. (Stores are considered "non-competitive" when they are situated a comfortable distance away in different towns or cities, giving each other little or no competition.)

Resident buying offices are located in the country's top fashion market centers. The majority are in New York City, with others in Los Angeles, Chicago, Dallas, and Miami. Some of those outside New York are branches of the larger New York buying firms. Some also maintain foreign branches in the important market centers abroad.

Resident buying offices have been in existence since before the turn of the century. In those days, the typical "office" consisted of one person who worked and lived in New York City, buying and covering the market for a single out-of-town store. During the 1920s—a period of rapid growth for New York's ready-to-wear industry—the number and size of buying offices multiplied. They enlarged their staffs, took on more clients, and, as a result, began to exert a new and powerful influence in the market. A few became large successful corporations, and some are still in business today.

Types of Resident Buying Offices

There are four types of resident buying offices: the independent office, the private office, the cooperative office, and the corporation office. The first is independently owned; the last three are store owned.

The Independent Buying Office. The majority of resident buying offices are independent enterprises that are run for a profit. These offices charge their member stores—their clients—a fee for services. The fee varies; generally it is based on the store's sales volume and on the amount and types of services used by a store.

The size of an independent office can also vary. Some are small, servicing as few as under a dozen stores. Others—like Independent Retailers Syndicate which handles about 205 stores in this country and 15 abroad—are huge complex businesses. Other well known independent buying offices include Atlas Buying Corporation, Mutual Buying Syndicate, and Felix Lilienthal and Company.

Independent offices strive to create a particular image and reputation. For instance, one successful office, Van Buren-Neiman Associates, caters to fine specialty and department stores and has developed a reputation as a buying office with fashion "savvy." Other offices have built their image or reputation on specialization. For instance, some offices expertly cover the "promotional" or low end of the market for stores that sell inexpensive goods. Others are even more specialized. These offices cover only one segment of the market—servicing retailers that deal exclusively in furs, children's wear, menswear or any other large single market category. Men's Fashion Guild, resident buyers for men's and boys' specialty stores, is a typical example of this type of office.

The Private Office. A *private resident buying office* is owned by a single retailing firm and services that firm exclusively. The cost of maintaining a private office is high and only giant chain, department, or specialty stores can afford to do so.

Two famous, but very different retailers with private resident buying offices are Montgomery Ward and Neiman-Marcus. Ward's has buying offices in New York, Los Angeles, Dallas, Miami, and Chicago—its home base—to help it expedite the enormous volume of its 500 stores and huge mail order business. Neiman-Marcus maintains its own New York buying office to support the kind of unique high fashion, top quality operation which made the Texas specialty store world famous. Although their needs are quite different, each of these retailing giants finds that the services of a private resident buying office are necessary to run their businesses.

The Cooperative Office. A *cooperative resident buying office* is owned by a group of non-related, non-competing, privately owned stores. It is also referred to as an "associated" office. Its stores support it on a joint basis.

Fees vary for each member depending on the store's sales volume and the services it requires.

When a cooperative office is organized, it tries to limit its membership to stores with similar characteristics. The merchandising policies, sales volume, and clientele of stores belonging to a cooperative office are usually alike. To maintain this similarity, new memberships in a cooperative office are by invitation only.

Although a cooperative office is not completely private, it does offer more personal service than an independent office. Its stores are usually of a high caliber, demanding—but willing to pay for—top service from their resident buying office. Furthermore, the similarity of the stores allows them to share and learn from each other's retailing expertise.

The best known office of this type is Associated Merchandising Corporation. Among its members are many of the country's leading retailers including Bloomingdale's of New York, Bullocks of California and Filene's of Boston. Another top cooperative office is Frederick Atkins, in which B. Altman of New York and John Wanamaker of Philadelphia are well known participating members.

The Corporate Buying Office. The fourth type of office is the *corporate residential buying office.* It is an office which is maintained and owned by a parent company for its stores. The parent company is usually a large corporation that has built a syndicate or chain simply by acquiring independent stores.

Many of the stores acquired by the large chains are very different from each other. Usually they vary in size. Almost all keep their original name and—assuming they are successful—their retailing policies. Consequently, a corporate buying office may find itself in the position of having to fulfill a broad variety of needs for dissimilar stores.

The corporate office is a well-staffed organization, which is deeply involved in the welfare of its stores and intent on providing almost unlimited service, making no profit on its own.

As part of the parent firm, the corporate office has the power to buy and distribute merchandise for its stores. Because of this power, it carries greater authority in the market place than the independent or cooperative office.

Typical of the large corporate buying offices are Allied Stores Marketing Corporation and Associated Dry Goods Corporation. Allied's buying office services 155 stores which belong to its parent company, the Allied Stores Corporation; while Associated handles the needs of the 168 stores in the Associated Chain.[1] Table 12-1 lists some of the top buying offices.

Organization of the Resident Buying Office

In essence, a resident buying office duplicates the buying and other executive staff of a retail store. Every department of a large store is represented in a buying office. Vice presidents head up the apparel, home furnishings, sales promotion, and financial divisions of a buying

[1] *1977 Sheldon's Retail and Phelon's Resident Buyers,* Phelon-Sheldon Publications, Inc., 32 Union Square, New York, N.Y., Directory of Largest Department Stores, Women's Specialty Stores, Chain Stores, and Resident Buying Offices.

TABLE 12-1

Some Top Buying Offices

Independent Offices
Independent Retailers Syndicate (IRS)
Felix Lilienthal and Company
Mutual Buying Syndicate
Van Buren-Neiman Associates
Private Offices
Sears Roebuck & Co.
Montgomery Ward & Co.
Neiman-Marcus Co.
Cooperative Offices
Asociated Merchandising Corporation
Frederick Atkins
Specialty Stores Association
Corporate Offices
Allied Stores Marketing Corporation
Associated Dry Goods Corporation
Macy's Corporate Buying

office. The fashion director, divisional merchandise managers, resident buyers, and assistants work directly under the merchandising vice presidents; while the art, display, advertising, and direct mail departments fall under the jurisdiction of the sales promotion vice-president. By duplicating the organization of a store and having one or more specialists to represent each department, a buying office is able to give all members of a store the help and guidance they need.

Services of the Resident Buying Office

To advise—that is the main function of a buying office. To fulfill that function, each day resident buyers, merchandise managers, and fashion office personnel thoroughly scour the market looking for new fashion trends and market conditions. During market weeks, when store buyers are in town, resident buying offices have the opportunity to present their findings to the stores personally. The rest of the year the buying office communicates with the stores via telephone and by sending them bulletins, brochures, and other written communications.

Resident Buyer. A specific area of the market is assigned to the resident buyer. Sometimes that market is limited, but by no means small. For instance, there are so many dress manufacturers in New York that a large office like Allied Marketing divides the dress market among six resident buyers—separating it by size and price. Each buyer covers one of the following classifications: Junior Dresses; Pacesetter and Budget

Career Dresses; Daytime Dresses; Bridal, Better and Designer Dresses; Moderate and Casual Dresses; and Women's World. This definitive breakdown does not include Basement Dresses or its Central Dress Buying operation, which fall under other divisions in the Allied organization.

The typical day of a resident buyer is long, full of hard work, sometimes exciting, and always interesting.

The morning may include meetings with visiting store buyers; meetings with manufacturers' representatives; receiving and making cross-country telephone calls; reading and answering mail; sorting orders; writing and proofreading bulletins; and setting up a day's schedule. By noon, the resident buyer is in the market where new lines are covered and older lines reviewed. Store orders and reorders are placed. In the late afternoon, the buyer rushes back to the office and between phone calls and meetings with merchandise managers and fashion coordinators—gets bulletins off to the stores on the new market developments of the day.

This pace becomes even more hectic during market weeks. In order to supply store people with a preview of the season's new fashion trends, prices, and market conditions, the buying office may hold meetings, fashion shows, and "clinics" in which each resident buyer participates.

These separate full-day meetings are held just prior to, or at the start of, the market openings. They are organized on a divisional basis. For instance, there are dress meetings, sportswear meetings, menswear meetings, and so on. Each division's merchandise manager presides over the meetings—and every resident buyer gives a report and interpretation on his or her segment of the market. To illustrate their recommendations, the buyers gather sample merchandise from their manufacturers and present it visually. Sometimes, they invite a manufacturer who has a special line or a new marketing or sales promotion program to speak before the stores. Often, a store buyer or merchandiser is asked to present a buying plan or promotional program which has proven successful for their store.

These sessions present a wealth of information to stores, making it much easier for them to organize the new season's buying plans.

In addition to informing stores on market developments, resident buyers also have the power to "buy." However, in most resident offices, buyers cannot place orders except when asked to do so by store buyers. Only buyers who work for a private or corporate resident office—where the buying office and store belong to one parent firm—have the money and the authority to place orders. These resident buyers are allocated an amount of money called an "open-to-buy," which gives them the option to ship merchandise they feel is right for their member stores without waiting for the approval of those stores.

It must be emphasized however that resident buyers are not substitutes for store buyers. It is their function to *supplement*—rather than replace—the work of a store buyer.

Because they serve as representatives for a store buyer, resident buyers are also called "market representatives." Regardless of his or her title, the resident buyer has one of the most challenging jobs in a buying office.

The Fashion Office. The responsibility of the fashion office in a resident buying office is to *research, analyze, and then define current and future fashion trends. The purpose of this is to incorporate these trends into a store's merchandising, promotion, and advertising plans.*

The fashion office is headed by a fashion director or coordinator who is assisted by one or several people. To determine the trends for a given season the staff starts compiling information more than six months before manufacturers present their lines to the retailers.

To better understand the timing of market coverage by a fashion office, assume the staff is working on a forthcoming fall season. The high priced manufacturers present fall lines in late May. The bulk of the market opens the first week in June. It is necessary for the fashion staff to have full knowledge of those fall trends *weeks* before the openings in order to prepare written material and the meeting agenda it will present to the stores. To obtain that information, a working schedule is prepared for that particular fall season. The following is a sample of a typical schedule for a fashion office staff working in New York City.

JANUARY	Analyze the swatched predictions of fall color and fabric trends from the editorial offices of fashion magazines, major mills, leather manufacturers, and fashion consultant firms like Color Association.
FEBRUARY-MARCH	Visit stylists at leading leather houses for their opinion on the direction of fall color.
MARCH-APRIL	Visit fabric houses. Begin with large mills like Burlington, Klopman, and Milliken for popular, overall color and fabric trends. Continue with the "pace-setters"—the small but high fashion fabric houses like Anglo Woolens, Concord Fabrics, and Eininger. Visit Wool Bureau, Cotton Council, and other similar fiber organizations. Visit and get forecasts from fabric editors of leading fashion magazines. As complimentary leather and fabric

	swatches come in from above sources, set up swatch boards in fashion office of each color and fabric in thematic fashion groupings for referral by staff members of buying office and store personnel.
JANUARY–MAY	Analyze ready-to-wear trends. Begin by studying European spring *couture* and ready-to-wear lines for new silhouette, color, and texture directions. Before the May openings, visit a few key ready-to-wear manufacturers for a "hint" of the direction they are taking.
EARLY MAY	Re-visit magazines. This time to see the merchandise editors for fall promotions they are offering to stores and for their analysis of the fall fashion trends.
MAY	Visit accessory market. Coverage of the accessory market will not only supply the new accessory trends, it will offer a confirmation of the top ready-to-wear trends as well.
MAY	Consult with resident office buyers and merchandisers to get opinions on trends and coordinate themes. For instance, if the fashion office endorses a new trend of "skirts that are soft and wide," store people will be much more receptive toward promoting that trend if it is also endorsed by buyers.

By following a schedule similar to the one above, a fashion office obtains a *total* fashion picture to present to the fashion directors, executives, merchandisers, and buyers of its member stores. It does so through:

an illustrated and swatched fashion brochure or book.

fashion promotion calendar with correct timing for presenting each theme.

a seminar or large meeting run by the fashion director.

Throughout the rest of the season the fashion office *follows through.* It sends daily bulletins, continually feeding the stores information on current and forthcoming fashion trends. To help train store salespeople, it may also provide stores with slides and taped commentary giving a seasonal fashion report. The quality and amount of material produced by a fashion office varies among the buying offices—depending upon the size, writing ability of its staff, and the production budget of the office. The store-owned firms generally allocate more money for a fashion office than the independents, and they produce more elaborate printed presentations.

Whenever it is required, the staff of a fashion office will visit member stores. Most often it is the fashion director who will be invited. He or she may be asked to serve as commentator at fashion shows both in and out of their store (country clubs, charity organizations, women's clubs, and so on); to speak to the store's teen and college boards; and to present the over-all fashion picture to its sales, advertising, and display staffs. As a visiting "personality," the fashion director might also be asked to do guest shots on local radio and television, publicizing the store's name.

This type of store sales promotion and public relations work, however, is a minor function of the fashion staff of a buying office. Its main resposibility is centered around the merchandising of fashion. It is by shopping and analyzing the various fashion markets and then imaginatively presenting those markets' most important fashion trends that a fashion office fulfills its prime function: to help member stores of a resident buying office merchandise the best and most saleable fashion.

The preceding description of the work of those in a fashion office will, we hope, dispel some long held misconceptions about the seriousness of that work. Much of it is creative, exciting, and fun, but a great deal of it is also intricate and arduous. The fashion director's job, for instance, does not revolve around attending or giving fashion shows—particularly in a buying office. A good fashion director is, in essence, a fashion merchandiser—one who has the talent and knowledge to analyze the fashion markets, identify the major trends, and then determine the saleability of those trends.

Centralized Buying. A centralized buying operation is one which buys for a specific department of its member stores. Each department supplies the office with a dollar budget and information on the colors, fabrics, and styles which sell well in its department. Equipped with these monetary and style guidelines, the resident office buyer selects and orders stock.

In place of a buyer, each store has a department manager who maintains sales and stock reports. These reports are sent to the buying office where the resident buyer uses them to reorder, replace, or discontinue merchandise.

Most resident buying offices have a centralized buying operation. It is used primarily in low priced or budget dress, sportswear, and accessory departments.

There are several advantages to a centralized buying operation—particularly for a smaller store. First, it eliminates the expense of maintaining a department buyer in the store. Instead, it offers the advantage of having a resident buyer who is in the market continually, supplying a department with a flow of fresh, new merchandise. And, because the resident buyer is buying for more than one store, it also gives the individual store price benefits that can only come from group purchasing.

Group Purchasing. Purchasing identical merchandise from a manufacturer at one time by a group of stores is called "group purchasing." Because of the large volume of the purchase, the manufacturer will sell the goods at a special reduced price.

Through group purchasing, a resident buyer may also develop an item with a manufacturer for exclusive distribution to a group of stores. It may be a new fashion item not yet available in the market; or an item for the Christmas, back-to-school, or seasonal catalog that buying offices produce for their stores. Stores also have the opportunity to take advantage of group purchasing when a resident buyer purchases closeout merchandise at the end of a season from a manufacturer who wants to clear out his inventory.

Other Fashion Services of the Buying Office. Although its prime function is to provide buying and fashion advice, a buying office also offers stores a variety of sales promotion services. Most of the larger offices maintain sales promotion staffs with visual merchandising (display), advertising, and direct mail departments.

A visual merchandising department in a New York buying office services the office's stores by providing fresh information on the new materials and price conditions appearing in the New York display market, and by supplying stores with illustrated suggestions for displaying new important fashion themes. The department's director and staff also service the New York office during market weeks, providing imaginative displays for the merchandise featured at buyer's meetings. The advertising staff of an office is responsible for preparing suggested ad layouts and copy for new fashion themes; and the direct mail department prepares a variety of brochures, catalogs, and many other mailing pieces a store sends to its charge customers.

As mentioned earlier, the degree and quality of service offered by resident buying offices varies. A store, however, considers its buying office—regardless of the office's size and type—"special." During market weeks, it represents a home away from home; a friendly, supportive place to check-in and get an all-important sense of direction before going into the market. During the rest of the year, it maintains a necessary physical and psychological link between the store and the market place.

Listed below is a summary of some of the services offered to stores by a buying office:

Cover and report on fashion trends and market conditions on a day-to-day basis through written and telephone communication.

Supply preview of new market trends at the beginning of a season through meetings, fashion shows, and "clinics."

Help stores organize seasonal buying and sales promotion plans.

Provide efficient and economical buying services through centralized buying and group purchasing.

Provide direct mail, advertising, display, and other sales promotion advice and material.

Fashion Consultants

Another important merchandising aid for the retailer is the *fashion consultant.* A fashion consultant is a person or independent firm who is retained by retailing firms to help them merchandise the fashion areas of their businesses. A consultant will research and evaluate the fashion markets, submitting their evaluations and recommendations to their client firms.

One of the oldest and most prestigious fashion consulting firms is Tobé Associates which was founded in 1927 by Tobé Coller Davis, a celebrated fashion personality with an uncanny ability to analyze fashion and predict trends. Hiring several young, but capable reporters, Tobé and her staff scoured the market for fashion "news." She died in 1962, but *The Tobé Report* continues under the capable direction of Marjorie Deane. Today, the staff covers all the fashion markets here and abroad. Their evaluation of those markets is presented in an 80-page weekly report which includes the price, manufacturers, and sketches of the recommended merchandise.

Every major retailing firm subscribes to *The Tobé Report.* Fees are based on the dollar volume of sales of a store, and for some, the fee may be as high as $25,000 a year for the service. Other fashion consultants who are smaller and less influential than Tobé, but who are nevertheless important sources of information are: Merchandising Motivation, Inc., which is known as MMI; Mildred Custin, former president of Bonwit Teller; I. M. Reports, Niegel French Report and Fashion International, a biweekly report of the "News and Views of the International Fashion World," published by Ruth Finley.

Consumer Fashion Magazines

Another help for the retailer is *consumer fashion magazines. Vogue, Harper's Bazaar, Glamour, Mademoiselle,* and *Seventeen* are the five fashion magazines most widely read by the American public. Naturally, the fashions they choose to present on their pages greatly influence the fashion preferences of their readers.

Retailers recognize the strong influence of these fashion periodicals; their customers often come into their stores to find a dress, an accessory, or even a "look" that they saw in the latest issue of *Vogue* or *Mademoiselle*. To anticipate those requests, retailers work very closely with the staffs of these fashion publications.

In addition to fashion editors, promotion editors, and fabric editors—magazines employ *merchandise editors*. It is their function to inform retailers of the merchandise, trends, and fashion themes which will appear in forthcoming issues. Throughout the year, retailers visit magazine editorial offices to meet with merchandise editors. There, they are shown "dummies"—rough paste-up replicas—of forthcoming issues. The dummies contain photographs and accompanying editorial copy of the fashions chosen from the wholesale market which, in the opinion of the fashion editors, represent fashion news.

At the same time, the retailers meet with the *fabric editors*. They are responsible for covering and evaluating the textile market, and provide an analysis of future fabric and color trends.

During the fall and spring market weeks, which take place in June and November respectively, magazines hold elaborate clinics and fashion shows to give the retailers a preview of the merchandise they will feature in forthcoming issues. For instance, in June *Seventeen* and *Mademoiselle* produce the most dynamic back-to-school shows in the industry. These shows present merchandise which will be featured in their July and August issues and are seen by almost 2000 retailing executives during the fall market weeks.

To supplement personal visits and "big-event" fashion shows, magazines periodically send retailers store kits. These kits include photographs and listings of editorialized and advertised merchandise appearing in forthcoming issues, and advertising, display, and other sales promotion suggestions.

To help them choose the type of merchandise which will be most appealing to their readers, magazines maintain research departments. These departments survey their readership, compiling data on age, life style, occupation, buying power, and buying habits. The magazines send the results of their surveys to retailers who also find it extremely helpful in servicing their markets. For instance, in 1974 *The Bride's Magazine* asked over 4000 readers their opinions on everything from wedding dresses to money management. As a result of that survey, manufacturers, retailers, and, of course, *Bride's* itself, revamped their thinking about the type of merchandise they would offer the two million first-time brides married yearly in America.

Trade Publications

There is a huge assortment of newspapers, magazines, and journals that are published for those in the industry which supply information on fashion and market developments.

The most famous of these trade periodicals is *Women's Wear Daily,* the trade paper for the wholesale and retail women's garment industries. Everyone in the industry—designers, manufacturers, salesmen, fashion editors, and retailers—reads *Women's Wear Daily.* Although read primarily for its industry news, many people outside the industry who are interested in fashion, also subscribe to the paper for its "fashion gossip." In *Wonderful World of Women's Wear Daily,* Katie Kelly calls WWD "a daily clothing industry/fashion newspaper rather than a trade paper."

Women's Wear Daily is published every weekday by Fairchild Publications, a publishing firm which was founded in 1890. They printed two industry publications: *Menswear,* a biweekly trade magazine, and the *Daily News Record,* a daily paper which now reports the business side of the men's and boys' clothing industry. In 1910, the brothers devoted a full page of the Saturday issue of the *Daily News Record* to the then-new, but growing women's wear industry. In a short time, the page grew into a separate publication: *Women's Wear Daily.*

For decades, it published dry, trade-oriented news. Then, in 1960, John Fairchild, grandson of one of the founders, became publisher, and forever changed the character of the paper. WWD began to report on what "fashion leaders" were wearing as well as the news of the trade. In reporting on fashion, it began to take it upon itself to edit the news, endorsing and presenting the looks it felt were and would be important.

By 1970, *Women's Wear Daily* had become an influential force in the fashion industry. Unfortunately, that year it used its influence to push the midi length (which it called the *longuette,* a French term), encouraging manufacturers to make it and retailers to buy it. The losses suffered by Seventh Avenue and retailers were enormous. Since then, though still informative and exciting, *Women's Wear Daily* has toned down its fashion endorsements.

Much of the "gossipy" type of fashion reporting which drew non-industry readers to *WWD* now appears in *W,* Fairchild's latest publication. Published every two weeks the newspaper was introduced to service the lay readership and it places a great deal of emphasis on "who is wearing what."

At the present time, Fairchild also publishes *Footwear News, Homefurnishings Daily, Men's Wear*—a fashion magazine on men's fashion, and the previously mentioned *Daily News Record. Footwear News* is a weekly which reports on every area of the shoe industry—from leather producers to shoe retailers. Since the leather industry works so far ahead of the other fashion industries, *Footwear News* offers the reader a marvelous preview of future fashion trends.

There are many other trade publications to help retailers in their merchandising activities. Most specialize in one area of the industry. Typical examples are *American Fabrics, California Apparel News, California Men's Stylist, Fur Parade, Handbags and Accessories,* and *Sew Business.* Other publications aimed at retail management include *Stores, Chain Store Age,* and *Visual Merchandising.*

Finally, a listing of important trade publications would be incomplete without *Fashion Calendar.* Although it neither advises nor reports on fashion, it is the one publication most considered indispensable. Published monthly, it offers a daily listing of upcoming events, market weeks, manufacturer's showings, trade shows, and all the other important happenings of the market. The time, place, number, and name of the person to call for information are conveniently included with each listing.

Other Sources of Market Information

There are so many sources providing pertinent market and fashion information that a buyer, merchandiser, or fashion director of a store would find it impossible to take advantage of them all. Most retailers pick and choose, extracting reading material and covering areas of the market which best helps them.

Manufacturers. Chapters 8 and 9 describe how individual fiber, fabric, and ready-to-wear manufacturing firms provide retailers with a steady stream of fashion and market information. Retailers find these analyses and predictions of color, fabric, and style trends indispensable aids in merchandising their stores.

Trade Organizations. There are several large organizations within the industry composed of manufacturers, retailers, and/or members of the press which provide helpful fashion and trade information.

The most specialized are the retail buyers' groups such as the National Association of Men's Sportswear Buyers and the New York Women's Buyers Club. Other associations and clubs have a much less specialized area of interest, dealing with problems in every area of retailing, and providing information on all important areas of the industry. Two examples are the National Retail Merchants Association—a dynamic organization to which most department and apparel specialty stores belong; and the Association of Buying Offices which represents most of the country's major buying offices.

FOCUS ON THE INDUSTRY

THE FASHION GROUP

A unique and exciting trade organization is The Fashion Group. It was formed in 1931 by seventeen women; among them were fashion giants like Dorothy Shaver, president of Lord and Taylor; Edna Woolman Chase, editor-in-chief of Vogue; Carmel Snow, editor-in-chief of Harper's Bazaar; Tobé of Tobé Associates; and Estelle Hamburger, vice-president of Jay Thorpe.

The original purpose of The Fashion Group was to increase the opportunities for women at the executive levels of the fashion industry. But since its inception nearly a half century ago, The Fashion Group has expanded its goals. It now offers a wide range of services, some of which are available to those outside the organization.

The group's most famous activity is its exciting fashion presentations. Through lavish fashion shows and fabric displays, the group offers all in the fashion industry—members and non-members alike—their expert analysis and evaluation of upcoming seasonal fashion trends. For its members, The Fashion Group offers career counseling workshops, fashion-career literature, and the automatic prestige which comes from membership in the organization. Composed of bright, well educated women, the group's range of interests has broadened to include the community, and The Fashion Group now also presents fashion and grooming clinics in hospitals and corrective institutions.

To be accepted for membership in The Fashion Group, an applicant must have at least five years of executive-level experience in the fashion industry, plus the sponsorship and recommendation of five Fashion Group members.

The original New York Group has multiplied many times over. The Fashion Group is now an international organization with thirty-one regional groups and chapters. They are located in Mexico City, Paris, Tokyo and many other cities throughout the world. Its main chapter, however, continues to operate in New York City, as the International Headquarters of The Fashion Group.

FOCUS ON THE INDUSTRY

TRADE PUBLICATIONS AND ASSOCIATIONS

The following trade publications and trade associations of the fashion industry provide various kinds of help to retailers in their merchandising operations.

Publications

American Fabrics, 24 East 38 Street, New York, N.Y. 10016

Boutique Magazine, 1300 Broadway, New York, N.Y. 10010

California Apparel News, 1011 S. Los Angeles Street, Los Angeles, CA. 90015

California Men's Stylists, 1011 South Los Angeles Street, Los Angeles, CA. 90015

Chain Store Age, 2 Park Avenue, New York, N.Y. 10016

Clothes, 380 Madison Avenue, New York, N.Y. 10017

Cosmetics Fair, 65 East 55 Street, New York, N.Y. 10022

Daily News Record, 7 East 12 Street, New York, N.Y. 10003

Department Store Management, 60 East 42 Street, New York, N.Y. 10017

Fabric News, 21 East 40 Street, New York, N.Y. 10016

Fashion International, 185 East 85 Street, New York, N.Y. 10028

Footwear News, 7 East 12 Street, New York, N.Y. 10003

Fur Parade, 3307 Park Avenue, New York, N.Y. 10001

GAP (French Ready-to-Wear) 24 East 38 Street, New York, N.Y. 10016

Handbags and Accessories, 80 Lincoln, Stamford, Conn. 06904

Hosiery and Underwear, 1 East 1 Street, Duluth, Minnesota 55802

Jeweler's Circular, 100 East 42 Street, New York, N.Y. 10017

Masculines, 1440 Broadway, New York, N.Y. 10018

Men's Wear, 7 East 12 Street, New York, N.Y. 10003

Modern Retailer, 10 West 33 Street, New York, N.Y. 10001

Sew Business, 350 Fifth Avenue, New York, N.Y. 10001

Stores, 100 West 31 Street, New York, N.Y. 10001

Style for Men, 1011 South Los Angeles Street, Los Angeles, CA. 90015

Visual Merchandising, 407 Gilbert Avenue, Cincinnati, Ohio 45202

Women's Wear Daily, 7 East 12 Street, New York, N.Y. 10003

Associations

Association of Buying Offices, 100 West 31 Street, New York, N.Y. 10001

Association of General Merchandise Chains, 1441 Broadway, New York, N.Y. 10018

International Council of Shopping Centers, 445 Park Avenue, New York, N.Y. 10022

Mail Order Association of America, 612 North Michigan Avenue, Chicago, Ill. 60611

Mass Merchandising Association, Inc., 100 Merrick Road, Rockville Centre, N.Y. 11570

Men's Fashion Guild, 353 Fifth Avenue, New York, N.Y. 10019

Menswear Retailers of America, 1290 Avenue of the Americas, New York, N.Y. 10019

National Association of Men's Sportswear Buyers, 185 Madison Avenue, New York, N.Y. 10016

National Retail Merchants Association, 100 West 31 Street, New York, N.Y. 10001

Shoe Retailers League, 60 West 32 Street, New York, N.Y. 10001

The Fashion Group, 9 Rockefeller Plaza, New York, N.Y. 10020. Also in major cities throughout the country and abroad.

TERMS TO REMEMBER

resident buyer
resident buying office
centralized buying
open-to-buy
group purchasing
fashion consultant
merchandise editor
fabric editor
trade publication
The Fashion Group

HIGHLIGHTS OF THE CHAPTER

- There are many people, organizations, and publications which help the retailer in the buying and selling of goods. The most valuable assistance comes from resident buying offices which serve as advisors and buying representatives for stores.
- A fashion consultant is a person or independent firm retained by retailers who want supplementary expert help in merchandising the fashion areas of their businesses.
- The fabric and merchandise editors of consumer fashion magazines help retailers formulate their merchandising plans by presenting their viewpoint on fashion and market trends. Similar information is available to retailers in the pages of *Women's Wear Daily, Menswear, Footwear News,* and other trade publications.
- A final source of information for retailers is that which comes from manufacturers, and various trade organizations. Combined with the auxiliary merchandising operations previously mentioned, these sources of information offer the retailer an enormous amount of help and advice. Most retailers find it impossible to utilize each and every one of these sources and will pick and choose those which are most helpful to them.

QUESTIONS

1. Describe the organization and basic function of a resident buying office.
2. Name the four types of buying offices and describe the differences in terms of ownership of each.
3. What is the main responsibility of the resident buyer? Which buying offices give resident buyers independent buying power?
4. What is the main function of a fashion office in a resident buying office? Summarize its method of operation.
5. What is centralized buying?
6. In addition to providing buying and fashion advisory services, buying offices provide stores with other services. What are they?
7. What methods do fashion consultants, fashion magazines, trade publications, and trade organizations use to provide fashion information to retailers?

13

PROMOTING TODAY'S FASHION

OBJECTIVES

After reading this chapter, you should be able to:

- Understand the importance of sales promotion in the retailing of merchandise.
- Identify the various departments under a sales promotion division and describe their functions and activities.
- Grasp the importance of sales promotion in the development and projection of a store's fashion image.

In the retailing business, getting the right merchandise into a store is only half the job; convincing the customer to buy that merchandise is the other half. The advertising, display, publicity, and other techniques used to induce those sales is called *promotion.*

All medium to large retail stores which advertise, display, and otherwise promote their fashion merchandise have a sales promotion division. The size of these divisions varies, depending on the size of the store and its promotion policies. For instance, a discount fashion retailer like Orbach's of New York limits its promotional efforts and therefore maintains a relatively small staff to handle its advertising, publicity, and display. On the other hand, Macy's, which has an aggressive promotion policy, employs three vice presidents and numerous other top echelon executives to direct its many promotional activities.

Typically, however, most stores have a sales promotion division which is headed by one sales promotion director and which has other key people managing the various promotional activities of the store. Usually an advertising director or manager runs the advertising department, and a visual merchandising director handles a store's display efforts. Stores that receive or seek a large amount of publicity generally have a publicity or public relations director. And, unless store policy places its fashion office in the merchandising division, the store's fashion director is also included as part of the sales promotion executive staff.

Together, these experts imaginatively communicate with the public, relaying a store's fashion message, and persuading its customers to buy.

THE FASHION OFFICE

One of the most important contributors to the promotion plans of a fashion store is the fashion director or coordinator. A *fashion director* or *fashion coordinator* is one who researches, analyzes, defines, and presents the dominant current and future fashion trends.

The job of fashion coordinator did not exist before the early part of this century. Until then, women "coordinated" their custom-made costumes by using illustrations in magazines or by consulting their dressmakers. As ready-made clothing became more acceptable, stores found it profitable to have someone coordinate displays and advertisements so that they reflected and promoted the latest fashion looks and trends. The coordinators were called "stylists," and their responsibilities were far less complex and diverse than the responsibilities of those in similar positions today.

Organization of the Fashion Office

Yesterday's stylist is now known as a fashion "coordinator" or "director." The titles are interchangeable and the choice is usually governed by the size of the staff of the fashion office and by the importance of the position in the estimation of the store. In some cases, the director may also be given the title of "vice-president," to further emphasize the prestige of the position.

For example, a large store which aggressively promotes fashion may have a fashion office staff consisting of a fashion *director* and several fashion *coordinators*. Each coordinator is responsible for covering one segment of the market under the direction of the fashion director who oversees and covers the entire market. The fashion office in a smaller store often consists of one key person and an assistant—in most cases that key person is called the fashion *coordinator.*

Traditionally, fashion directors have been women. The situation is rapidly changing, however, as many young men with a talent for fashion are also considering—along with the more traditional jobs in buying, merchandising, and design—careers as fashion directors.

Responsibilities of the Fashion Office

The fashion office of a store has three basic responsibilities: *merchandising, sales promotion,* and *sales training.* It is the only department of a store which functions both in merchandising *and* promotion. The activities connected with fulfilling these two functions are closely related; and although this chapter is concerned primarily with promotion, it is necessary to include a description of the merchandising activities of a fashion office in order to fully understand those which deal with promotion.

Merchandising. The previous chapter describes how the fashion director and staff of a typical resident buying office carry out their merchandising responsibilities. Briefly stated, they research, analyze, and then define current and future fashion trends for the purpose of incorporating their findings into their firm's merchandising and promotion plans. The merchandising responsibilities of a store's fashion office staff are identical, but the method of operation is slightly different.

For instance, out-of-town fashion directors do not have daily access to the market, and therefore, their market information is obtained through seasonal market trips. A good portion of those trips is devoted to covering (viewing) the store's resources (manufacturers) by attending showings with their buyers and merchandisers. Further research includes those areas not covered by the buyers. The fashion director visits leather, fiber, and fabric houses; confers with the merchandise editors of consumer fashion magazines; shops the New York department stores for ideas on interior and window display; and visits museums, the theatre, and any other places in the city which are of interest from a fashion point of view.

Using this kind of research, the fashion director is in a position to advise store management and buyers alike of the overall direction of market trends. She or he can also evaluate which looks are most suited to the store's clientele and image. In short, the fashion director becomes an editor of the market, extracting trends that are good for a particular store and rejecting those that are not.

It must be stressed, however, that the role of the fashion director is an advisory one. It is up to the store management to support recommendations of the fashion director and to encourage store buyers to follow those recommendations when they make their merchandise purchases.

Promotion. Once its merchandising responsibilities are completed, the fashion office undertakes its most time-consuming task: promotion. As was stressed at the beginning of this chapter, getting the right type of merchandise into the store is only half the job—the other half is getting it sold. The fashion office is just as involved in promoting, or selling, merchandise as it is in helping to choose it.

One popular promotional activity handled by the fashion office is the fashion show. The basic goal of a fashion show is to sell merchandise; but a good show also tries to educate the consumer by presenting the store's authoritive opinion on current fashion. A great deal of time and thought, therefore, is devoted to a show's preparation. The fashion director is responsible for planning the theme, choosing the merchandise, and writing and making the commentary. The staff, meanwhile, does most of the leg work such as hiring models, gathering the merchandise, producing the program, and—in essence—taking care of all the mechanics involved in organizing a fashion show.

A second promotional responsibility of the fashion office is special events. Some of these special events are yearly occurrences, such as the back-to-school promotions run in conjunction with magazines like *Seventeen, Mademoiselle* and *Glamour.* But most special events are one-time store-wide promotions like import fairs, anniversary celebrations, branch openings, and so on. These store-wide efforts are organized by the sales promotion department; the fashion office participates through various activties which reflect the theme of the event. During an import fair, for instance, the fashion office may organize and run a boutique featuring some of the most unique merchandise the store has imported for the event.

A third responsibility of the fashion office is to supply the merchandise used in a store's window and interior displays. In a medium-size store, one of the assistant fashion coordinators is given this responsibility as part of her or his duties. In a large store, this activity is a full-time job; a display coordinator is usually employed as part of the fashion or display office staff.

A fourth responsibility of the fashion office is providing direction to the store's advertising department. Although key advertised items are chosen by buyers, the fashion office gives advice on accessories, skirt lengths, hair styles, and other particulars which will help the ads project up-to-the-minute looks.

Sales Training. Stores hold periodical training sessions to keep their sales help informed of the latest fashion trends. These meetings are often organized and presided over by the fashion director. After merchandising and promotion, sales training is the third and final large area of responsibility of a store's fashion staff.

There are additional minor, but nevertheless important, activities which are performed by the fashion director. These include making public appearances on local radio and television; lecturing at local schools and civic organizations; getting editorial coverage for the store in the local press; and, in general, serving as the store's fashion spokesperson whenever necessary.

ADVERTISING

Buying space or time in the print or broadcast media such as newspapers, magazines, radio, and television is known as *advertising*. It is the most important means of communication between a retail store and its potential customers. Almost every major store which advertises has a director who heads an advertising staff of copywriters and artists. Together, they produce or help produce the ads a store places in both the printed and broadcasting media.

The Printed Media

Newspapers. Retailers spend more money on advertising than on any other form of sales promotion. And the majority of their advertising budget goes towards buying newspaper space.

Men's clothiers were the first to use newspaper advertising as a sales promotion tool. During the early 1800s, they discovered that it was better to advertise in newspapers than to hire "hawkers" to stand outside their doors and announce or "hawk" their merchandise to the passing public.

Originally, the ads were composed solely of copy. Joseph Schaffner, a founder of the Hart Schaffner and Marx menswear firm, is credited with introducing illustrations into advertising when, in the late 1890s, he began to use a "copy plus pictures" advertising technique. The ads immediately increased his business and were widely copied by retailers and manufacturers alike.

Hart Schaffner and Marx also introduced several other, then unheard-of, advertising premises. They were the first to promote the wisdom of *purchasing better merchandise during bad times,* successfully convincing the public that in the long run, a purchase of quality was more economical than a purchase of cheaper but inferior goods. During the recession of the mid-1970s, present day fashion retailers used the same technique—promoting classic, quality fashions which would have a long fashion life as "Long Term Fashion Investments."

Hart Schaffner and Marx also pioneered "non-advertising" *institutional* advertising. An *institutional* ad does not sell merchandise. Instead, it publicizes or "sells" the store. Ads of this type may present a general fashion message, announce a community event, or even salute an unusually famous personality. The firm's first institutional advertising consisted of booklets on "courage," "enthusiasm," and "cooperation," setting a pattern for the type of institutional ads many stores, including Wallach's—Hart, Schaffner and Marx's own retail outlet—have done (see Fig. 13-1).

Although most advertising costs come out of the retailer's pocket, a good portion of their ads are subsidized through "co-op" advertising. *Cooperative advertising* is the arrangement where manufacturers and re-

speaking of arbiters

We have just been reading "The New Emily Post's Etiquette," published by her granddaughter-in-law Elizabeth L. Post. Curiously, the word "courtesy" doesn't appear in the index. But that is what, like its predecessors, it is all about. Consideration, leading to a sense of self-respect.

Somehow, we had a feeling that Emily had been etiquette's arbiter at least as long as we had been clothing's ditto. In fact, she was only 14 years old when we first opened our doors, and she didn't publish her first Etiquette book until 1922, when we were 35.

The new compendium is brought very much up to date with the social customs of the 1970's, yet it retains the grace of an earlier age.

The original work has been revised, improved and modernized several times as its author saw fit. We have had a slight advantage there. For Wallachs is open every working day, and each day is a gradual new edition. Both clothing and courtesy have a daily opportunity to adapt and to improve. We try to see that they do.

FIGURE 13-1. Wallachs famous institutional ads are still being used for special promotions
Courtesy: Wallachs, Inc., New York

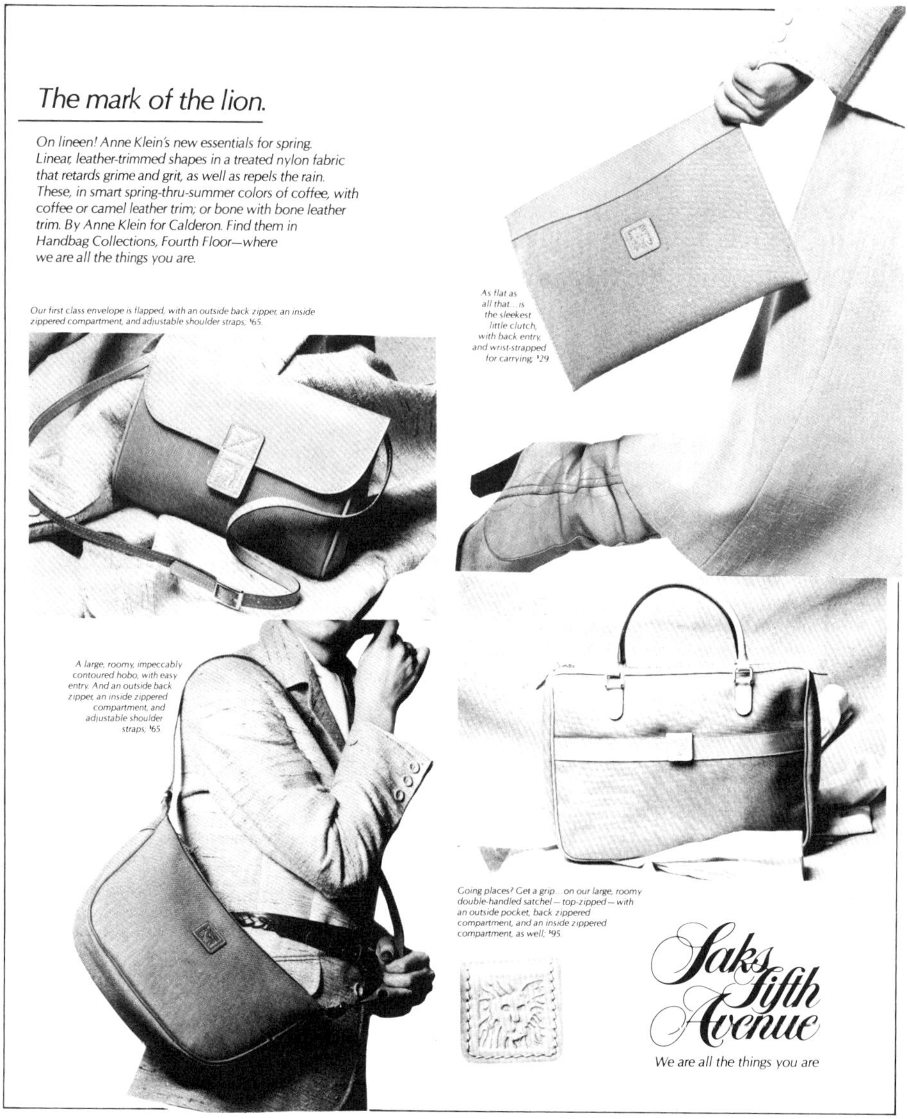

FIGURE 13-2. This Anne Klein-Saks Fifth Avenue ad illustrates designer and store participation in co-op advertising
Courtesy: Saks Fifth Avenue, New York

tailers share the cost of featuring the manufacturer's merchandise in the store's ads (see Fig. 13-2).

Retailers now consider newspaper advertising their greatest business builder. In 1976, the Newspaper Advertising Bureau sponsored a research study which confirmed the value of this medium as a retail sales booster. The study indicated that consumers who were pulled into a store by an advertised item, went on to buy additional merchandise elsewhere in the store. On the average, it was found that for each dollar people spent on an advertised item, another dollar was spent throughout the store.

Retailers generally advertise in local newspapers, choosing the one which most appeals to their customers. In New York, for instance, the stores which sell better high fashion merchandise advertise in *The New York Times,* a newspaper which has an affluent fashion-conscious readership. New York stores who wish to advertise less expensive fashion merchandise choose *The Daily News,* a popular tabloid which appeals to a broader segment of the people.

Fashion Magazines. *Godey's Lady's Book* was the first fashion magazine in America to gain nationwide recognition. It was published between 1830 and 1879 and, as the only source of fashion information available to most women, was known as the "Victorian Bible of the Parlor." Along with illustrations of the latest fashions, the magazine presented poetry, fiction, recipes, and assorted bits of advice on fashion and the social graces. Sara Josepha Hale became famous as Godey's talented editor, but because of her influential editorials on the acceptance of women in the medical, teaching, and missionary professions, she is also remembered as one of the first exponents of women's rights.

Although the slick fashion magazines of today are much more sophisticated, Godey's was responsible for developing the format all present-day magazines follow: fashion plus interesting reading matter. *Vogue, Harper's Bazaar, Glamour, Mademoiselle,* and *Seventeen* are the "big five." Except for some fiction or timely article, all devote their pages to the subject of fashion. Each, however, has its own fashion philosophy and image which is tailored to appeal to different segments of the population. *Vogue* and *Harper's Bazaar* cater to the woman who is interested in expensive high fashion. *Glamour* and *Mademoiselle* gear their fashion presentations for the sophisticated, well-educated college, career, or young married woman. And *Seventeen* edits its magazine to please the tastes of the American teen-aged girl. Although there are some fashion editorials and a good deal of fashion advertisements in *Playboy* and *Esquire, Gentleman's Quarterly* is the only magazine exclusively devoted to fashion for men.

When magazines feature an item on their editorial pages, the magazine supplies its readers with the name of one or more stores throughout the country which will carry the featured item. This free bit of advertising for the store is known as an *editorial credit.*

In terms of sales, magazine advertising is not as important for a store as newspaper advertising. Most of a store's business comes from its local customers; retailers do not expect to get unusual sales results from a nationally distributed magazine ad. They do feel, however, that national exposure in one of the country's leading fashion magazines adds valuable prestige to their store and, for that reason, are willing to give part of their advertising dollar to magazines.

Retailers also find magazines to be extremely cooperative and eager to help a store sell its goods. Magazines gladly provide posters and handtags for merchandise which is advertised or featured editorially in their pages, and they encourage stores to use their name when the merchandise appears in local ads and store displays.

Direct Mail. Advertisements which retailers mail directly to the consumer are known as *direct mail.* Direct mail comes in many forms—from simple postcards, leaflets, and brochures to elaborate catalogs. When a piece of direct mail is inserted with the customer's monthly financial statement, it is known as a "statement enclosure." These enclosures are provided to the retailer by the manufacturer. Eager to publicize their products, manufacturers swamp retailers with offerings of enclosures, but mailing costs prohibit stores from taking advantage of many of their offers.

Brochures, catalogs, and any other mailing pieces which feature items from more than one manufacturer are produced by the retailer. Manufacturers, however, are agreeable to contributing toward most or all of a store's production costs for the privilege of having their merchandise included in these mailing pieces.

The first mail order catalogs were introduced during the 1800s by city retailers who wanted to service customers who were unable to travel to their stores. However, these retailers did not extend their offerings to people living in the rural areas. To reach that untapped market, in 1872 Aaron Montgomery Ward produced a one-page "catalog" which introduced the concept of selling exclusively by mail.

That concept was copied by others, including Sears, Roebuck and Company, who, in 1893, organized what is now the world's largest retail company. As the country expanded to the west and the demand for ready-made clothing grew, the mail order business flourished. But in the 1920s, the introduction of the automobile improved rural transportation, and small independent stores began to spring up close to the rural areas. To meet this new competitive threat, Sears opened its first retail store in 1925, and other mail order firms then followed suit.

Although buying-by-mail continued to retain its popularity throughout the years, mail order business enjoyed a spectacular increase several years ago when, in 1975, gasoline became scarce and expensive. To keep the business of the customer who was reluctant to travel, stores increased their direct mail offerings. The huge success of these direct mail efforts has prompted stores to continue with those efforts. In addition to the traditional back-to-school and Christmas catalogs, stores are now sending their customers exquisitely prepared "magazine" type mailings which feature each season's newest merchandise.

The Broadcasting Media

Radio. In order to appreciate fashion, it must be seen. Newspapers, magazines, and direct mail are appropriate for fashion advertising because each presents fashion visually. Radio cannot. And because it cannot, stores have used a limited amount of radio advertising to promote fashion.

Cosmetics such as shampoos, face creams, and so on—which need not be seen to be appreciated—are the only fashion products which are heavily promoted on radio, and then usually by their manufacturers. Retailers reserve their radio fashion advertising for the announcement of special fashion sales and promotions which, like cosmetics, do not require a visual presentation.

Television. Television is, of course, a visual media. But it was not automatically accepted by retailers for fashion advertising. To most, television represented an unfamiliar advertising medium whose ads took too much time and money to prepare. Until recently, stores still preferred to sell their fashion in print.

But in 1977, the television industry began to pursue the fashion advertising dollars of retailers. Using the New York metropolitan area for its research, television executives estimated that out of the $300 million New York stores spent on fashion advertising in 1976, only 2 to 3 percent (or 9 million dollars) was spent on television.[1] By offering retailers expert help and guidance, television felt it could make that New York figure jump to 20 percent in just 5 short years.

By the end of 1977, Abraham & Straus, Bloomingdale's, Gimbels, and most of New York's other leading fashion stores had increased their fashion advertising on television. Gimbels thought so much of their television advertising that they publicized it in print (see Fig. 13-3). And Korvette's, the well-known discounter famous for its hard lines, began to upgrade its fashion image with a battery of television ads which introduced the "fashion half" of Korvette's.

Thus far, retailers have preferred to launch these short television campaigns for the purpose of upgrading their image or announcing an important sale. Most of these one-to-three week campaigns cannot—unfortunately—be used to accurately measure the effectiveness of ad-

[1] *Women's Wear Daily* (July 12, 1977), p. 1, col. 1.

FIGURE 13-3. Gimbels boasts of its TV advertising in an exciting newspaper ad
Courtesy: Gimbels, New York

vertising on television in terms of fashion sales. There have been, however, some positive examples of TV's pulling power. One of the most impressive has been the claim by one retailer that by adding television to his newspaper advertising, the sales of fashion wigs jumped from 1,200 to 22,000 per promotion. Examples of this type are encouraging more and more retailers to experiment with television, and most have made plans to include the use of TV in their future fashion promotions.

PUBLICITY

When a person, product, or firm receives free and voluntary mention in any media, that mention is known as *publicity.* In order to obtain publicity, retailers must provide the media with information that will be considered "news." In most cases the "news" pertains to special events that are taking place in a store. These may include the opening of a new branch store, the visit of an important designer or fashion editor, the opening of a new fashion department within the store, or any other "happening" which might be of interest to the local reading and listening public.

There are many publicity agencies that handle fashion accounts. Eleanor Lambert (the creator of the Coty Fashion Award), Ruth Hammer Associates, and Rosemary Sheehan are three of the best known. But the clients of these New York based agencies are fabric and apparel producers, rather than retailers.

Large stores prefer to employ a staff publicity director who has contact with the local media. It is his or her function to publicize a store's name and—in the case of a fashion store—the store's fashion leadership.

Publicists use several methods to pass "news" along to the printed and broadcasting media. The most popular method is to use *press releases.* A press release is a written description of a product, personality, or event. Press releases are written by a store's publicity department, but they are also made available to a store by manufacturers who wish to publicize their merchandise. Often, manufacturers will include accompanying photographs with their press releases. Many local newspaper fashion editors rely on these press releases and photographs to provide them with most of the news they print on their fashion pages.

The telephone serves as another means of communication between a store and the media. Sometimes, particularly in the case of simple announcements or short bits of information, a phone call can take the place of a press release. It is in these instances that a close liaison between a store's publicity director and members of the media becomes extremely useful and important.

Local newspaper editors and broadcasting producers will often invite a representative from a store to speak on current fashion subjects. The expert may be a store's owner, a store's fashion director, or even a visiting designer or magazine personality, and these personal appearances are always extremely effective in gaining publicity for a store.

Although a store does not pay the media for publicity, publicity is not cheap. It is expensive to maintain an expert publicity department and to produce the fashion events which bring a store publicity. But leading retailers justify their publicity expenditures by insisting that their publicity efforts invariably improve their businesses.

A major exponent of this theory is Stanley Marcus, son of the founder of Neiman-Marcus in Dallas, Texas. One of the great modern pioneers of sales promotion in retailing, Marcus displayed his flair for sales promotion early in his career when he created two retailing classics: the luncheon fashion show in 1926 and the bridal fashion show in the 1930s. The success of these ventures prompted Marcus to introduce many other fashion promotions. One of the most successful has been the famous *Fortnight in Dallas* which, in its two week celebration, annually honors a foreign nation. Publicity from this event has enhanced the store's national and international reputation. But, according to Marcus, "the fundamental purpose of the *Fortnight* was to help us overcome a historical business lag of mid-October."[2] The event turned October into a peak traffic month, even surpassing Christmas, and netted the largest sales increases for that month in the store's history. Publicity, Mr. Marcus has proven, does pay.

VISUAL MERCHANDISING (DISPLAY)

The presentation of merchandise in a store is known as *visual merchandising*. Until recently, the activity was simply called "display." But as window and interior store presentations became extremely effective in *selling* merchandise and fashion ideas to the public, the industry felt that "visual merchandising" was a much more accurate description of this activity.

Merchants did not always consider presentation of their merchandise to be important. In fact, until the 1890s, stores were bare and unattractive—not at all like the stores of today. Merchandise was never "displayed"; stock was simply piled high on tables. At the turn of the century, retailers entered into their "plate glass period," replacing the large old barn-like stores with places which were faced with huge plate glass windows. Store interiors displayed new stock cabinets, while ladies' tea rooms, men's barber shops, shoe polishing facilities, and rest rooms were added as conveniences.

The first manikins were primitive dolls when compared to today's life-like creations. They were made of wax, extremely delicate, and posed a special problem in hot weather. As the temperature rose, window trimmers had to periodically pour cold water into the heads and hands of the manikins to prevent them from melting. Over the years, the quality of the manikins and all other display materials was rapidly improved; and by the 1930s, store display—fashion and otherwise—had become firmly established as a creative art.

[2]Stanley Marcus, *Minding the Store* (Boston: Little, Brown and Company, 1974), p. 210.

Presently, window and interior displays are used for two basic purposes: to sell merchandise, or to present a special "message" from the store. Stores use display as a selling tool simply by dressing windows and store interiors with merchandise which entices customers to stop, look, and in many cases, buy. There are times, however, when windows and some inside areas of a store are merchandise free and are used solely as a means of transmitting the best wishes of a store to the community on the celebration of a holiday, or an important local anniversary or event.

Until the introduction of suburban shopping centers, most stores were located in cities or large towns—places where people walk and window shop. In order to attract the attention of the many passersby, the stores built large street-level windows, which showcase the most exciting merchandise and ideas a store has to offer.

Suburban store branches, however, are usually located in shopping centers which do not cater to a walking public. Most of these stores have windowless facades. The few which have front windows are usually part of a shopping mall, places where store fronts are viewed by pedestrians as they saunter from store to store along the enclosed promenade of the mall.

But even these mall stores have a comparatively reduced amount of window space and, as a rule, suburban store display departments concentrate most or all of their efforts on the interior displays of their stores.

The competition from the new attractive suburban stores has forced many of the older city stores to reevaluate their appearance. Ordinary wear and tear has made periodical redecorating necessary in most—but some of the more outdated city stores have decided to undergo extensive renovation. As a result, the traditional, often dull interiors of these older stores have been transformed into exciting, chic selling areas which are attracting the business of many former customers.

The emphasis by both city and suburban stores on interior appearances poses a challenge to today's visual merchandising director. More than ever before, displays are relied upon to complement and enchance the overall appearance of a store. If a store has older, traditional interiors, its displays must help to tastefully bring its appearance up to date. On the other hand, should a store have new non-traditional open space, then its displays must be equally innovative and used imaginatively within that space.

DEVELOPING A FASHION IMAGE

Sales promotion has two functions. One is to sell merchandise; the other is to project what is now commonly called a store's "image."

In retailing, the word "image" refers to the mental impression the public has of a store. The *fashion image* of a store then, may be defined as the impression the public has of a store's fashion expertise.

As tools of sales promotion, advertising, publicity, and display can help to project a store's fashion image. But these sales promotion activities cannot, by themselves, create that image. To develop a fashion image, a store must: (1) decide on who it wants as customers; (2) offer fashion merchandise which will appeal to that group of customers; and (3) promote that merchandise with sales promotion techniques which will be most effective with that clientele.

When choosing the type of people it wants as customers, a store simply looks for that portion of the public which it feels it can service most profitably. The type of merchandise a store sells is determined by the tastes of those customers. For instance, if a store has customers who prefer expensive high fashion clothes, then its merchandising policies will be based on obtaining the best available selection of high styled, quality clothes.

Once a store has established its clientele and merchandised its inventory accordingly, the store promotes and presents that merchandise in a manner which will most appeal to that clientele.

Since the fashion image of a store is determined by the type of merchandise it sells and the characteristics of its sales promotion activities, stores which sell little or poorly styled fashion apparel and employ unimaginative sales promotion techniques automatically project a "poor" fashion image. As the American consumer becomes increasingly fashion oriented, retailers are consciously trying to maintain or upgrade their image. Changing an image, however, is a huge and difficult task, and successful transformations are few and far between. Bloomingdale's is one of the few, and probably the most impressive example of how a store can systematically change and improve that very important ingredient known as a store's fashion image.

FOCUS ON THE INDUSTRY

FROM BLOOMINGDALE'S TO "BLOOMIE'S" (CHANGING A FASHION IMAGE)

Manhattan's Bloomingdale's is one of the country's most exciting fashion trend-setters. It draws people from all over the world and it is not unusual to see international film, television, and political celebrities mingling with the public as each looks at and buys one of the thousands of exciting items alluringly displayed throughout the store.

Although it has been in business over 100 years—it celebrated its centennial in 1972—Bloomingdale's did not always enjoy its current reputation as an international fashion pace-setter.

The original store is located at 59th Street and Lexington Avenue in what is now an affluent area of high rise apartments and office buildings. At the end of World War II, however, it was surrounded by tenements and small shops, and a lot of its business was in low-end, low priced merchandise.

When the post-war building boom began to upgrade other parts of the city, Bloomingdale's realized that, in time, its neighborhood would also be upgraded into a district of affluent residents and high-income career people. To attract these two groups, the store began to alter its image, introducing three ingredients into its merchandising policies: quality, fashion, excitement.

The change involved every aspect of the store—merchandise, advertising, publicity, display, and service. The transformation took place in stages, department by department. As the quality of the merchandise in one department was improved, attention was directed to the next. Once a department's merchandise was upgraded, it was imaginatively displayed and advertised to the public. Displays became "showcases." Ads stressed fashion. Even the store logo was changed. The "new" Bloomingdale's was aggressively and expertly promoted to the public.

Although the changes began as early as the late 40s, it was not until the 60s that Bloomingdale's new image wholly crystalized. The revolutionary fashion of that period provided the store with just the type of material it needed. Fashion was young and avant-garde; life styles unrestricted. Immediately, Bloomingdale's aligned itself with these trends, and soon every department in the store—from designer dresses to stationery—was successfully catering to its upper income target market with the newest, trendy merchandise. By the 70s, the store had become "Bloomie's"—the "in place" to shop.

Today, Bloomingdale's reputation as a fashion leader is firmly established. It draws customers from the city's outlying suburban areas as well as from its own posh neighborhood. The store's fame as a trendsetter also attracts Seventh Avenue manufacturers and the country's retailing executives who "shop" the store religiously for trends that are usually six months ahead of the rest of the country.

The store itself has become a sort of "social gathering place." An after-hours charity fashion show or an afternoon wine-tasting party promoting a $45 book on *The Joys of Wine* are daily, rather than rare occurrences. Many of these activities take place on Saturdays, and "Bloomie's" has become a Saturday social hangout for the young and affluent New Yorker—a place to meet old acquaintances or develop new ones.

Although Bloomingdale's has won fame because of its fashion leadership, the store's success in changing and upgrading its image to cater to a changing clientele has also made retailing history. Its methods are now known as the Bloomingdale's formula: identify your customer, and then woo that customer by presenting distinctive merchandise in imaginative displays, with a great deal of showmanship.

TERMS TO REMEMBER

special events
media
institutional ad
editorial credit
direct mail
publicity
press release
visual merchandising
fashion image
co-op advertising
The Bloomingdale's formula

HIGHLIGHTS OF THE CHAPTER

- The advertising, display, publicity, and other techniques used by retailers to induce sales is called promotion. All medium to large stores employ promotion activities to sell fashion merchandise, but those activities vary depending on the promotion policies of a store.
- The fashion office of a store has many fashion promotion responsibilities. They include presenting fashion shows, participating in store special events, coordinating fashion promotions with maga-

zines, supplying merchandise for store displays, and advising on the fashion "look" of store fashion ads.

- Buying space or time in newspapers, magazines, radio, and television is known as advertising. Fashion retailers use all mediums for advertising, but retailers consider newspapers their greatest business builders.
- The brochures and catalogs stores mail to customers' homes are known as direct mail. The gasoline shortages of the mid-70s prompted stores to increase mail-order offerings. This form of solicitation was a great success and continues to be widely used.
- Free and voluntary mention in the media is known as publicity. To obtain publicity, retailers maintain expert publicity departments which supply the media with interesting information or "news" about their stores.
- Visual merchandising is also known as "display" and refers to the presentation of merchandise in a store.
- The fashion image of a store refers to the impression the public has of a store's fashion expertise. Most present day retailers spend an enormous amount of time and money to maintain a favorable fashion image for their store.

QUESTIONS

1. Describe the structure of a sales promotion division in a retail store, and explain the function of each department.
2. Name and describe the three basic responsibilities of a fashion office.
3. On paper, organize a typical store fashion show, using newspaper and magazine pictures as merchandise. Group the merchandise thematically in the order you think it should be presented and write a simple commentary.
4. How and when did newspaper fashion advertising originate in this country? Define an institutional ad.
5. What are the "big five" fashion magazines in the United States? Describe the fashion philosophy of each. What is an editorial credit in a magazine?
6. How do stores pay their direct mail production costs? Obtain several pieces of direct mail sent to your home and debate the sales provoking qualities of each.

7. What do you think is the effectiveness of the fashion advertising retailers are presenting on television? Explain.
8. How do local retailers transmit information or "news" of their store to the media for the purposes of publicity?
9. Visit several large stores in your area and "shop" their windows and interiors, looking for the fashion themes each store is trying to project through their displays. Rate the efforts of the stores and explain your ratings.
10. Name the three factors a store must consider in developing a favorable fashion image. Rate the fashion image of one of your local stores. How do you think that image could be improved?

BIBLIOGRAPHY

ANSPACH, KARLENE, *The Why of Fashion.* Ames, Iowa: Iowa State University Press, 1967.

GRACE, EVELYN, *Introduction to Fashion Merchandising.* Englewood Cliffs, New Jersey: Prentice-Hall, Inc., 1978.

HAMBURGER, ESTELLE, *The Fashion Business—It's All Yours.* San Francisco: Canfield Press, 1976.

———, *History of the menswear Industry 1890–1950,* Men's Wear 60th Anniversary Issue. New York: Fairchild Publication, 1950.

JOHNSON, LAURENCE A., *Over The Counter and On The Shelf: Country Storekeeping in America, 1620–1920.* New York: Bonanza Books, 1961.

KELLY, KATIE, *The Wonderful World of Women's Wear Daily.* New York: Saturday Review Press, 1972.

KITWELL, CLAUDIA B., AND MARGARET C. CHRISTMAN, *Suiting Everyone: The Democratization of Clothing in America.* Washington, D.C., published for the National Museum of History and Technology by the Smithsonian Institution Press, 1974.

MAHONEY, TOM, AND LEONARD SLOAN, *The Great Merchants.* New York: Harper & Row Publishers, 1966.

MARCUS, STANLEY, *Minding the Store.* Boston: Little, Brown and Company, 1976.

———, *1977 Sheldon's Retail and Phelon's Resident Buyers,* 93rd ed. New York: Phelon, Sheldon & Marsar, Inc., 1977.

PINTEL, GERALD, AND JAY DIAMOND, *Retailing,* 2nd ed. Englewood Cliffs, N.J.: Prentice-Hall, 1977.

TROXELL, MARY D., *Fashion Merchandising.* New York: McGraw-Hill, 1976.

WITTKIN, HERBERT, "An Image is a Multi-Faceted Thing," *Readings in Modern Retailing.* New York: National Retail Merchants Association, 1969.

VI

THE ENVIRONMENT OF TODAY'S FASHION

Since the overall direction of the fashion industry is rooted in the wants and needs of the fashion consumer, the success of those in the industry depends largely upon their ability to analyze consumers and define those wants and needs. This final section begins by reviewing some of the methods and techniques of consumer research which help the fashion industry indentify and anticipate the demands of its customers. It concludes by offering observations on the future direction of some aspects of the fashion industry.

14

ANALYZING AND UNDERSTANDING THE CONSUMER

OBJECTIVES

After reading this chapter, you should be able to:

- Define the "marketing concept" and describe the phases firms pass through before reaching it.
- Understand what it means for a firm to be "marketing oriented."
- Explain the four steps in consumer fashion research.
- Define "demographics" and "psychographics" and show how they are used in market segmentation.
- Describe the American fashion consumer of today in demographic and psychographic terms.

THE MARKETING CONCEPT

Before presenting a product to the public, fashion manufacturers and retailers spend a great deal of time and money analyzing its potential user: the consumer. This was not always so. The American fashion industry went through two previous periods of development before it became consumer oriented and made the consumer the focal point of its marketing decisions.

During its first stage of development, the industry emphasized the acquisition of technical know-how and machinery. Termed *the production phase,* the major concern of the industry was to "set up shop" through the development of land, labor, and capital. As discussed in Part Two, this production phase began shortly after the American Revolution and lasted through the early 1900s.

By the 1900s, the fashion industry's sophisticated production techniques were able to produce huge quantities of ready-to-wear. In order to distribute these goods among America's expanding population, the industry entered into its second stage of development: *the distribution phase.* During this phase, manufacturers were primarily concerned with developing inexpensive, but efficient methods of distribution and on finding the right type of retail outlets for their goods.

Once the industry was equipped with efficient production and distribution facilities, it was able to provide the American consumer with a wide array of fashion merchandise. However, the industry assumed a dictatorial position on the styling of that merchandise. Designers, magazine editors, and other industry "fashion authorities" set strict guidelines for "proper dress." For years consumers accepted and wore the styles the industry created; as a result the industry believed that the fashion consumer needed and, in fact, demanded specific fashion direction.

In 1970, the industry's dictatorial power over consumer fashions abruptly changed. That year, there was a literal consumer revolt against the industry's imposed midi (longuette) look. The rejection of the mid-calf length skirts by consumers was an expensive and disastrous marketing lesson for some fashion firms. But it made the industry realize that it now had to observe and listen to the consumer. It had to produce the type of fashion the consumers wanted—not the type of fashion the industry "experts" dictated to be "right." Manufacturers, retailers, and others in the industry began to focus on the needs and wants of the consumer—signaling the kind of approach necessary for phase three: *using the marketing concept.*

In Chapter 1, *fashion marketing* was defined as directing the flow of fashion goods from producer to consumer in order to profitably satisfy consumer needs. A company which functions under this marketing concept, plans its entire operation around the idea of satisfying the consumer. It begins by defining its customer and identifying the unfilled needs and desires that customer has. It then goes on to develop products and sales strategies which will cater to those needs and desires while yielding a profit for the company. A firm of this type is considered *marketing oriented.* It produces the "right" products and distributes them in the "right" location, at the "right" price, and at the "right" time—by using the consumer (its market) to help it define "right." Now we can see why it is essential for those in the fashion industry to know as much as there is to know about their perspective customers.

FOCUS ON THE INDUSTRY

DIANE von FURSTENBERG— A MARKETING STORY

Growing up to become a beautiful and wealthy princess is a common fantasy among little girls. Actually having the dream cone true is exceptional.

But Diane von Furstenberg is exceptional. She is by no means a typical storybook princess. Instead, she is an ambitious and effective entrepreneur. She works hard and long hours managing her fashion apparel empire which began in 1970 with a $30,000 investment. Today, that empire generates over $130 million in sales each year.

Dubbed the "designer who put women back into dresses," the von Furstenberg empire was built on marketing a simple little jersey wrap dress. Although unable to sew and untrained in designing, the 22-year-old Diane worked closely with Italian fabric manufacturer Angelo Ferretti and created several sample dresses. She brought the dresses to New York and they were featured in *Vogue* magazine, thanks to then editor-in-chief Diana Vreeland.

As business began to increase, Diane went to Seventh Avenue to find a manufacturer who would handle volume dress production. After being turned down by such companies as Jonathan Logan and David Crystal, Diane decided to open her own showroom on Seventh Avenue and a factory in Como, Italy.

Today, the von Furstenberg empire consists of much more than the little wrap dress business. There is Diane von Furstenberg Importing—the division which handles cosmetics and fragrances, and Diane von Furstenberg Creative Services Inc., which handles advertising and promotion of her products. The *Diane von Furstenberg Book of Beauty*, published in 1976, has added additional revenues to the empire as do the many franchised products bearing the von Furstenberg name. These include: stationery, costume jewelry, furs, handbags, lingerie, patterns, raincoats, scarves, shoes, sunglasses, table linens, tops, umbrellas, and rainhats. These products alone generate close to $90 million a year in sales.

How did Princess von Furstenberg become such a successful fashion marketer? The success of this story is not in a name or in a title. Diane is, above all, an astute business woman. She is fully aware of the most important marketing rule: know your customer's needs and fill them.

She began her dress business at a time when everyone was wearing pants. Diane sensed women were ready for a change—for something new.

Her dress was designed for a specific customer: an older woman looking for a sophisticated look. A woman who wanted to feel sexy without feeling like a sex object.

The dress was wearable by a variety of figure types. It felt comfortable, was packable, and suitable for anytime, anywhere. Costing under a hundred dollars at retail, the moderate price was also right.

Because of her name, the dress could be sold in high fashion stores. Because of the price it could also be sold by moderately priced retailers. And moreover, Diane was willing to make an all out effort to personally promote the dress. She spent much of her time visiting stores, giving lectures, being photographed by trade and consumer magazines, and simply shaking hands with salespeople and customers. To supplement her efforts, co-op advertising was carefully planned with retailers to promote both the dress and the von Furstenberg name.

The Diane von Furstenberg story is not a fairy tale. Instead, it is an account which demonstrates what effective marketing is all about: knowing the customer and offering the right product, at the right price, time, and place, with the right promotional methods.

CONSUMER FASHION RESEARCH

In order to obtain detailed and specific consumer information, firms in the fashion industry cannot rely on casual observation or guesswork. Instead, they must turn to the structured, analytical, and formal approach used in all types of consumer research, obtaining information rationally, honestly, and objectively—so as not to contrive results. The best and most often used consumer research approach is based on the *scientific method.*

Following the guidelines of this method, consumer fashion research can be organized into four steps: (1) identify the potential market; (2) gather statistical data about the market and its sales potential; (3) segment the market in terms of existing and potential needs; and (4) determine and develop products which will best satisfy those needs—testing the products on a sample group before distributing them to the public.

For example, having identified its market as a group of fashionable, affluent, status-conscious consumers, a firm that makes expensive handbags can develop merchandise which will cater to the needs of that type of consumer. It will produce highly styled, high quality, expensive items—introducing the all-important "status" ingredient through the use of unusual materials and styling, or through the popular touch of a designer signature.

Identifying the Potential Market

The term "market" can have many meanings, all of which connote a gathering of people for the purpose of exchanging goods and services. Specifically, the market for fashion goods may be defined as a group of people who have the money and the desire to purchase fashion merchandise. These people may be identified and described by using two kinds of data: *demographic* and *psychographic.*

Demography is the use of statistics to describe people. Some of the most common ways to describe population demographically is through breakdowns of age, income, location, occupation, and so on. The information is categorized numerically, making use of the principles of statistics. For example, "in 1976 the median age of the U.S. population was 28 years" is a statistic which means that of all the people living in the U.S., 50 percent were older than 28 and 50 percent were younger.

Since the definition of a market for fashion goods includes the desires or motivations of people, additional data about their psychological concerns is needed. The kind of statistical data which evaluates a person's attitudes, values, and beliefs as it affects behavior is called *psychographics.* Less exact than demographics, it tries to measure how a person's life style influences his attitude toward a certain product, affects his evaluation of the product, and contributes to his purchasing decisions.

Although obtaining this kind of consumer information is difficult and prediction methods are complex, it is generally agreed that understanding and analyzing the consumer is incomplete without psychographic data.

Gathering Data

Basically, data gathering for any kind of research is done in three ways: (1) by *observation* of the subject; (2) by a *survey* of the subject (through face-to-face, telephone, or mail interviews); and (3) by *conducting experiments* with the subject. These experiments take place under controlled scale-model circumstances set up by the researcher.

The information obtained through any of these three data gathering techniques is labelled either *primary* or *secondary* data. Primary data is first-hand information which is collected from scratch, and which has not previously been available to the researcher from any other source.

Primary data is very specific and detailed, causing it to be somewhat limited in its application, as well as rather expensive to obtain. Secondary data on the other hand, is readily available material which has been gathered and published by others. It is often free or inexpensive and can be obtained from such suppliers as the U.S. government, magazines, periodicals, industry trade associations, and year-end company reports; or it can be purchased from marketing research firms, computer companies, or advertising agencies at nominal cost. Usually, secondary data offers general information and is lacking in certain particulars needed for sound decision making. Therefore, most companies gathering consumer data use both kinds—primary and secondary. Customarily, they begin by culling needed information from secondary data sources. If the information they require is unavailable or if they need more detailed information, they then revert to gathering primary data.

Segmenting the Market

Once a firm has collected and categorized demographic and psychographic data on the total fashion market, an analysis of that data begins. Hopefully, the analysis will reveal "sub-markets" consisting of groups of people with similar characteristics, financial means, and motivations who are potential users of the fashion producer's product or service. Each of these sub-markets or market segments is called a firm's *target market.*

Upon identifying its target market, a fashion firm will make a further analysis into the characteristics of that market looking for answers to several key questions. For example, does the target market have similar or different psychographic and demographic characteristics from the overall fashion market? Is the target market going to increase or decrease in size during the next several years? The more a firm knows about its target market, the easier it is to identify and profitably cater to the needs of that market. Should a firm choose to satisfy more than one target market, it does so simply by diversifying its product line.

FOCUS ON THE INDUSTRY

SEGMENTING THE FASHION MARKET

Using people's life styles, attitudes, and beliefs to help determine the products which should be manufactured is not yet a widespread practice in the fashion industry. Some have hesitated to try market segmentation because they feel it is too difficult, too inaccurate, or even not at all necessary.

However, a most successful application of market segmentation was undertaken by Warner Slimwear, a division of Warnaco, Inc., and it proved how valuable market segmentation can be.

The company was interested in producing a new line of bras. Unsure of the type of customer it could most profitably service, it undertook an extensive marketing research program. It obtained information both demographic and psychographic and which, when analyzed, revealed a variety of attitudes and preferences in reference to bras.

The research revealed five distinct target markets, as follows: 1) conservative, 2) fashionable, 3) brand conscious, 4) outgoing, 5) home/price oriented. Further research enabled Warner to evaluate the size and financial potential of each segment on a national scale. They uncovered that the most profitable segments were: 2) fashionable, 3) brand conscious, 4) outgoing. Thus, the company was able to eliminate segments 1 and 5 as unprofitable markets. It was already catering to segments 2 and 3, so segment 4 became the focus of its attention.

As a result, a sheer stretch bra named "Starkers" was specifically designed for and marketed to this segment. Reorders were three times the normal level. Both Warnaco and participating retailers enjoyed welcome additional profits. In their estimation, segmenting the market for the development of saleable fashion goods is possible, sometimes necessary, and certainly profitable.

Testing

After a product is developed, the last step in the research process is to test a target market's reaction to that product. There are several ways to test a product; the methods vary with each type of business. For instance, apparel manufacturers may produce sample runs—small quantities of specific styles—and place them with select retailers for careful monitoring of consumer reaction and sales. Textile firms may survey their apparel manufacturer accounts by sending them fabric samples for their reaction. And magazines may conduct surveys to obtain feedback from their readers on newly advertised products.

Regardless of the method a firm uses in its testing, the critical testing factor is the selection of a sample group of users which is truly representative of a firm's target market. Those surveyed and analyzed must be an exact, albeit miniature, duplicate of the target market. The closer a sample group comes to accurately representing a target market, the more accurate are the test results. Careful selection of a sample group, therefore, is the most important factor during the testing phase of market research.

The idea of "know your customer" is not new to the fashion industry. But much of the consumer research of the past was informal and perhaps subjective. Today—especially since the emergence of the giant textile, apparel, publishing, and retail companies—many firms have full-time consumer research and product development programs which use sophisticated and elaborate computer systems to precisely and objectively get to "know their customer."

PROFILING THE AMERICAN FASHION CONSUMER

We will now examine how demographic and psychographic data on the American consumer is utilized by the fashion industry to develop fashion products and services for their consumer.

The demographic data includes statistics on population size, age, and location; educational achievement; occupation; and purchasing power. The psychographics describe attitudes towards affluence; materialism; marriage and the family; the quality of life; and the importance of self.

Demographic Characteristics

Population Size. Population size is controlled by four factors: births, deaths, immigration and emigration. Between 1776 and 1976, the population of the United States jumped from 2.5 million to 216 million. There were tremendous increases in the country's birth and immigration rates. At the same time, death and emigration rates declined. (Virtually no emigration has taken place since few people wish to leave the United States.) Each of these factors contributed to the extraordinary population growth of the United States during its first two hundred years.

Past experience has made the fashion industry keenly aware of the effect changes in the size of the population can have on its business. For instance, the clothing demands of the great waves of immigrants who came to this country during the late 1800s literally built the foundation of America's ready-to-wear industry. Subsequent population increases—such as the post-World War II baby boom which created tremendous business for maternity and children's wear firms—continued to have a profound impact on the growth of the industry.

During the 1960s and 70s, population growth conspicuously slowed down, making these years known as the "zero population growth period." The era is characterized by the lowest recorded birth rate in the country's history.

Most demographers agree that the slow-down in population growth will continue. They project that the country's population will increase from its present size of 216 million to about 240 million through the 1980s—a relatively small increase when compared with the great population explosions of the past. Aware of this projection, the fashion industry no longer expects population expansion to be an important determining factor in the future of its business (see Fig. 14-1).

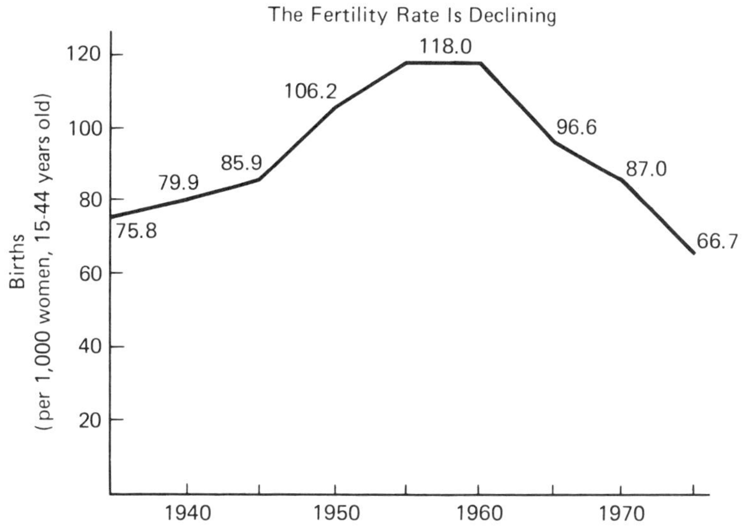

FIGURE 14-1. Population growth rate, 1935-1975
Data based on statistics from the Bureau of the Census

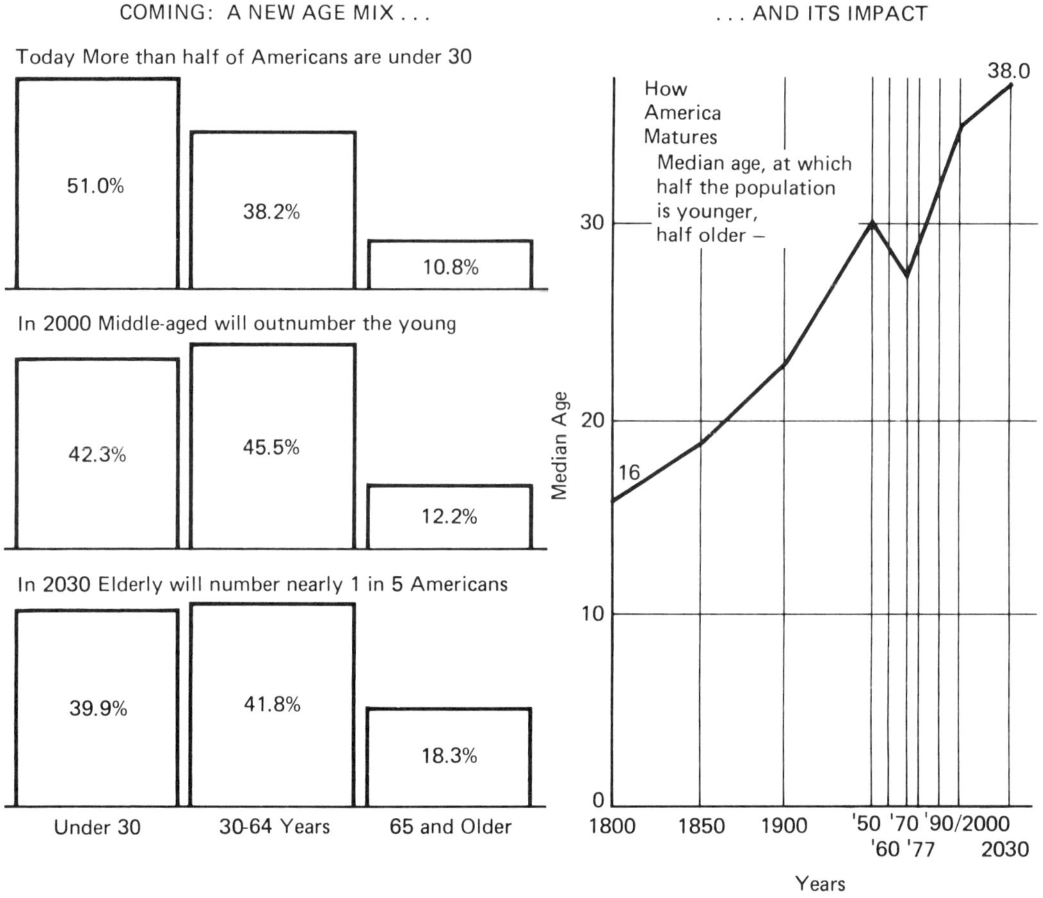

FIGURE 14-2. Shifts in the median age of the population
Source: U.S. Department of Commerce

Population Age. Lower birth rates and increased life expectancy have also affected the average *age* of the country's population. In 1976, the population's median age[1] was 28 years, 9 months. By 2036, the median age is expected to jump to 36 years, 9 months. This "graying" of America is more obvious when expressed through the following statistics. Between 1976 and 1991—a mere 15 years—the number of people 35 to 49 years of age will increase by an unbelievable 76 percent; the number who will be 50 to 64 will increase by 23 percent; and the number in the over 65 age group will increase by 30 percent. By contrast, the under 35 age group will grow a mere 17 percent. In essence, these figures project two

[1]Median age means that 50 percent of the population is older than a certain age and 50 percent is younger than that same age.

important market trends: the emergence of larger "middle age" and "senior citizen" markets; and the decline of the "youth" market (see Fig. 14-2).

Because of these trends, the fashion industry has recognized that the majority of its future business will come from increasingly older groups—and it began to shift from the youth-oriented styling of the 60s. It is now creating merchandise which tends to be more sophisticated and which appeals more to those older groups.

Location. What people wear and how they buy is very much affected by *where* they live. It is therefore extremely important for the fashion industry to know exactly how the American population is distributed throughout the country.

Americans are not, of course, evenly divided among the fifty states. In fact, nearly half of the present population is located in ten states. But

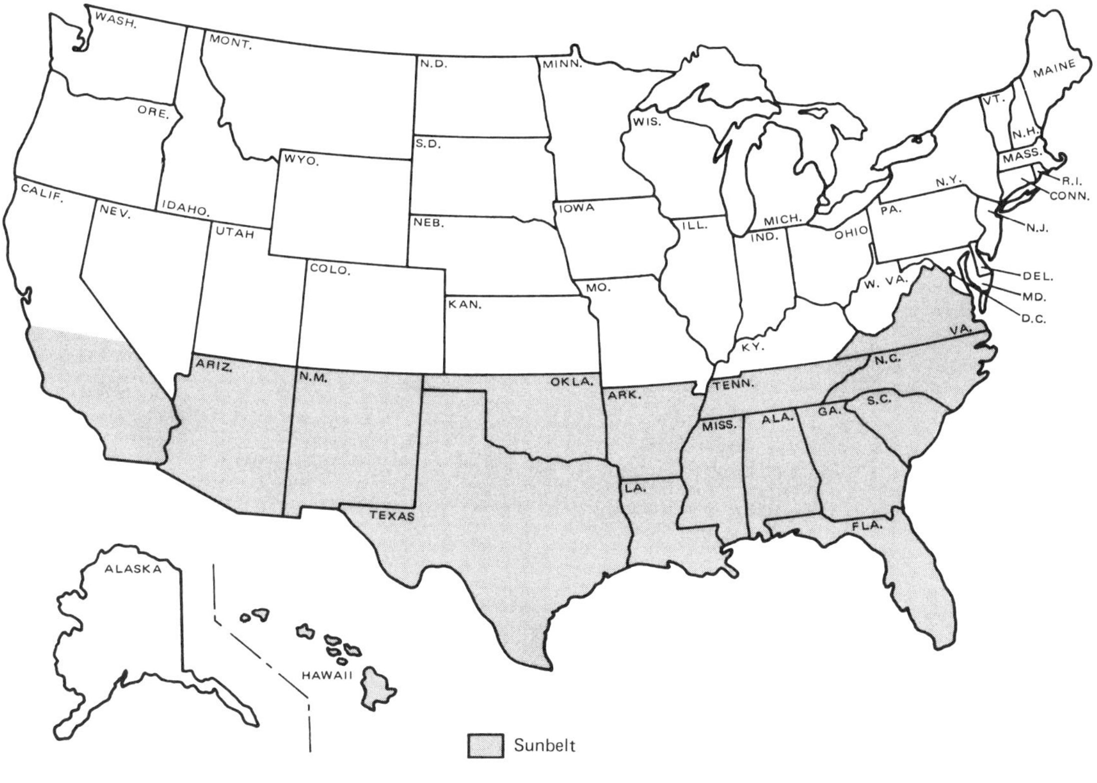

FIGURE 14-3. Sunbelt states

Americans have become an increasingly mobile group and the country's population is very much on the move. By the 1990s, substantial population shifts are expected to take place, drastically increasing the number of people in some states while decreasing the number of people in other states.

Presently, the greatest population growth is in the southern and southeastern part of the United States. Known as the "sunbelt" region, this area is attracting people from the older and colder northeastern states; its population is expected to continue to increase at a tremendous rate (see Fig. 14-3).

Within the states, there have been other profound population shifts. Both rural areas and central cities have been losing their populations to suburban areas. Most of these areas are within commuting distance to jobs in the inner cities and are often referred to as the "urban sprawl."

As Americans change their location from city to suburb, north to south, even state to state, they automatically change their life style. The more drastic the move, the more drastic the change in their clothing needs, their tastes, and their buying patterns. In order to successfully service the needs of a mobile population, the fashion industry studies population shifts and plans its marketing strategies accordingly. Manufacturers, for instance, translate a population increase in the "sunbelt" into an increase in their production and sales of warm weather clothes, while retailers see the shift to the suburbs as a signal for them to open store branches to meet their moving customer's needs.

By closely monitoring these and other trends in population shifts, the fashion industry has much better opportunities to keep existing markets and capitalize on new ones.

Education. The average amount of education an American receives increases every year. In 1960, for instance, all Americans over the age of twenty-five had an average of ten years of education. By 1976, that average had gone up to twelve years, with nearly 17 percent of the population completing four years of college. The trend toward higher education continues—not only for recent high school graduates, but for women and older adults as well, and these educational achievements have made the United States the most educated country in the world.

Presently, clothing expenditures represent only 8 percent of a consumer's disposable income (amount of money left after taxes to spend on necessities and luxuries). Since, in most cases, the motivation toward higher education is "a better paying job," to the fashion industry a better educated consumer represents a more affluent consumer—one who has more money for clothing expenditures. The industry cannot overlook the fact that a better educated consumer is also a more discriminating one, however, and it has been increasing both the quality and the appeal of its fashion merchandise in order to meet the high demands of the better educated consumer.

Occupation. Perhaps the most significant result of America's higher educational achievement has been the tremendous changes which have taken place in the country's labor market over the last thirty years.

Two major changes have occurred. The first involves a shift from blue collar to white collar jobs. The number of blue collar jobs which require manual or physical labor has decreased—while the number of white collar jobs requiring technical skills and specialized services has increased.

The second change pertains to an increase in the number of women who work. By 1977, women made up 49 percent of the United States work force. They were, and are, performing all kinds of jobs—from laborers to corporate executives. Many are "career" oriented, remaining on the job for longer periods of time and refusing to drop out after marriage or while raising a family.

Both these occupational changes in America's population have directly affected the fashion buying habits of the consumer and the fashion offerings of the industry. For instance, even with relaxed dress codes, the suit remains the required office uniform for men, while tailored business-like apparel is considered proper for women. As the number of both male and female white collar workers increases, the demand for suitable "on the job" apparel intensifies, expanding the industry's production of men's and women's tailored business clothing.

Purchasing Power. The purchasing power of a consumer is determined by three factors: personal income; accumulated or net worth; and available consumer credit. In spite of present inflationary conditions, Americans now have more purchasing power than they have ever had. But over the years, the percentage of that purchasing power used to buy apparel has decreased. In 1950 for example, Americans spent 12 percent of their income on apparel while in 1976 that percentage declined to 8 percent.

Most fashion firms define their competitors as those who produce similar goods. There are other firms, however, which believe that in order to capture a large share of the American dollar, the fashion industry will have to re-define its competition and vie with those outside the industry for the consumer's "discretionary dollar." (The "discretionary dollar" is the amount spent on luxury items.) Apparel, long classified as a necessity, must be presented as a "necessary luxury"—upgraded through promotion so it is considered an exciting and important part of "the good life."

Psychographic Characteristics

As defined earlier, psychographic data presents a person's attitudes, values, and beliefs. An analysis of that data can reveal how those attitudes, values, and beliefs will influence a person's purchases.

Attitudes toward Personal Spending. Purchasing power may enable the consumer to buy goods, but the attitude of a consumer toward spending actually determines whether or not that consumer will buy those goods. That attitude is governed by two factors: (1) a consumer's past economic experiences, and (2) the current economic conditions or affluence of the country.

Remember the Great Depression of the 1930s? Those over fifty years of age do, and those difficult times have greatly influenced the attitude of that age group toward personal spending. Conservative and cautious, many reject credit or impulse buying and consider job security and financial solvency ("a little something in the bank") most important. For the younger, under-fifty age group, these considerations are not so important. Raised in an affluent society, they consider easy credit and free spending a way of life—and place relatively little importance on savings and job security.

The condition of the country's economy, however, can alter the established spending attitudes of both groups. When the United States' economic system is healthy, both jobs and goods are plentiful. America appears to be a "land of plenty." Under those conditions, the older generation is encouraged to relax its normally cautious attitudes and increase its personal spending. Should the economy slow down—making jobs and goods scarce and expensive—the free-spending young generation tightens up its purse strings and becomes more concerned with the stability of a job.

From a fashion marketing perspective, a positive attitude on the part of the consumer toward personal spending is absolutely essential. If consumer confidence is shaken, even slightly, fashion purchases are among the first to be curtailed. The use of psychographic surveys recently developed on consumer confidence allows the fashion industry to monitor any changes in the attitude of the consumer which might have a subsequent effect on consumer spending.

Attitudes toward Materialism. Americans have always used appearance, possessions, and purchases as expressions of affluence (status symbols). During the 60s there was much talk about a trend toward "antimaterialism" but in reality the trend was not against materialism as much as it was against the old, established "status symbols." Materialism continued to exist; only the symbols changed. Obvious signs of wealth became unpopular and distasteful—and were rejected in favor of understated possessions. For instance, the Cadillac and the mink coat of the 60s were replaced by customized vans, foreign cars, and a wardrobe of casually styled fur coats.

On the surface, these and other present-day status symbols appear to be unpretentious. But their high cost—which makes them available to a fortunate few—automatically makes them materialistic expressions of affluence and position.

Attitudes toward Marriage and the Family. Although there has been much discussion on the rise of communal arrangements, living together relationships, open marriages, and childless marriages—surveys indicate that the traditional monogamous marriage continues to be adopted by the majority of people; and that most married couples will have children. There have been, however, observable changes in some of the attitudes surrounding the basic institution of marriage.

To begin with, people are now deciding to marry later. Before they marry, they establish one of several types of living arrangements. Some live alone or with one or more members of the same sex. A few live with a member of the opposite sex and, in their case, the decision to marry is usually prompted by the desire to have children.

Attitudes toward children have also changed. The preference toward large families has dissappeared and most couples now consider one or two children "ideal."

Because of the increase in the divorce rate—one out of every three marriages end in divorce—the outlook on divorce has also changed; it is now considered an acceptable solution to an unsatisfactory marriage.

These changes in the attitude toward marriage and family have been reflected throughout different segments of the fashion industry. A delay in marriage and children for working women has caused the industry to increase their production of suitable "nine to five" business clothes. A decline in the birth rate has meant a reduction in the production quotas of children's wear. And since the social values of a society are always reflected in the fashion trends of its apparel, the liberalized attitudes towards marriage and the family have created an equally permissive attitude on the part of both the consumer and the industry toward choice of dress.

Attitudes toward the Quality of Life. As people become better educated, make more money, and have more leisure time—they expect more from life. Their pursuit of the "good life" increases. They take a greater interest in music, theatre, dance, and other cultural arts; they develop a keener appreciation for quality and beauty; and, in general, they seem to show a deeper appreciation of the finer things in life. This appreciation extends itself to food, environment and, of course, clothes.

Clothing, as described in Chapter 2, serves many purposes. In addition to offering protection and comfort, it serves as a tool for expressing one's affluence, personality, and taste. For those who have developed keen fashion tastes, clothes serve as a personal statement.

As more and more Americans improve their life style, the fashion industry has been increasingly pressed to produce finer fashion products that will satisfy both basic needs and esthetic tastes. As a result, most current fashion reflects an improvement in quality and taste, adding enormous to the overall quality of the American life style.

Attitudes toward the Importance of Self. When people begin to upgrade the quality of their life style, it is natural for them to become much more introspective—to concentrate on themselves. Self understanding and self-beautification become prime objectives. The success of countless how-to books, offering advice on improving one's emotional, sexual, and physical state is directly related to the increasing interest people have been taking in themselves.

Psychographic surveys which reveal how consumers are satisfying their search for self-improvement are important to the fashion industry. For instance, efforts toward physical self-improvement have resulted in a growing pre-occupation with jogging and tennis, as well as a surge in the popularity of health and beauty spas. As survey data informs them of these trends, manufacturers are able to provide the consumer with sportswear that is suitable to wear for these activities.

Demographic and psychographic characteristics of the United States population are constantly changing. In order to correctly identify consumers and their needs, consumer research must be continuously updated through an ongoing, uninterrupted process. Only the most accurate data can help the fashion industry properly profile and evaluate the American consumer so that it may provide them with the "right" product at the "right" place, price, and time.

TERMS TO REMEMBER

marketing concept
scientific method
demographics
psychographics
segmenting the market
primary data
secondary data

target market
purchasing power

HIGHLIGHTS OF THE CHAPTER

- Before becoming marketing oriented, the fashion industry passed through two phases: the production phase and the distribution phase.
- Being marketing oriented means using the marketing concept which begins with defining the customer and identifying unfulfilled needs.
- To learn about the consumer, consumer fashion research is done using the principles of the scientific method.
- The market for fashion goods is defined in terms of both demographic and psychographic characteristics.
- Demographics is the use of statistics to describe a population.
- Psychographics refers to describing people's attitudes, values, and beliefs as they affect behavior.
- Demographic and psychographic data is gathered by observation, survey, or conducting experiments.
- The data is analyzed to determine potential market segments or target markets.
- The final step in the consumer research process is testing.
- The American fashion consumer is changing demographically in terms of population size, age, and location; educational achievement, occupation, and purchasing power.
- The American fashion consumer may be described psychographically in terms of attitudes towards affluence, materialism, marriage and the family, the quality of life, and the importance of self.

QUESTIONS

1. What are the three stages of development that the fashion industry has passed through? What was the concern in each phase?

2. What happened in 1970 which caused the end of fashion dictatorship?
3. What does *using the marketing concept* mean in the fashion industry?
4. List the four steps of organization used to obtain consumer fashion research.
5. What are demographics? Give four demographic characteristics which the fashion industry can use to identify a market.
6. Define the term psychographics. Give four psychographic characteristics which the fashion industry can use to identify a market.
7. List three ways to gather data for fashion consumer research.
8. What is a firm's "target market"?
9. What is the critical concern in testing a new fashion product?
10. What is happening to the size, age and location of the U.S. population? Specifically, how will the fashion industry be affected?
11. How do education and occupation influence consumer spending for fashion merchandise?
12. What is meant by the term "purchasing power"? What has happened to the amount spent on fashion goods since 1950?
13. How does consumer confidence affect consumer spending for fashion goods?
14. How have changes in marriage and the family affected fashion?
15. Attitudes towards the quality of life and oneself have changed. How has the fashion industry responded to these changes?

15

FUTURE DIRECTIONS OF THE FASHION INDUSTRY

OBJECTIVES

After reading this chapter, you should be able to:

- Name some sources of inspiration for future fashions.
- Discuss how the role of the designer is changing.
- Discuss the problems facing American producers and retailers. Suggest what can be done to solve them.
- Describe the fashion consumer of the future.

In this final chapter of *Marketing Today's Fashion,* the authors will focus on the future of the fashion business. From the primary markets to the ultimate consumer, the watchword is *change.*

Fashion marketing in the 1980s and 1990s will be different than it is today. New products, new technologies, new methods of distribution and promotion, as well as new consumer needs will replace many existing ones. In this chapter we will examine some of the specific elements of the business which are likely to undergo the greatest transformations. Other elements are not yet predictable. But the student of fashion should learn to expect and look for a constant stream of innovations and changes, for they will most assuredly occur.

WHERE WILL FASHION COME FROM?

A long-term forecast of specific future fashion trends is largely impossible and, for the purposes of this text, unnecessary. But it is safe—and pertinent—to make some observations on the future *source* of fashion trends. More than ever before *fashion will continue to mirror the times.* It will reflect society's prevailing preferences, satisfactorily meeting the wants and needs of the wearer . . . Specific styles will originate from all levels of society. Some will trickle-down; some will travel "bottom-up," while some will move horizontally. This democratization of fashion will be further encouraged by the fact that more people—from all levels of the social strata—are finding fashion affordable and thus increasingly available. . . . Thanks to the power of the mass media, specific style changes will continue to develop quickly—but *the life of overall fashion trends will continue to last a span of several years.* In summation, fashion will come from all areas of society—influenced by the people, the arts, the economy, politics, and the social environment; and overall trends should continue to have the seven to ten-year life span they have been having during the past several decades.

THE CHANGING WORLD OF THE FASHION DESIGNER

The 60s and 70s saw the professional world of fashion designers change drastically. They became the "stars" of the fashion business, with a celebrated status that evolved from more than just their designing activities. Today's top designers are heads of designing empires who, in addition to apparel, offer the public all types of fashion merchandise from fragrances to home furnishings. This trend toward diversification is growing and most designers will continue to concentrate on creating a *total* environment for the consumer. They will invade other markets and, as some have already done, style everything from automobile interiors to luggage, carpets, and even appliances in order to expand their areas of creativity. . . . In their efforts to reach a wider segment of the public, designers will enter into *world-wide activities,* establishing *international* networks of sales, production, and distribution centers. Through these foreign operations, designers will achieve world-wide recognition and, in essence, will become internationalized. A recent example of this trend was the naming of Pierre Cardin as special fashion consultant by the government of China. . . . Although designers will expand their creative and business activities, the recent democratization of fashion will prevent them from wielding a dictatorial influence on mass fashion. Most designers agree that their future role will be to *interpret—not dictate—fashion trends*. . . . Because of its unprofitability, the future of the French couture has long been uncertain and debatable. But most couturiers will continue with their couture operations, defending their existence by pointing to the enormous amount of publicity and prestige they get from the news-making collections. That publicity, they maintain, strongly propels the sales of their ready-to-wear operations. It is safe to assume then, that as long as the couture remains *news-worthy,* it will continue to exist. . . . "Picking up pins" at a designer house was once a way young, talented people got started in the fashion business, but manufacturers no longer have the time to train the unschooled and inexperienced. Moreover, as the role of the designer continues to broaden, design aspirants need the kind of advanced and intensive training which is only available academically. In the future, aspiring designers will have to *choose school over on-the-job training* as a means of learning their craft.

FUTURE TRENDS FOR AMERICAN FASHION PRODUCERS

For those American firms which produce textiles, leather, fur, and all manner of wearing apparel, the future contains several similar, overlapping problems. The most overriding of these problems is the ever-increasing *competition from imported goods.* Although the government has tried to relieve the situation by convincing some foreign countries to reduce their shipments to the United States, the problem is by no means solved. The situation cannot be corrected by simply imposing quotas and tariffs on imports. These steps would most likely lead to retaliatory measures which would hurt the exports of the United States. The fashion industry therefore, is considering—and will undoubtedly take—several alternate steps as part of the solution. First, they will try to increase consumer awareness and *demand for American goods* by upgrading the fashion excitement and quality of those goods. This step has already been successfully taken by the fur industry, and similar upgrading efforts will definitely be taken by most American fashion producers. . . . American producers will also try to increase their sales in *new, emerging foreign markets.* Around the world, countries are improving their standard of living and their people are increasingly able to afford more than just the living essentials. Astute, agressive American manufacturers intend to advantageously service the needs of these new markets. . . . With a larger, greatly diversified multinational market, producers will also undoubtedly *broaden their product lines.* Many firms are adding—and will continue to add—new lines and new products to increase their share of the market. . . . The most successful products and lines will be those which *combine fashion and practicality.* Along with fashion, consumers now expect fabrics that are easy to care for and clothes that are comfortable to wear. The future will belong to those who incorporate both factors into their fashion merchandise. . . . The recent trend toward a *separation* of operations in the manufacturing process will continue to grow. More and more manufacturers will change to an "outside shop" method of operation, turning the production process of their business to contractors in low-cost labor centers here and abroad. Designing and marketing activities will remain in New York, Los Angeles, and other fashion centers of the country . . . All in all, the future success of American fashion producers depends heavily on their flexibility, adaptability, and their readiness to respond to changing consumer demands. Fortunately, from the beginning, most American manufacturers have considered these three qualities a part of the industry's "way of life."

FUTURE TRENDS IN RETAILING

Gone are the days of planning and running a retail operation on guesswork and intuition. Present and future retailers will *rely more and more on sophisticated marketing research* methods to secure information that will help them with their decisions during the merchandising process. They will also increase their dependence on *computer technology* in order to upgrade the efficiency of their stores. Already in use are such computerized technological advances as point-of-sale registers (cash registers which are computer terminals and provide instant merchandise control), credit authorization systems, and optical scanners which can "read" information from merchandise tickets. But retailers are looking forward to enjoying many other new applications of the computer. Among these is the process of direct billing, whereby funds are automatically transferred from a customer's checking account to a store's account, eliminating the need for payment by personal check. Retailers also hope to increase the use of computerized merchandise control which provides invaluable up-to-the-minute computerized data on the sales performance of every piece of merchandise. Although retailers have been relatively slow in incorporating marketing research techniques and computer technology into their operations, the increasing competitiveness of the fashion business is certain to soon make these concepts routine in both large and small retail operations. . . . Greater *competition between retailers will increase the vulnerability of the small retailer.* Large corporations and conglomerates have the marketing expertise most small retailers lack and, under extremely competitive conditions, can win a larger share of the retail fashion dollar. Moreover, large firms are better equipped to absorb the financial losses which are often a part of the temperamental fashion business. The *small retailers that will survive are those who complement rather than compete with the giants.* Customers will continue to shop in boutiques and small specialty stores which offer the type of exciting, unique merchandise not easily found in large stores. They will also be drawn to the small retailer who is known for personalized one-to-one attention, custom alterations, special orders, and other services not usually given by large retail operations . . . As the competition between stores sharpens, stores will battle to obtain the best available help. Stores of all sizes will require—and demand—people with proper academic credentials, innovative ideas, and dynamic ability. They will need these people to attract those who can represent future success or failure to a store: tomorrow's fashion consumer.

TOMORROW'S FASHION CONSUMER

For retailer and manufacturer alike, clothing the fashion consumer of tomorrow promises to be extremely challenging. Fashion consumers will expect much *more for their money* in terms of product performance and wear. To meet those expectations, the industry must continually upgrade their merchandise and provide top quality control. . . . But consumers will also demand additional protection from sources outside the fashion industry. They have already prompted government agencies like the FTC (Federal Trade Commission) and FDA (Food and Drug Administration), who are charged with the responsibility of maintaining competition and honesty in the market place, to introduce such requirements as care and content labeling, product safety standards, and truthfulness of advertising claims. These government activities will no doubt be expanded as consumers press for greater protection . . . Because tomorrow's fashion consumer will be older, better educated, have more discretionary income, stay single longer and, when married, have fewer children, *he or she will be more self-conscious, comfort conscious, and fashion conscious.* In the June 1977 issue of *Vogue* magazine, designer Geoffrey Beene analyzed the fashion consumer. Although he was speaking of women, his opinions also apply to the attitudes of men. Both sexes have developed an independent, sharp, individual approach to fashion, one that promises to continue and intensify in the future. Quoting from Mr. Beene:

> . . . It used to be compulsive buying, but that isn't the case anymore. The way women are dressing today is extremely thought out—their

whole point of view, their wanting to be individual, their wanting the best of everything. As designers, we're doing our best to give it to them. They deserve it, and they have reached the point where they demand it.[1]

[1]Edith Gross, ed., "How You Look," *Vogue,* Vol. 167, No. 6 (June, 1977), p. 198. Copyright © 1977 by the Condé Nast Publications Inc.

BIBLIOGRAPHY

GROSSACK, MARTIN, *Understanding Consumer Behavior.* Boston: The Christopher Publishing House, 1966.

McCARTHY, E. JEROME, *Basic Marketing: A Managerial Approach,* 3rd ed. Homewood, Illinois: Richard D. Irwin, 1968.

PACKARD, SIDNEY, AND ABRAHAM RAINE, *Consumer Behavior and Fashion Marketing.* Dubuque, Iowa: Kendall/Hunt Publishing Company, 1977.

SCHWARTZ, DAVID, *Marketing Today—A Basic Approach.* New York: Harcourt, Brace, Jovanovich, 1973.

GLOSSARY

Accessories items which accompany basic items of wearing apparel. Examples are gloves and jewelry.

Adoption Process the flow of fashion from one class or group to another.

Adornment Theory contends that clothing originated as a result of the human desire to enhance one's self concept and sexual image among peers and the opposite sex.

Advertising the paid mention in any media of a person, product, or firm.

Bottom-Up Fashion fashion which originates with the masses and then moves to the upper classes above.

Boutique small shop selling unusual, fine merchandise. Also refers to an innovative method of merchandising and displaying merchandise.

Branch Store a suburban outlet under the direction of the main store; often carrying a modified line of merchandise.

Caution French term for deposit. Refers to a fee which is sometimes required of those attending a couture showing.

Chain Store two or more stores which are similar in physical appearance, carry the same merchandise, and are centrally owned and operated.

Chambre Syndicale de la Couture Parisienne organization which represents the French haute couture.

Classic style or design which remains in fashion year after year.

Collection a group of original designs presented by a designer or a manufacturer.

Color a phenomenon of light which, in a visual sense, distinguishes one object from another.

Combined-Need Theory contends that the origin of clothing was multidimensional, filling several human needs at the same time.

Conglomerates corporations which control a variety of enterprises in unrelated fields.

Consignment an arrangement between a manufacturer and a retailer whereby unsold goods are returned to the manufacturer along with monies from sold goods.

Conspicuous Consumption the wearing of certain clothes or the purchase of certain objects for the sake of improving one's status in the eyes of others.

Contractor a firm that does sewing and pressing for manufacturers on a contract basis.

Converter a firm that makes unfinished (greige) goods into finished fabric.

Corporate Retail Group single company made up of large department and specialty stores that were once independently owned.

Coty American Fashion Critics' Awards annual awards given to American designers for excellence in women's wear and menswear fashion design.

Couturier (male) or Couturière (female) French word for "dressmaker"; in the fashion business it is used to identify designers who create and sell the finest high-fashion, custom-made apparel.

Custom-Made an item of apparel made to individual specifications.

Demography the use of statistics to describe the characteristics of people such as age, income, education, and so on.

Department Store a store which offers both hard and soft lines of merchandise, and employs at least twenty-five people.

Derived Demand a need for primary products which originates with the ultimate consumers.

Design a unique version of a style. Designs consist of the elements of silhouette, texture, color, detail, and trim.

Detail various components or parts within a silhouette. Examples include collars, cuffs, and sleeve types.

Direct Mail printed matter featuring merchandise offerings which retailers mail directly to the consumer.

Discount Store stores which emphasize low prices and high volume, and de-emphasize store decor and display.

Display (see Visual Merchandising.)

Dry Goods Stores stores which carried wearing apparel and accessories for women.

Dual Distribution sale of goods by a manufacturer at both the wholesale and retail level.

Editorial Credit getting free mention as the retailer or manufacturer of an item which is featured editorially in a publication.

European Common Market an organization of nine European nations who are bound together in free trade and economic unity.

Fabric Editor one who evaluates and provides an analysis of textile and fabric fashion trends for a publication.

Fabric Libraries places which display fabrics which are currently in production or are slated for production in upcoming seasons.

Factoring a process used by manufacturers to raise cash.

Fad styles or designs which gain and lose their popularity within a short period of time.

Fashion the imitation and general acceptance of certain apparel and accessories which are produced and marketed by the fashion industry and are reflective of prevailing individual and societal values, attitudes, and beliefs.

Fashion Appeal an illusive ingredient in a design which makes it desirable to the consumer.

Fashion Consultant a person or firm who is retained by other firms in the fashion industry to help merchandise and promote fashion merchandise.

Fashion Coordinator (see fashion director.)

Fashion Designer one who conceives or interprets styles of wearing apparel.

Fashion Director (or Fashion Coordinator) one who researches, analyzes, defines, and presents current and future fashion trends.

Fashion Forecasting the ability to recognize or predict current and future fashion trends.

Fashion Image the impression the public has of a store's fashion expertise.

Fashion Life Cycle a graphic presentation of the four stages of the acceptance of a fashion.

Fashion Marketing directing the flow of goods from producer to consumer in order to profitably satisfy consumer wants and needs.

Fashion Movement the overall direction of fashion.

Fashion Seasons selling seasons used by manufacturers and retailers.

Fiber a natural or synthetic hair-like filament from which yarn is made.

Finishing a process which dyes, bleaches, prints, or otherwise treats unfinished (greige goods) fabrics.

"Fords" styles which catch on immediately with the public and sell in great quantities.

Franchise a store in which a compnay provides its name, merchandise, management, and marketing expertise in return for an initial payment from the merchant and a share of the profits.

Fulling a process which cleans and presses unfinished woven woolen cloth to create "finished" cloth.

Garment Center wholesale fashion district located in midtown New York City.

Greige Goods fabric which has not been dyed, bleached, printed, or otherwise treated. Also known as unfinished fabric.

Group Purchasing the purchasing of identical merchandise from a manufacturer at one time for a group of stores. This type of transaction is usually done by a buyer in a resident buying office.

Hard Goods non-apparel merchandise such as appliances, luggage, housewares, linens, china, silverware.

Haute Couture the finest, custom-made high fashion clothing.

Haute Couturier designer who produces the finest, custom-made high fashion clothing.

High Fashion new and extreme fashion.

Hot Number a style which receives sufficient orders to go into production.

Independent Store one which is privately owned.

Inside Shop refers to a manufacturer who performs all the steps involved in designing, producing, and selling apparel merchandise.

Institutional Ad an advertisement which "sells" a firm's name by presenting a general message instead of merchandise.

Jobber manufacturer who designs and sells apparel, but has the sewing and pressing operations performed outside the premises by other firms known as contractors.

Knock-off a copy of a style or a design.

Leased Department a department within a store which is operated by an outside independent firm.

Licensee a firm which pays for the use of a well-known name on its product.

Licenser one who agrees to lend his or her name to a product for a fee.

Licensing an agreement between a designer and a manufacturer whereby the manufacturer pays the designer a fee or royalties for the use of the designer's name on a product.

Mannequin French term for a model or one who wears and displays apparel. American term (manikin) for the figure used to display apparel.

Marker large piece of paper on which pattern pieces are arranged and traced as a guide for cutting fabric.

Market Weeks periods of time when manufacturers show and sell their lines.

Marketing Oriented refers to a firm which plans most or all of its entire operation around the idea of satisfying consumer wants and needs.

Media methods of communication such as newspapers, magazines, radio, and television.

Merchandise Editor one who works closely with manufacturers and retailers, supplying retailers with the trends and fashion themes which will appear in their magazine.

Minimum French term used to indicate the minimum purchase required of a customer who wishes to attend a couture showing. In reality, a minimum is a fee.

Model in France, a term for a sample of a design. In the United States, one who wears and displays apparel.

Modesty Theory contends that clothing originated as a result of the humans' shame over their bodies.

Multifiber Textile Agreements pacts between the United States and foreign countries which control the amount of textile/apparel goods imported to the United States from foreign countries.

Natural Fiber fibers which come from animals or plants. They are cotton, wool, linen, and silk.

Outside Shop term used to identify a firm that does sewing and pressing for a manufacturer on a contract basis. Since the work is done outside the manufacturer's premises, the contractor's firm is called an outside shop.

Piece Rate the amount paid to workers for each piece of completed work.

Planned Obsolescence the deliberate outmoding of merchandise by the subsequent introduction of other newer products.

Press Release a written description of a product, personality, or event which publicists send to the media for free mention of the described subject.

Prêt à Porter French word for ready-to-wear.

Primary Data information which is collected from scratch and not previously available to a researcher from any other source.

Primary Markets those which provide the fashion industry with raw materials for fashion goods. They are the textile, leather, and fur producers.

Protection Theory contends that the human need for shelter and protection of the body is the basis for the origin of clothing.

Psychographics statistical data on one's attitudes and beliefs.

Publicity the free and voluntary mention of a person, product, or firm by the media.

Purchasing Power the amount of money a consumer can spend. Consists of three factors: personal income, accumulated net worth, and available consumer credit.

Rebate a price discount given by manufacturers or governments to encourage a customer's business.

Resident Buyer one who works as a buyer in a resident buying office.

Resident Buying Office an organization which serves as an advisor and buying representative for one, several, or many noncompetitive retail firms.

Runners styles which are heavily reordered.

Sales Promotion the techniques used to encourage sales.

Scientific Method of Research a structured, analytical and formal approach toward research.

Secondary Data readily available information which has been gathered and published by others.

Seventh Avenue main thoroughfare of New York city's Garment Center. Also called Fashion Avenue.

Showing a presentation of a collection of fashion merchandise.

Silhouette the general outline or shape of a costume. In fashion there are three silhouettes: the bell, the tube, and the bustle.

Soft Goods merchandise which is classified as wearing apparel.

Special Events activities such as fashion shows, anniversary celebrations, or import fairs, undertaken by a store in order to promote business.

Specialization (or Piece Work) dividing labor by using one worker to work on only one piece of a garment, such as a sleeve, collar, or cuff.

Specialty Store a store which offers one type of goods as opposed to a variety of products. Specialty stores carry either single (footwear, ski apparel, etc.) or limited (complete assortment of either soft goods or hard goods) lines of merchandise.

Spinning drawing out and winding of loose filaments of fibers into thread or yarn.

Style characteristics indigenous to a specific person, place, or thing. In fashion, style refers to basic characteristics of clothing.

Style Piracy term applied to the copying of another's styles or designs.

Stylist in France, often used to identify ready-to-wear designers. In the United States, one who adapts current styles into new ones is often called a stylist.

Sumptuary Law law which prohibits lavish dress by regulating personal expenditures on extravagant and luxurious items.

Sweatshop turn-of-the-century apparel factories with unsanitary conditions, long hours, and low pay.

Synthetic Fibers man-made fibers which are either cellulosic (made of wool and cotton linters by-products) or non-cellulosic (made chemically).

Target Market a sub-market or market segment consisting of potential users of a product or service.

Task System dividing labor by using a team of workers—a baster, operator, finisher, and presser—to work on one garment.

Textile Converter machine used to print or chemically treat unfinished fabrics (greige goods).

Texture the appearance or feel of fabric.

The Fashion Group professional organization of the fashion industry's top women executives.

Toile French term for muslin replica of a design.

Trade-up to increase the quality and therefore the price of goods one sells or manufactures.

Trading Post places where early American settlers and trappers exchanged furs and supplies; oldest form of retailing in the United States.

Trend the direction fashion is taking. Trends are either incoming or outgoing.

Trickle-Down Fashion fashion which originates with the upper class of a society and then moves to the classes below.

Trim decorative additions to a garment which are not part of its general construction. Examples include buttons, belts, lace.

Utilitarian Function the serviceable and practical features of a garment.

Vertically Integrated Company one which handles all phases of production necessary to make a finished product.

Visual Merchandising the visual presentation of merchandise in a store. Also referred to as "display."

Women's Wear Daily the fashion industry's major trade publication on women's wear.

INDEX

Exam —

Chapters 6,

7, 9, 10, 12,

13